The Novels of Walter Scott and his Literary Relations

Also by Andrew Monnickendam

CLAN-ALBIN A NATIONAL TALE (*ed.*)

BACK TO PEACE: Reconciliation and Retribution in the Postwar Period (*ed. with Aránzazu Usandizaga*)

The Novels of Walter Scott and his Literary Relations

Mary Brunton, Susan Ferrier and Christian Johnstone

Andrew Monnickendam
Universitat Autònoma de Barcelona, Spain

First published 2013 by
PALGRAVE MACMILLAN

Palgrave Macmillan in the UK is an imprint of Macmillan Publishers Limited, registered in England, company number 785998, of Houndmills, Basingstoke, Hampshire RG21 6XS.

Palgrave Macmillan in the US is a division of St Martin's Press LLC, 175 Fifth Avenue, New York, NY 10010.

Palgrave Macmillan is the global academic imprint of the above companies and has companies and representatives throughout the world.

Palgrave® and Macmillan® are registered trademarks in the United States, the United Kingdom, Europe and other countries.

ISBN 978–1–137–27654–4

This book is printed on paper suitable for recycling and made from fully managed and sustained forest sources. Logging, pulping and manufacturing processes are expected to conform to the environmental regulations of the country of origin.

A catalogue record for this book is available from the British Library.

A catalog record for this book is available from the Library of Congress.

10 9 8 7 6 5 4 3 2 1
22 21 20 19 18 17 16 15 14 13

Printed and bound in Great Britain by
CPI Antony Rowe, Chippenham and Eastbourne

To Carmen

Contents

Acknowledgements

Much of this book was written and many of its ideas took form during a stay at Venice International University, located on the island of San Servolo in the middle of the lagoon. Although for centuries a madhouse, it provided a peaceful and fruitful atmosphere for reading and writing. I would like to thank Ilai Alon, Joseph Shatzmiller and Ulrich Metschl for a series of informal but instructive exchanges on scholarship, which were friendly, useful and productive.

The greatest single acknowledgement must go to all the readers, writers and critics whose names appear in the bibliography and whose work I greatly admire. I am particularly grateful to Dorothy McMillan who, some years back, asked me to edit *Clan-Albin* for the Association of Scottish Literary Studies. A special word of appreciation goes to Murray Pittock for having had sufficient confidence in my ability to ask me to write on Scott, Burns and the national tale. I would like to express my gratitude to Simon Edwards for our conversations about literature in general and Scott in particular, which have made me feel that I might have something worthwhile to say. My gratitude is extended, in no uncertain terms, to the Palgrave Macmillan reader for giving me the green light.

Introduction

A new volume on the Scottish national tale might meet with one of two reactions. The first would be 'a study of three of Scott's contemporaries is of interest only to a tiny minority of students and scholars' and the second would be something akin to 'yet another book about Scott and his contemporaries'. The first reaction might have made some sense several decades ago, but it fails to recognize the extent to which the canon of romanticism has increasingly admitted national tales into its pantheon, a situation that would not have been necessary in most European countries where the demotion of the historical romance to the level of children's fiction would be baffling. The second response recognizes those efforts, but suggests either that the work has been somewhat repetitive or else there is little more of value to be said. Obviously, I do not share such opinions because this critical study hopes to contribute to the burgeoning interest in the national tale precisely by adding to work undertaken by prominent scholars in the field over the past two decades or so, as I shall now go on to explain.

Its contribution comprises two major exercises. Although there have been two short studies of Ferrier (Grant 1957 and Cullinan 1984), this is the first volume which draws together the work of Mary Brunton, Susan Ferrier and Christian Isobel Johnstone with the aim of analysing their fiction on its own grounds. It uses two original strategies: the first is, as a point of departure, the examination of contemporary memoirs, correspondence and views of their life and work in order to assemble a literary persona. Second, it is only once their fiction has fully been examined that their relationship to Walter Scott can be best determined. In other words, the underlying hypothesis is that, by giving the three novelists critical independence, a more complex and diverse picture of their writing is produced, as we are no longer fettered by their supposed subordinate position which predetermines, or at least foresees, where criticism is going to take us in the end. That in itself would perhaps be interesting, but it could never be considered anything approaching innovative or ground-breaking. However, what I propose in the final chapter would, if successful, require a re-engagement with the way that Scott, the Scottish novel and, in a few cases, the history of English fiction are read. I will argue that if we look at Scott after close examination of these supposedly secondary writers, it is possible to see a rather different Great Unknown than we have been accustomed to. In purely abstract terms, it is logical to assume that the works of contemporaries would influence one writer as much as the works of this one writer would influence the others. As we all know, in practice, the dominant role of Scott has made this well-nigh impossible, and, until recently, would have been deemed pointless. Now, the situation is somewhat different. In other words, rather than a question of foolishly trying to overturn literary history, the objective is to remove the blinkers that have impeded a wider look at the sides, or, in the terms of this study, at Scott's contemporaries.

Before explaining how this book is organized, I would like to trace the recent development of our understanding of the national tale. In 1991, Peter Garside published his influential article 'Popular Fiction and National Tale: Hidden Origins of Scott's *Waverley*'; its findings and procedure have laid the foundations for numerous critical publications, of which this is simply the latest one.

It is worth reminding ourselves both of what Garside proposes and how he builds up his argument. As the title suggests, he is looking for evidence that will fix the date of composition of the early chapters of Scott's first novel. His approach is empirical: he collects his material clues before drawing up his proposal. In the 1829 'General Preface' to the Waverley Novels, Scott explains that he had started writing the novel in 1805, then abandoned the project, before taking it up again when he discovered the manuscript while searching for fishing tackle. The greater part of the novel was therefore written between October 1813 and the following June. However, Garside points out that *Waverley* had been advertised for publication by John Ballantyne in his 1809–10 catalogue. Consequently there is no correlation between Scott's own account, this advertisement and the other documentary evidence that Garside outlines; in short, '[n]one of this fits' (33). This healthy scepticism towards grand pronouncements smoothes the way for a completely new project, namely a reappraisal of contemporary fiction, as the way the fishing-tackle story is written indicates two crucial features of modern Scottish literary history. First, that Scott strove successfully to dominate the novel not only commercially but also through the careful creation of his own literary persona: the fishing-tackle story locates him as the founding father who had really invented the national tale as far back as 1805. The date is of paramount importance, as Scott is insinuating that he had more or less formulated the national tale before the publication of, say, Mary Brunton's *Self-Control* (1811), which I discuss, as well as other similar novels, like Jane Porter's *The Highland Chiefs* (1810), which I do not. Scott's desire for aggrandizement, I would propose, is evident even in such a familiar term as 'the Great Unknown', which primarily fosters stature: however known or unknown his identity, he is automatically depicted as great. In other words, even though grammatically 'great' could qualify 'unknown', in practice it qualifies Scott alone, by suggesting that only the name of the great genius is missing; that we are dealing with a genius is irrefutable. Indeed, the mundane nature of the discovery of his sporting equipment additionally suggests that casualness, but only the casualness of a great master, was sufficient to engender a literary revolution. To determine what Scott's motives were for the fishing-tackle story is open to debate; some evidence is circumstantial, other suggestions are merely speculative, but what is indisputable is that it underlines his attempt to consolidate his number one slot at the expense of his contemporaries. Such a situation emerges, and in logical terms I would say inevitably, from an awareness – immeasurably greater than that of his many critics since 1814 – of their existence-cum-status as writers. If there were no rivals on the field, there would have been no need to be so assertive.

Garside's scientific caution leads him to conclude that possibly the mysterious birth of *Waverley* may never be completely clarified, yet there is enough information to suggest that Scott was part of a continuum and it is precisely there that '*Waverley*'s position in relation to other contemporary novels invites reappraisal' (48), as one research question leads on to the next. The extent of the reappraisal is patent when we briefly consider three cases. Garside points out that before accepting *Waverley*, Constable had 'turned down works of fiction on Scottish subjects by both James Hogg and John Galt' (47). Their destiny has turned out to be radically different. Chiefly through the auspices of the late Douglas Mack, Hogg has emerged as a major figure, evident in the magnificent Stirling–South Carolina edition of his collected works, a scholarly biography by Gillian Hughes (2007) and the journal *Studies in Hogg and his World*. John Galt has not enjoyed such aura, despite the appeal of his political novels, like *The Member* (1832), and satirical novels of manners, like *The Entail* (1823), both of which have been recently published by mainstream companies. Galt is not greatly unknown, but has not benefited greatly from reappraisal. In the field of the national tale, one writer who certainly has taken on a status only superseded by Jane Austen is Maria Edgeworth. This is a result which, arguably, has less to do with the revaluation of the national tale along Garside's lines and more to do with the attention she receives from women's studies. As we shall see, Ferrier did not think highly of Edgeworth, and Johnstone subjected her to a ferocious attack (Monnickendam 2000). That said, the national tale is arguably as open a field as ever it has been since its heyday; the differing fortunes of Hogg, Galt and Edgeworth show how the situation has shifted.

A vital part of our understanding of the national tale derives from inquiries into gender. As an example, Dorothy Blakey's *The Minerva Press* (1939) goes so far as to suggest that 'reviewers were sometimes known to temper their criticism to the fair sex' (52) and that in the early days so great was the demand for fiction that occasionally titles and covers changed, but not the content (29–32)! Ina Ferris's *The Achievement of Literary Authority: Gender, History, and the Waverley Novels* (1991) is the major exponent of how crucial the change from biology to culture – from sex to gender – has become. In fact, Blakey's example of extreme behaviour fits neatly into Ferris's now classic distinction between female reading and feminine writing. The former is defined by being 'an act of the body rather than the mind. More specifically, it typifies it as a form of eating, hence as part of the material realm repudiated by the republic of letters' (37). This reinforces the firm distinction between body and mind, the emotional and the rational, that which requires control and that which controls, and a lengthy list of other gendered polarities. Only a small movement is required to extend the metaphor into one of an eating disorder, something which really calls for stern remedial treatment after bingeing on fiction. Feminine writing is defined as 'the proper novel that directly functioned as a corrective counterfiction' (52). 'Proper' indicates something moral, didactic or instructive, or a combination of all these interlocking elements.

Two examples of what borders on literary schizophrenia are provided by Jane Austen and Ann Radcliffe. *Northanger Abbey* (1817) is well known for its intertexual discussions of popular fiction: it might not be great literature, but the reading public's appetite – to continue Ferris's metaphor – for it is insatiable across gender and social classes, extending to Austen's own reading practice as evident in her borrowing habits from circulating libraries. The heroine's education consists in learning that the drama of popular fiction, dark secrets, castles and despots does not correspond, thankfully for all concerned, with reality: hence Tilney's patriotic defence of Western civilization, despite its neighbourhoods of voluntary spies: 'Remember that we are English, that we are Christians' (199). Minerva-style fiction is a pleasant form of entertainment, nothing more, nothing less, only once its potential for distortion is held firmly under control. Radcliffe's *A Sicilian Romance* (1790) has a marked split in form: on the whole, it operates as a Gothic tale, but it is often interspersed with brief lectures on education, for example on elegant conversation, which is sufficiently important to be included in the form of a disquisition in chapter 1 (1998: 7–8). These two examples provide clear proof of how female reading and feminine writing may inhabit the same pages of the same texts. Similar cohabitation is evident in the three novelists under consideration. The most blatant example is Ferrier: quite often a humorous scene is rounded off by a moral statement, or a string of humorous scenes is followed by an extended lecture on morality, for example the notorious 'The History of Mrs Douglas' section of *Marriage*. Diners (or readers) after enjoying a series of tasty dishes topped with a frothy chocolate mousse do not take kindly to a dose of castor oil. Instead of entering into an argument as to how well or badly the pieces fit together, it is sufficient to note that these two forms of literary expression are yoked together, hence, first, the diagnosis of schizophrenia is not as incongruous as might first seem, and second, conceivably it was not judged as such in that period.

The value of Ferris's analysis derives in part from the lucid manner in which she defines and illustrates the binary opposition and in part from the realization that it has a venomous sting in its tail. Male equivalents to female reading and feminine writing might exist, but in no way can we ever approach a situation equivalent to separate but equal: the subordinate position is evidently that of the female. Following Jean-Jacques Rousseau's belief that nature is more powerful than nurture, feminine writing has a privileged access to feeling, but this wild zone is an entity whose shapelessness cannot be reined in by formal methods; consequently, feminine writing is definitely writing but it will definitely never be art. These parameters have an easily identifiable source, the reviews: as arbiters, they are responsible for moulding taste. Ferris points out that Jeffrey, as a representative example of a powerful reviewer, sees Edgeworth as a limited author because of her didacticism and gender (65), which turns out be a completely circular argument since Edgeworth, as an individual author, could be substituted by the generic term feminine writing; again, it might be excellent writing, but it could never aspire to art. As a consequence, the importance of Scott is that, from the reviewers' angle, he rescues fiction by infusing it with the virtues which female reading and feminine writing did not, or, more likely, as a taxonomic category, could never possess. His fiction has the stamp of quality that female writers lack. This description of Ferris's study is admittedly brief, given that its impact is enormous. For, as a consequence of her terms of reference, it is virtually impossible to talk about the national tale without entering into the arena of gender. The literary schizophrenia, in addition, highlights the fact that questions of gender and form are inseparable. A graphic and sadly ironic illustration of the latter is Walter Scott's fall from literary grace in the terms used by E.M. Forster in *Aspects of the Novel* (1927); it shares similarities to the arguments used by Scott's contemporary supporters in enthroning his superior fiction far above the sensational Minerva novel. For Forster, the Waverley Novels had become little more than a form of cheap entertainment for unsophisticated readers; they were definitely not art. The wheel had come full circle: he saw Scott as a supplier of something akin to female reading, the very thing he had supposedly superseded.

Katie Trumpener's *Bardic Nationalism: The Romantic Novel and the British Empire* (1997) starts off with an exploration of how 'the bard symbolizes the central role of literature in defining national identity' (xii). The bard is a traditional, aristocratic figure, embedded in antiquarianism, yet is able to break free from what might be seen as an extremely limiting context to become a supra-national figure. By this, I mean that not only does the bard represent one culture, not only are songs and poetry vital to one dominated group, but that Trumpener is able to extend the coverage of the national tale; in brief, the question of imperialism enters the equation. Relationships, whether cultural or political, between Ireland and Scotland, for example, are always going to be tricky, as religion and emigration (in both directions) complicate the picture; Johnstone's *Elizabeth de Bruce* (1827) is probably the novel that shares greatest awareness of these complex issues. However, Trumpener, as the title of her work suggests, is able to extend the implications of the debate across the Atlantic, consequently not only into the empire as a whole but into the very concept of imperialism. Trumpener emphasizes affinity and common experience. She sees 'the constant copying and cross-pollination between the Irish and Scottish novel' (1997: 17) as standard practice. What they share is not simply a series of national symbols with the bard at the centre, but they are both products of a similar historical situation: that of the imposition of English, 'coercively imposed on the British peripheries' (16). The new immigrants take with them the experience of occupation, though memory tends to chip away at its most unsavoury and violent events and manifestations. Trumpener's ideas are backed up by a meticulous and thorough examination of many national tales, such as Johnstone's *Clan-Albin*. Although this side of her work is generally recognized, perhaps other aspects, crucial to this study, have not received as much attention or acceptance. Trumpener stresses that the national tale undergoes a transformation into the historical novel. This affects its three key motifs: the journey, the marriage and national character, as they sometimes do not take easily to the change. Trumpener states that '[t]he culminating acts of union become fraught with unresolved tensions, leading to prolonged courtship complications, to marital crises, and even, in two of Susan Ferrier's novels, to national divorce' (146). What is put under strain or into quarantine is the strength of the love-plot to sustain the arguments for national identity which the bardic figure, *ipso facto*, represents. This will be one of my central concerns.

Trumpener highlights the importance of Scott in providing a solution to – or perhaps an escape route from – what seems the insurmountable problem of the private and public sphere purportedly acting in unison but in fact misbehaving. Trumpener proposes that 'with the historical novel, a progressivist history of linear progressions, paradigm shifts, and epistemic breaks seems to have gained a clear victory' (151). The progressions, shifts and breaks all point to a major change of perspective which probably cancel out the note of caution carried by 'seems'. Of course, in no way is this a seamless argument, starting with the very terms of reference, as it is debatable to what extent the two overlapping literary genres can be so easily separated. Yet, the emphasis on progressive history is not just a reference to Scottish Enlightenment historiography but to the importance of Georg Lukács as Scott's most influential reader. It serves as a timely reminder that much, if not the majority of, Scott criticism centres on discussion of the political implications of his tales, or, in Trumpener's terms, the strength of bardic resistance or the degree of national capitulation. In her hypothesis, these implications spread all across the empire, aided by a collective amnesia of the bitter struggle originally chronicled by bards, old and new. In the latter category lies Scott's unobtrusive, ubiquitous narrator (151) who preaches progress rather than resistance. Trumpener's evolutionary model might seem to contradict my earlier statement that gender and genre are inextricably linked, but it is clear that same evolution requires the removal and extinction of those tiresome problems that could lead to national divorce. It was Scott himself who, by placing the marriage in the last-but-one chapter and the political postscript as the conclusion, must take the responsibility for lessening the potential friction that the marriage of his heroes and heroines might otherwise produce. The order of these final two chapters necessarily quashes gender difference. If that appears to be an unwarranted blanket statement, let us consider whether *Waverley* would have been a different book and Scott criticism a different discipline if the novel had closed differently, if the last two chapters had been switched round, with the postscript on Scotland's progress in the previous centuries coming last-but-one. Were the final scene to depict Waverley and Rose chastely kissing to seal their marriage, we would surely have given that wedding photograph more attention.

If there is an ur-text for the idea of union, we have to move, temporarily, several centuries back, to William Shakespeare's *Henry V*, a popular play in the nineteenth century. It beams a strong light on the structure of military codes and strategies, and the incorporation of peripheral national character in the minor roles of Gower, Jamy, Macmorris and Fluellen, who complement the virile, heroic figure of the Christian Prince. The concluding act is a courtship scene, an act of union, in which the stripping of royal titles for Hal and Kate does not obscure the real nature of power and gender questions. Scott's Rose (*Waverley*) or Lady Morgan's Glorvina (*The Wild Irish Girl* (1806))[1] would never say anything like 'Is it possible dat I sould love de *ennemi* of France?' (5.2.166) nor would Waverley speak in terms like 'I love France so well that I will not part with a village of it, I will have it all mine' (5.2.169–70). And yet these surely are the central issues which are located but somewhat hidden in national tales and historical novels. In addition, Kate's marked French accent shows an awareness of how important language is in marking difference and subordination. We are earlier shown her taking some bizarre English instruction in 3.4 which is so burlesque in nature that it subverts the language of occupation through projecting its potential for double entendres of a sexual nature. There are two major differences between the Shakespearean drama and fiction. One is that the former is considerably blunter or honester in its cultural representation of power struggles. The second is that whereas Shakespeare identifies national identity in terms of dynasty, in the national tale, despite its aristocratic origins, it is the more bourgeois Waverley and his peers who accrue wives and territory.

Trumpener concludes that a process of homogenization takes place whereby a fictional model more than smoothes away rough edges of conflict; in the end, it erases them through 'collective amnesia'

(246), which might read as a resounding defeat for the old bard: resistance seems to have been pointless if not a complete waste of time. Trumpener's assignment of monumental power to the Waverley Novels ironically confirms the much-commented remarks by Scott himself in the 'General Preface' when he proposes that Edgeworth's fiction has 'done more to completing the Union than perhaps all the legislative enactments by which it has been followed up' (Scott 1985: 523). For if Trumpener is correct, Scott enthroned not only Edgeworth as cultural Empress of the Union but himself as her successor, with the additional distinction of Cultural Supremo of the British Empire. However, we should not lose sight of the fact that Trumpener would never deny that this is anything other than a temporal title. Just as the bard had his moment of glory, ditto, the Waverley Novels. In addition, Trumpener's thesis correlates the co-existence of a change from content to form: from resistance to inclusion; from the bard to the ubiquitous narrator. Furthermore, as Wolfgang Schivelbusch points out, Scott was a powerful figure not only in the empire but in the United States, more concretely in the South, Twain's famous denouncement of Scott being the most famous example. Schivelbusch argues that 'Scotland was the model of an anti-England that young America could emulate in its struggle to form itself into an independent nation' (2003: 48). What I am emphasizing is that fiction was an important vehicle for political cohesion as Scott, Trumpener and Schivelbusch all recognize in an explicit fashion. Schivelbusch also insists that the defeated rapidly recover in cultural terms, as they instinctively believe that they are culturally superior to their victors; the conquered might not be Romans, but the victors certainly look like barbarians. The apocryphal cry from a member of the audience – 'Whaur's yer Wullie Shakespeare noo?' – during the first performance of Home's tragedy *Douglas* in 1756 makes better sense when we consider that this incident took place only ten years after Culloden. Home is perceived not as being the artistic equivalent to Shakespeare (one would hope), but as having the equivalent standing as Scotland's bard; in other words, he is not necessarily a superior bard but the bard of a superior culture, which, in the end, is a much more potent political message than any which could be produced by comparing individual authors or their works. The adage that the best English literature at the end of the nineteenth century and beginning of the twentieth century is Irish – the Abbey Theatre, Oscar Wilde, William Butler Yeats and James Joyce for starters – is similarly an argument that skips between asserting superior literary quality on the one hand and bardship status on the other.

These final illustrations lead to the ongoing arguments about national identity. Where did Brunton, Ferrier and Johnstone see themselves with regard to that rather old-fashioned but useful term? Is their position any clearer than Scott's? These questions are better understood if we briefly note where the tensions or contradictions stem from. If Scott is languorous in his fiction, to use a term close to Thomas Carlyle, then Scott's *Letters of Malachi Malagrowther* (1826) are certainly thunderous in their defence for Scotland's claim to take major decisions over its own affairs; after all, what is more important than banks and currency? That highly vocal Scott does not have much in common with the Scott who institutionalized tartanry by stage-managing the 1822 royal visit of George IV to the land of (oat)cakes (known as the 'King's Jaunt'). The former promotes independence, if not politically, at least at certain moments, while the latter promotes total assimilation. How can a sense of Britishness and Scottishness co-exist? Epistemologically, what is at stake are two ways of identifying allegiance: the older way centred on religion, dynasty or empire, and the more modern vision of the nation state. That said, the co-existence of allegiance to England and Scotland is always going to be potentially uneasy. In Ferrier, particularly in *Marriage*, there are satirical portraits of Scotland from various viewpoints, and harsh pictures of England from others. In Johnstone, a similar unforgiving array of critical postures is discernible; I will discuss in particular her use of the term 'national prejudice'. This might seem a case of having your cake and eating it, but, in the case of Ferrier, it emerges that relentless puns and fun-making indicate that, in the end, inconsistency does not trouble her.

If that is the case, then perhaps one explanation is that the ubiquitous term 'imagined community' has been used very freely or even irresponsibly, simply as a discursive term void of specific historical or political content. Benedict Anderson's *Imagined Communities: Reflections on the Origin and Spread of Nationalism* (1991) sets very clear parameters on this subject, as far away as possible from the general use of the 'imaginary' as romantic vaporousness. Actually, one of his central arguments is that Marxist revolutions after World War Two used a national term to delineate their national revolution; for example, the Kurdistan Workers Party (PKK) defines itself in these very terms. However, Anderson's contrastive analysis of the power of language and religion as community markers sheds great light on Brunton in particular.

One recent outstanding monograph is Caroline McCracken-Flesher's *Possible Scotlands: Walter Scott and the Story of Tomorrow* (2005), whose third chapter 'Chancing Scotland' analyses the 1822 visit. McCracken-Flesher emphasizes the role of Scotland as a land of origins, of essences, which then gets the Royal thumbs-up. The motif running through this study is that of exchange: in general, the Scottish fiction market enhanced a 'swap between Scottish signs and English money' (116), the former a synecdoche of that much greater exchange the *Waverley* postscript prescribes. Left as such, this firmly enthrones Scott as the champion of the new bardic nationalism. However, her analysis of *The Talisman* (1825) shows Richard I confronting a whole series of others, a process which removes the lustre of the novel's thematic predecessor, *Ivanhoe* (1819), as it has been traditionally received. While Sir Kenneth, future King of Scotland, wears several disguises, there is little doubt that its military potential – 'Kenneth manifests the idyllic vision of military Scottishness' (118) – is its primary contribution. In this process of alienation, the role of the Highland regiments returns to us in a fresh light. This late Scott novel displays a military enterprise which has brought together a whole series of European leaders. It identifies and articulates European stereotypes, but due to the umbrella term of Crusade, the other is more likely to be identified in Saladin, a historical figure as much a subject of glamorous romanticization as Richard I. It is Saladin, not Richard, a grotesque parody of military bluffness, who therefore takes on the role of father-tutor, leading McCracken-Flesher to posit that 'Scott recommends Saladin's more creative strategy. Saladin teaches Kenneth to accept his otherness, and thus neither to reject the boundary between himself and the crusaders, nor to transgress it' (126). Consequently, even on the edges of Christianity, differences and boundaries are conceivably accommodated within a greater political entity, which to Scott's contemporaries can only be Britain and its empire. The sophistication in this argument stems from its ability to identify the other both in what is distant, the Holy Land, what is nearer home, the European Crusaders, and what is next door and therefore uncanny, England and Scotland. This again highlights the Waverley model. I would surmise that in *The Talisman* a meeting with the other surely uncovers instability or doubt as well as the need for understanding and cohesion, and perhaps the novel is somewhat bleaker in its vision of the collective history than it is in its handling of the meeting of cultured individuals. After all, the third Crusade self-destructs; Saladin does not need to do anything to bring about its defeat.

Ian Duncan's *Scott's Shadow: The Novel in Romantic Edinburgh* (2007) takes up the tantalizing suggestion made by Trumpener that '[f]or a brief moment in the early nineteenth century (as Edinburgh becomes a major centre for novel publishing and reviewing) the intense mutual influence of Scottish and Irish novelists and their influence on novel readers of both nations begin to constitute a transperipheral Irish–Scottish public sphere' (Trumpener 2007: 132). Although both critics centre their attention on a specific time and location, they incorporate the major findings of the Russian formalists that novels, despite all the heteroglossia available in multiple guises, instruct their readers how to live in the new bourgeois society that their fiction often describes, whether in terms of the magnificence of its roots or for its bustling modern transformation. As evident from this brief citation, the reviewer acts almost like a superego, formulating the social rules, or, in Duncan's words, 'novels rhetorically unified a modern reading public [...] whereas magazines and reviews politicized its social divisions' (2007b: 28). Again, as in Trumpener and McCracken-Flesher, homogenization is crucial. Duncan is particularly incisive on the implications of hygiene in Elizabeth Hamilton's *Cottagers of Glenburnie*. After all, the cottagers are called MacClarty, and clarty is the Scots word for dirt, therefore hygiene begins in the mouth, with language and culture. Duncan likewise makes highly perceptive critical judgements on Ferrier and Johnstone. I will later make substantial use of his analysis of the latter's *Elizabeth de Bruce* in his article 'Ireland, Scotland, and the Materials of Romanticism' (2007a).

Of the many valuable contributions made by *Scott's Shadow*, I would stress two. The first is his analysis of the debate on the Republic of Letters as it cedes to 'the new figure of national culture' (Duncan 2007b: 49). This emphasis on change permits the setting up of parameters that go far beyond the unionist or nationalist, Lukács or anti-Lukács debates, whose binary models remain extremely influential. The advantage of shedding this straitjacket, if that is not too strong a word, and using more flexible and productive critical models is illustrated by a penetrating interpretation of *Rob Roy* in which Scott's Glasgow anticipates Alasdair Gray's by being 'hypermodern and Gothic' yet 'set just below the Highland line' (109). In short, they are neighbours, and attempts to distance them in time and space should logically rebound. The second major contribution, and greater in terms of its impact, is Duncan's ability to bring a series of writers out, as the title of the book suggests, of Scott's shadow and into the limelight. The fact that Scott, Hogg and Galt all wrote a covenanting novel and that, in addition, Hogg and Scott's exchanges are available from Hogg's point of view in *Anecdotes of Scott* enhances the persuasiveness of Duncan's argument. Although Hogg typically identifies Scott through his shaggy eyebrows, in this instance it is another physical attribute, Scott's voice, which stands out here, as much as for its message – his critique of *The Brownie of Bodsbeck* for being false and exaggerated – as for its form, Scott's literary English as against Hogg's literary Scots (50–1). Through a contrastive analysis of the three writers, questions of subordination to the Great Unknown yield to the new picture of three writers involved in a fictional rivalry over the depiction of this crucial period of Scottish history. The replacement of the binary model, Hogg versus Scott, by a richer setting of three contemporaries, means that each reflects back and forth on the other two, thus providing new insights into previously shadowy parts of literary history. This is precisely what I intend to do in the three central chapters and particularly in Chapter 4, when I discuss what Scott himself looks like after reading the fiction of his contemporaries. As these novelists wrote on different subjects in different styles, the structure of the book will have to be, in its initial stages, a little more descriptive, as a certain amount of dispersed and little-known material has to be gathered together and given shape; therein lies the challenge. The fact that a profound contrastive analysis of Scott, Hogg and Galt as they write on a common theme was still something of a novelty in 2007 gives a good illustration of the minimal status of Scottish novelists – other than Scott – inside the academy.

Linda Colley's highly influential *Britons: Forging the Nation 1707–1837* (1992) forcefully argues that a common sense of identity is a highly successful construction based on Protestant nationalism (Hanoverianism) and a sense of empire. Scotland's role in this enterprise was highly significant; campaigns against the influence of such politicians as the Earl of Bute, orchestrated by Wilkes and his followers in the 1760s, were principally a reaction to the presence of Scots in the ruling elite, a replay, in some ways, of the events that followed James VI's accession to the English throne at the beginning of the previous century, as satirized in Chapman, Marston and Jonson's infamous comedy *Eastward Ho* (1605). 'Forging' is a curious word due to its double meaning: that of taking form, from metallurgy, and that of forging, in the sense of falsifying. This very same word appears in the last-but-one entry in the diary in the final chapter of Joyce's *A Portrait of the Artist as a Young Man* (1916), 'Oh life! I go to encounter for the millionth time the reality of experience and to forge in the smithy of my soul the uncreated conscience of my race' (276–7). The denseness of Joyce's metaphors, mixing the spiritual and the volcanic, should not divert us from the ambivalence of race, in other words whether upper in his mind he places Ireland or the race of modernists. As Dedalus is on the point of leaving and as he has already shown a marked aversion towards essentialism, evident in Davin's story (197–8), the latter is a more likely candidate. That link between Colley and Joyce hopefully foregrounds the success or failure of Colley's thesis.

For, Colley does not integrate Ireland into her analysis or discuss it in any great detail. As Murray Pittock puts it, with another Joycean note, 'in fact, it [Ireland] is deliberately excluded, as incremental history must exclude it, for it is an embarrassment to "Britain". "It seems history is to blame", as Haines says to Stephen Dedalus' (1994: 2). This anticipates some of the subjects I will later go on to look at in greater detail. It is clear that rather than there being simply an Irish question, the presence of Ireland undermines the basic assumptions about *Britons*, Britons and British romanticism in particular. At the very least, it would show up a certain inconsistency. Scott and Edgeworth are paired in critical accounts through their work, friendship and correspondence, but it does not necessarily follow that Scotland and Ireland marry with the same ease; the chinks in the argument are more clearly displayed once greater attention is paid to the points at which they diverge, which I hope to demonstrate is evident in the writings of Scott's and Edgeworth's contemporaries.

In *Scottish and Irish Romanticism* (2008), Pittock tackles these problems head-on. He argues that we have to make several vital distinctions. One is evident from the title: romanticism might arguably be a pan-European movement, but the Scottish and Irish models and experience are markedly different. To which we have to add a more important one, '[w]hat in continental Europe became Romantic nationalism [...] remained in Scotland Romance' (59). In other words, Alessandro Manzoni's *The Betrothed* (1827) or the much later Ivan Vazov's *Under the Yoke* (1888) are both literature and platforms for the unification of Italy and its language in the case of the former, and the liberation of Bulgaria from Ottoman rule in the case of the latter, which have no parallel in Scottish or Irish romanticism. Byron's life and works would show him to be the one exceptional figure, a Scottish or British continental Romantic, aware of the limitations of Romance and willing to spend vast amounts of money and his time in the fight for Greek independence. Historians might argue back that there is a simple historical explanation. The English beheaded their monarch very early on, in 1649; the dynastical question in Scotland was really over either in 1688, 1715 or 1745 at the latest; and Wales does not even enter the equation, so there is consequently little need for a Manzoni or Vazov. At the risk of repetition, Ireland is always going to be problematic. We can leave it out or include it, but if we take the latter path, as its literature represents a radically different set of experiences and narrative voice, its romanticism reflects and modifies our perception of Scottish romanticism.

A brief illustration is provided by Pittock's discussion of the ascendancy's 'incentive to make themselves as different as possible to carve

out their own identity' (2008: 102), as to highlight their English origins
and culture would identify them so openly as colonizers. This same
problem trickles into the big-house novel as a whole and into the fiction
of twentieth-century authors such as Molly Keane or William Trevor, to
name but two. Waverley and his descendants do not face this problem,
as they may fancifully decorate their homes with Highland memorabilia.
In short, bracketing the cultures leads to unwarranted generalizations
that need inspection. Or to abuse a well-known formula, not all Celts
are equal, and some are even less equal than others. Of great interest
to this volume must inevitably be Pittock's account of Edgeworth and
Scott. For Pittock, questions of language are crucial in all Edgeworth's
work; in *Castle Rackrent* we are narrated 'the learnt speech of a people
stigmatized as barbarous, and hence more contemptible still in the
anglopetal world of stadial development towards Teutonic liberty and
its metropolitan grammar' (171). Of course, in the Scottish case, it is
ironic that another Irishman, actor and elocutionist Thomas Sheridan,
is famed for eradicating unmetropolitan expression from James Boswell
and his Edinburgh contemporaries. Again, this looks like something
both similar and different. But in the case of Scotland, it is basically a
social and educational problem that leads at most to diglossia and deep
cultural angst; the stigma stops there instead of extending into communal violence. Pittock's view of Edgeworth's fiction must therefore query
Scott's remarks in the 'General Preface': as Pittock so neatly puts it, 'it is
a true "literature of combat", posing as a literature of reconciliation; yet
how, in an age of union, can a national tale be anything but political, as
Edgeworth withstands her own ancestral "settler history" claim to con-
vert Irish history into British identity?' (2008: 185). Scott's 'muffling the
triumph of Bannockburn in the *Lord of the Isles*' (187) and the even more
notorious muffling of Culloden provide part of the answer. Pittock's persuasive argument centres on, other than the writers cited, Moore, Burns,
Hogg and Maturin, whereas I aim to see whether similar situations are
identifiable in the work of this trio of Scottish women writers.

Pittock's final chapter discusses the concept of 'fratriotism' which he
defines as the way in which colonized nations express 'reservations con-
cerning the nature and development of empire' (2008: 238). One way
this operates is through the 'transmutation of patriot discourses from
the first to the third person' (240). This harmonizes with Trumpener's
stress on the switch to a ubiquitous narrator and the historical novel
at the expense of resistant bard and national tale. At the same time,
a discussion of fratriotism rather than patriotism leads inevitably to the
legitimacy of describing Scotland and Ireland as colonized countries

whose literature is meaningfully understood through the language of postcolonial theories. One of the foundational texts of postcolonialism, Ashcroft, Griffiths and Tiffin's *The Empire Writes Back* (1989), expresses certain caution:

> A model such as Dorsinville's also makes less problematical the situation of Irish, Welsh, and Scottish literatures in relation to the English 'mainstream'. While it is possible to argue that these societies were the first victims of English expansion, their subsequent complicity in the British imperial enterprise makes it difficult for colonized people outside Britain to accept their identity as post-colonial. (33)

First of all, the polemic is displaced onto another writer, the Haitian Roger Dorsinville, then shrouded by the doubting 'while it is possible' to finally reject the suggestion with the very forceful term 'complicity'. To this we should add that the bundling together of Irish, Welsh and Scottish literatures is precisely what the work of Duncan and Pittock have identified as a strategy which steamrolls the union wherever needed. Surely it would not take a great deal of persuasion to propose that Conrad's *Heart of Darkness* and its attendant horror could be adapted to Irish history and literature with as much ease and success as Coppola's translation to Vietnam in *Apocalypse Now*? But could Inverness convincingly become the Central Station and the Caledonian Canal the treacherous waterway with threatening natives lying witchingly in the heather?

Part of the answer to these absorbingly complex questions comes from Mack's *Scottish Fiction and the British Empire* (2006). Initially, it might seem odd that the distinguished Hogg scholar should turn his attention to postcolonial theory, but that turns out be a perfectly logical development once we consider Hogg's literary persona, first as he portrays himself in his own writings, such as *Anecdotes of Scott*, in his journalism for *The Spy*, and in the buffoonish portrayal provided by both John Gibson Lockhart's biography and the carnivalesque figure of 'Noctes Ambrosianae'. Hogg is thus the subversive, the spokesperson of the subaltern Scotland that receives little from imperial expansion. Mack does not use the term exactly, but his portrait of Hogg corresponds to Henry Gates's 1988 formulation of the signifying monkey whose linguistic trickery subverts the language of officialdom through mimic; subsequently, the greater the profanity, the greater the subversion, and, most important of all, the greater the power of the popular culture that trickster is immersed in. Other evidence of the trickster comes from parallel narratives in James Hogg's novel *The Private Memoirs and Confessions of a Justified Sinner* (1824), the stress on the importance of orality and, I believe most importantly, in Mack's disquisition that the *Three Perils of Women* (1823) narrates the events of 1745–46 from 'a subaltern perspective' (Mack 2006: 104). Consequently, the questions of right and wrong, or tradition versus progress, are put on hold if not rendered rather secondary to that Conradian concept 'ludicrous, destructive horror' (105). It is one thing to stress the powerful presence of Hogg, but there is clearly not as strong a trickster tradition in Scottish literature as there is in the African-American context, so not everyone would take initially to the daring suggestion that Buchan's *Prester John* is really Waverley in Africa (195). However interesting a suggestion that is, of greater importance is the realization that within this period dominated by Scott, literature played out a series of tropes which later became part of postcolonial discourse and which are now easily identifiable in hindsight.

The year 2010 saw the publication of Juliet Shields's *Sentimental Literature and Anglo-Scottish Identity 1745–1820* and Pam Perkins's *Women Writers and the Edinburgh Enlightenment*. Although reaching rather different conclusions, both volumes deal with some of the writers and some of the issues of this project; as the titles themselves suggest, Johnstone, examined by both scholars, would represent the twilight of the Enlightenment, and Ferrier, the twilight of sentimentalism; questions of classification refuse to go away. This is not a question of pedantry, but simply another indication of how the fiction of this period has a remarkably unstable identity. In stark contrast, Pittock's study, covering approximately the same timeline, as its title indicates, *Scottish and Irish Romanticism*, suggests more of the Romantic century – 1750–1850 – than the Enlightenment, plurality rather than one movement. Claudia Johnson (2000) and several notable critics argued the case for this denomination in a special number of the *European Romantic Review*.

Shields begins her study with a firm declaration that '[g]ender functions in their writing symbolically, by signifying relationships of power, and literally, by negotiating between an older but still current understanding of the nation as race or consanguineous community and a newer concept of the nation as sentimental community' (2010: 8). The 'signifying relationships of power', arguably the keystone of her approach, reach from the days of Ossian down to Hogg and Galt, whose apparent failure to live up to the standards of the Great Unknown led to their relegation in the league of literary success to be expressed in 'gendered terms' (152). Perhaps her most controversial and thought-provoking idea concerns *St Ronan's*

Well, Scott's only contemporary novel. Shields argues that Scott is again appropriating acknowledged female territory: with *Waverley*, he latched on to the national tale; in this case, the novel of manners of such writers as Brunton, Ferrier or Johnstone.

Johnstone's adoption of the persona of Scott's Meg Dods, of the Cleikum Inn, as the penname for her best-selling *The Cook and Housewife's Manual* (1826) is an intertextual move, certainly, and, arguably, a back-handed compliment to Scott and his pervasive influence in publishing. In similar fashion to the fishing-tackle story, Shields regards Scott's strategy as anything but homage to his contemporaries: he wishes to describe a rather lacklustre, dull contemporary world, in comparison to the heroic potential of the past, something which interpretations of the wavering hero of historical fiction partly predict.

Perkins's study has, what is to me, a striking title in that women and romanticism are nowadays acceptable stablemates, whereas women and the Enlightenment are not usually linked so often in this way. After all, classical Athens is a place and culture where female presence is conspicuous by its absence, so, one wonders, what about the Athens of the North? Her study concentrates on the figures of Elizabeth Hamilton, Anne Grant and Johnstone. The analysis of the symbiosis of domesticity and intellectualism, and the private and the public sphere, provides persuasive arguments that the binary opposition of the same concepts cannot manage. To take a simple but productive question, in reference to the identity of Johnstone, what exactly are the implications of her use of 'we' in her strongly worded journalism, as Perkins so pertinently asks (251)? Her account of Hamilton, and particularly her novel *Memoirs of the Life of Agrippina, the Wife of Germanicus* (1804), would suggest that the latter is a text where all the concerns of the period meet: classicism versus romanticism, gender and genre, just to begin with.

At this point, I will explain how, in response to this critical development, I have chosen these texts, how the following chapters are organized and what they hope to achieve.

The choice of Brunton, Ferrier and Johnstone corresponds to their importance within literary history, fiction and the national tale. Although that is taken for granted, there are three individual instances, in fact exclusions, which require more explanation. The first is the absence of Hamilton and particularly her highly influential *Cottagers of Glenburnie* (1808), a text that ran to several editions in the years subsequent to publication. Its mix of manners and didacticism place it somewhere near the front as candidate for the earliest major national tale. This might all be true, but there are two points to be made. First of all, it is a text which is well analysed by Ian Duncan in *Scott's Shadow*, by Susan Egenolf (2009) and Pam Perkins (2010), who has also edited the novel for the Association of Scottish Literary Studies. The lucid introduction highlights the polemical issues of her writing, such as her views on equality and inequality. I have made several brief additional remarks in my chapter on the national tale for the Edinburgh University Press *Companion to Scottish Romanticism* (2010). I do not think I can contribute more other than stressing that its vigorous plan for reform, outlined both in the fictional creation of her cottagers' lives and in the concluding treatise of education, is at variance with the central features of a national tale. Mrs Mason, certainly, and possibly her creator, both feel that national character is in need of hygiene. I do not perceive of it as a celebration of either past or present Scottish life.

Jane Porter's *The Scottish Chiefs* (1810), an account of the life and death of William Wallace, has enjoyed considerable popularity in the United States, as well as looking very much like the template for Kilt Movies. Heroism, valour and patriotism are all highlighted as crucial to a national platform. From a historical perspective, as stated previously, its date indicates very clearly that it could be one of those texts that Scott had in mind when he used the fishing-tackle story as a strategy to leapfrog his contemporaries. It deals with two literary subjects which are not given much importance by Scott: these are, I would argue, homoeroticism and questions of female desire, displayed in the relationship between Wallace and Edwin in the case of the former, and in the lengthy story of Lady Mar in the latter. It is a story set in Scotland, but its concerns seem to me to connect more directly to a different set of parameters than those generally associated with the national tale: these are basically two. One concern is with the universal – rather than national – qualities of the Western epic. As I have argued in my chapter on the national tale for the Edinburgh University Press *Companion to Scottish Romanticism*, Wallace's Christian virtues and Christ-like love of his people are highlighted as being incomprehensible to the other Scottish chiefs; thus, he becomes a saintly martyr. In second place, the highly rhetorical, epic language has very little to do with the dynamics of a national tale. It is perhaps a translation of perceived Shakespearean rhetoric, the figure of Henry V again springs to mind, and if it is tushery it leads very easily into the language of those long Victorian narrative poems which are now almost forgotten, such as Matthew Arnold's 'Sohrab and Rustum' (1853) or Thomas Babington Macaulay's *Lays of Ancient Rome* (1842). In short, it shares common ground with the national tale, but many of its major components are at odds with it.

The third and final elucidation concerns the novel *The Saxon and the Gael; or, the Northern Metropolis: Including a View of the Lowland and Highland Character*, published in Edinburgh in 1814. In this particular instance, the problem surrounds authorship. Is it by Johnstone or not? I simply do not know. The British Library catalogue assigns no author to the novel whereas the National Library of Scotland does. The current *Oxford Dictionary of National Biography* does not list it as one of her publications. Dorothy McMillan states it is 'presumed' (1999: 133) to be Johnstone's text. Perkins pertinently reminds us that 'it was published anonymously and was not subsequently claimed by Johnstone' (2010: 211). I have opted for caution, in part because there is no sure way of knowing the truth, and in part because some more openly didactic books, which were previously assigned to Johnstone, are no longer credited as hers. The almost ethnographic title signposts the direction her fiction would take in the two novels that I do go on to analyse; all three share common interests. In contrast, the prose itself is unlike the later works: it is syntactically much simpler, also lacking the philosophical inroads that are very much Johnstone's imprint. Perkins affirms that even 'if Johnstone did not write it, the novel indicates that from the very beginning of her career she took a sophisticated interest in some of the era's main literary and political debates' (2010: 212). My personal appraisal, which cannot compensate for hard evidence, would be that either it is not her work at all or else, at most, it is a much earlier attempt at writing fiction than its year of publication indicates.

I have structured the central chapters in a series of common themes. The first of these is the author's literary persona, which might appear to hark back to an outmoded model of impressionistic criticism, but this is not the case. Garside's findings indicate that Scott's fishing-tackle story is nothing less than an attempt to create a literary persona through a very reader-friendly recollection of events and ideas. With Lockhart's biography several decades off, it is surely no exaggeration to say that the anecdote might be a minor item but its impact has been enormous. Whether Lockhart's monumental work had a greater knock-on effect than the story is, at the very least, an open question.

Brunton's posthumous fragment *Emmeline* is accompanied by a memoir written and compiled by her husband, which clearly strives to create a literary persona who likewise faces a major problem: the status of fiction. Alexander Brunton portrays his wife as someone so deeply religious that in the end the obvious question we have to ask ourselves is how she ever conceived of writing for pleasure in the first place. However, close attention to the pieces assembled for the memoir display someone rather different from a tightly corseted Presbyterian: nothing less than someone with a particular interest in religious art. The next section of each chapter is titled 'heroinism'. This word is discussed in detail in the chapter dedicated to Johnstone, who introduces this term in *Clan-Albin*. To the criticism that it is a vague term to describe the function of a heroine, two replies automatically suggest themselves. First, the same could be said of heroism, an answer which takes us nowhere, and second, as it is a term applied by a contemporary to the literary characters her fiction represents, it certainly has significance. Brunton's particular take on heroinism stems from the uncomfortable co-existence of deep religiosity, which is attested to by all readers and scholars of her work, and by a deep preoccupation with sexual desire, an issue barely dealt with in criticism other than to suggest that she represses it at every turn. I put forward the idea that *Emmeline*, a fragment dealing with a second marriage, becomes a requirement in assessing her views of female sexuality.

Shorter sections are dedicated to two concerns, parents and education, and locations. Although the spirit of Samuel Richardson's *Clarissa* and *Pamela* pervades much of Brunton's writing, she does not follow her literary mentor by placing mother–daughter relationships as a central issue; in fact, all three novelists have little at all to say about this subject. Consequently, we have to try and understand where, in the light of reformers like Mary Wollstonecraft, educational instruction is to come from. As the national tale is about national character, then location must play an important role. In Brunton's case, her landscapes are rather peculiar, ranging from ideal parochialism to transatlantic kidnapping.

The three central chapters each close with a discussion entitled 'cul-de-sac'. All three authors stopped writing fiction; in the case of Brunton, death truncated her career, whereas Ferrier and Johnstone gave up on fiction before completely abandoning writing in the case of the former and concentrating on journalism in the case of the latter. One of the central arguments of this study is that their fiction displays a deep concern with its own terms of reference, that there is such marked distrust in the nature of fiction itself that in the end writing becomes an almost impossible task. In the case of Brunton, this inquiry begins with an analysis of a lengthy review of *Emmeline* that pinpoints the difficulties that led Brunton, according to the review, to create characters who could never have existed.

In moving on to Ferrier, we encounter a completely different writer, a novelist greatly admired in the nineteenth century and the only one whose fiction is currently published by a mainstream company, namely the Oxford World Classics edition of *Marriage*. I will argue that perhaps no nineteenth-century Scottish novelist other than Scott has ever received such wide praise. This strikes a contrasting note with her very low current status. One reason why this sea-change has occurred can again be traced back to the creation of her literary persona, in this case by her great-nephew and editor of her correspondence, John Doyle. He asserts right at the beginning that her life was so dull and her fiction so artless that we are begged the question of why he went on to edit her correspondence at all. In the section on heroinism, I argue that Ferrier's harsh satirical spirit has brought about an irreconcilable divide between her humour and her more serious side, a pattern which can be traced back to the impact that the early chapters of *Marriage* have had over her interpretations of her work. Put bluntly, if her subsequent writing does not have the spring of these early pages, then heroine and novel are discarded. I therefore try and rectify the situation by suggesting a harder, more pensive frame of mind produces a serious heroine in the figure of Gertrude in her third novel *The Inheritance*, seen often as being a dull book. As to concerns with parents and education, there is little doubt that Ferrier is deeply influenced by Wollstonecraft, and one of the more convincing critical accounts of *Marriage* is that it is a fictional translation of the latter's work. Ferrier also describes a different landscape from that of the romantic Highlands, above all in *The Inheritance*. There are castles, there is folklore, but the atmosphere is definitely more sombre, a word that in part defines why Ferrier enters into a fictional cul-de-sac. More specifically, I will argue that the personal sphere, the love-plot, the metaphor of union, cannot be accommodated in such a bleak world.

Johnstone's literary persona, in fact much of her life, is an odd affair. This stretches back to the very place of her birth to the inexistence of a will. While her journalism is catalogued in *The Wellesley Index to Victorian Periodicals*, she strives to remain as anonymous as possible. Portraits of Susan Ferrier and Mary Brunton can be found at the beginning of several editions of their work, yet there is no extant portrait of Johnstone. In short, what Alexander Brunton did to his wife and Doyle to his great-aunt – that is, almost erase their presence – Johnstone does to herself. This sits at odds with a very lively and polemical mind that grapples with the great liberal causes of the day and which lies behind the lengthy handling of heroinism in *Clan-Albin*. The novel suggests that in the end men are the emotional beings and so are more deeply implicated in war than their more rational partners. Johnstone's take on parents and education is a product of her strong eighteenth-century cast of mind, reason being its basic ingredient. But unique among fiction of its time, is her defence of Gaelic, or if that might later turn out to be an exaggeration, she certainly provides a different angle. Johnstone provides us with an ethnographic account of Highland life before the Clearances. For Johnstone, the Americas will provide freedom and opportunity to such an extent that even when fortunes are reversed and the glens offer a new life, the ex-clansmen will not return to their homeland. Into this predictable set of circumstances, Johnstone insists that her ideal hero should be given a bilingual education and that the final blessing in the novel will be given in Gaelic; in brief, if handled properly, there is a future outside the dictates of *Britons*.

Elizabeth de Bruce is remarkably different. Lacking the centrifugal drive of its predecessor, instead of roaming around the world, it focuses on a narrower geography and a narrower set of concerns: the relationship between Scotland and Ireland. The journey, such a central trope in Scott's fiction, is generally from South to North, from metropolis to periphery, but here the journey is from Scotland to Ireland, or, in abstract terms, from one periphery to the next. This change of compass is precisely what precipitates the shape of Johnstone's impasse. The union of hero and heroine, Scotland and Ireland, can surely be only coherently interpreted as an alliance between the victims of unionism, and therefore Johnstone begins to call into question the very nature of the national tale itself. It has become a literary blueprint that can no longer fulfil its major role as a means of cultural and political assimilation.

The final chapter draws these wide-ranging ideas together and returns us to the Waverley Novels and more concretely to *Waverley*. It is the Scott text I will refer to most often for two basic reasons: the first is that it is foundational, the second is that it is published after Brunton's first tale, and coincides, more or less, with the first novels by Ferrier and Johnstone. Its contemporaneity is evident in the remarks made by the authors on his work and personality in their own writings. The aim here is to see Scott anew, not completely, but in certain interesting aspects. In other words, my conviction is that their texts illuminate, inform, engage with, influence – or whatever term we would like to put in place – the works of the Great Unknown. The interplay manifests itself at two levels, one more specific, one more like a superstructure. Heroism is a central subject to the trio yet their heroines' activities have been judged, on almost all occasions, as conventional, predictable and therefore typical of fiction of the time. A close examination shows that this is not always the case: for example, Emmeline, in the eponymous novel, has married for a second time and her own fears and the reactions to other people's behaviour point towards a deep concern or even scepticism in the narrator's voice which belies the staunch Presbyterianism that makes up her literary persona. As a result of such analysis, a return to *Waverley* does help clarify some of the questions posed by Scott himself or Lukács or more contemporary voices, on the woodenness and basically nondescript nature of his heroes. Other subjects dealt with include the question of desire, religion and, above all, the knotty question of union accompanied by progress, which forms the hearty, optimistic message of *Waverley*'s closing paragraphs. All-in-all, the women writers certainly have different opinions about key matters, but what they all share is a high degree of certainty about what is and what is not right or wrong, about how society should and should not respond to violence, and so on. The end result is that when we return to Scott, such ideological certainties contrast markedly with the aptly named wavering hero.

1
Mary Brunton: From the Soul of the Baroque to Tron Church

'It is virtue and goodness only, that make true beauty.
Remember that, Pamela.' (Richardson 1984: 52)

Literary persona

Mary Brunton (1778–1818), author of *Self-Control* (1811), *Discipline* (1814) and the posthumously published *Emmeline and Other Pieces* (1819), is a writer whose fiction is dominated by a deep religiosity. This is self-evident from the titles of her first two novels which seem more appropriate for sermons than fiction. The unfinished *Emmeline* deals with the disastrous consequences of a second marriage; its interest for contemporary readers lies in whether Brunton is able to make the text coherent and relatively homogeneous, in other words whether the development of the tale follows or veers away from the censorious pen of its narrator. Brunton's intensely moral world-view might make her fiction out of place in a more secular literary tradition where love-plots and bible-thumping are not bedfellows. That in itself is a phenomenon which merits attention, but I believe that her writing not only examines the role of the heroine in Scottish fiction, but also reaches the conclusion that certain fictional subjects are simply too awkward to handle. Why these questions have received scarce attention is greatly the result of the literary persona her husband designed.

One of the pieces that accompanies the unfinished *Emmeline* is the memoir written by her husband, Alexander Brunton, which would later be included in the Standard Novels editions of *Discipline* (1832, 1842 and 1849). He rose to become Professor of Oriental Languages at the University of Edinburgh, publishing a grammar of Persian for his students in 1822. The memoir, 116 pages in all, begins with a self-deprecatory admission that he is not up to the task, before giving a brief biographical sketch of his wife's early years. Much of the memoir consists of her letters on a varied subject matter, before concluding with two religious texts. The first consists of four pages on her religious character: 'her piety was not of an ostentatious or obtrusive kind' (Brunton 1819: cxiii). Apart from the Bible, we are informed that her favourite reading comprised John Newton's *Messiah*[: *fifty expository discourses on the series of scriptural passages, which form the subject of the celebrated oratorio of Handel*] (1786) and his *Cardiphonia*[: *or, the Utterance of the Heart*] (1781), Jeremy Taylor's [*The Rule and Exercises of*] *Holy Living* (1650), presumably Richard Allestree's *The Whole Duty of Man* (1659), and Richard Baxter's *The Saints' Everlasting Rest* (1650). The only item which is literary, in the more widely accepted term of the word, is Cowper's poetry which is itself informed by deep religious angst. Conspicuous in its absence is any reference to the genre his wife is remembered for: fiction. Brunton does not himself write the final lines of the memoir; instead, insisting that he has written only a 'feeble sketch' (cxvii), he uses part of a sermon preached by Dr Inglis, 'one whose good opinion was dear to her, for she loved and reverenced him'. The only connection, if it is one at all, with Brunton, is that it was 'the first which was preached in the Tron Church after her interment' (cxvii). It makes no specific reference at all to either her life or her work; it is a sermon on piety, which ends with a brief exhortation on how salvation should erase our fear of death. Then, *Emmeline* follows.

The volume concludes with extracts from her journal, stretching to 69 pages, which describes her travels in England and Scotland. This is followed by 'Helps to Devotion Selected from the Holy Scriptures', 22 pages in length. Addressing her dear young friends, she informs them that the author of these pious pieces is 'a woman in the prime of life, as cheerful, as happy' (179).[1] That said, the final pages are dedicated to six 'Examples of Praise'. It is helpful to see this volume as consisting of a risqué story, *Emmeline*, sandwiched between a pious prologue and a pious epilogue. There can be no doubt that Brunton presents his wife as a deeply religious reader in order to present her as a deeply religious writer, as devoid of irony, humour or creativity as he himself shows himself to be.

That final comment is intentionally critical, but, in marked contrast, *The Edinburgh Monthly Review*, in a review of *Emmeline and Other Pieces* published in July in the year of her death, wrote of Alexander Brunton's writing in the following eulogistic terms, '[i]n judgment, taste, and feeling, on the one hand, and elegant and faultless composition of the other, we question if it is surpassed by any biographical writing in the language' (Rev. 1819: 73). This rhetorical question is followed by a disquisition on what and what should not be included in a biography:

> We dreaded, we confess, before we opened the volume, the traces of overwhelmed feelings, unmeet for the public eye; we feared that there might be too much or too little on a theme with which few in the author's situation might be trusted; but we were soon relieved, and readily formed the opinion, that proof of finer tact, or more skilful calculation of the foundations and the limits of others' sympathies, has not been afforded by any writer who ever ventured to give his thoughts to the world in circumstances of equal trial and difficulty [...] It is eminently calculated to better the heart – to inspire a love for talent and worth, for true greatness and true humility. (74)

This is written exclusively in abstract terms, as, logically, it has to be. Unless we know part of or the full story of her life, we can never know what the public eye should discern. The strong emphasis on propriety, what is or is not 'unmeet for the public eye', might initially indicate the importance of gender. However, very similar concerns are evident in the initial reception of Lockhart's biography of Scott (Hart 1971: 164–75) and may also account for his dislike of Hogg's revelations, a subject which I discuss in Chapter 4. We shall soon see that one subject that was not dealt with in great depth was her ancestry, and one that received no mention at all was their marriage. It is impossible to know whether the anonymous reviewer knew anything about the latter, but it is more likely that he is simply uttering a generalization on what represents good taste, 'finer tact', and what represents greatness, 'true humility'. At the same time, on closer inspection of this passage – and of the review as a whole – a strategy is divined which ensures that Alexander Brunton himself emerges as the hero of the narrative. Mary Brunton might have written good, instructive fiction, perky journal entries and absorbing guides to prayer, but they are not assigned terms like elegance, faultless and unsurpassed, as is the memoir. *The Review*, perhaps aware of this bizarre situation which it has created by praising Alexander Brunton up to the skies, tries to refute that suspicion by pointing out that the memoir is so perfect because it 'places *her* in so prominent a point of view' (Rev. 1819: 78). Initially, it seems odd that such a comment should be necessary in the first place, as memoirs focus on the virtues of the recently departed, especially so when one spouse is mourning the loss of the other.

In this particular instance that is doubtful, to say the least. It is clear that not only has Brunton himself gone through his own vale

of sorrows after his wife's tragic death in childbirth, but has successfully emerged to write a faultless memoir; in addition, he is given
considerable credit for his wife's talent. How much, depends on how
we tease out and unravel comments like the following: '[a]fter her marriage, Mrs. Brunton's whole leisure was devoted to the improvement
of her mind; in which her husband had a much larger share than he
himself can properly record' (74). The reviewer claims to know more
about the couple than the husband himself! We are told that she was
particularly interested in languages and in the writers of the Scottish
Enlightenment, which is possibly a gloss on Alexander Brunton's own
comment that 'in the evening, I was in the habit of reading aloud to
her, books chiefly of criticism and Belles Lettres' (Brunton 1819: ix). Her
literary taste was partly the result of this education; she did not turn to
writing for some years after their marriage, or, in other words, for some
years after this instruction had begun. *The Edinburgh Monthly Review*
has one bone to pick with Brunton: his wife's failure to master maths.
Alexander Brunton is not very explicit about this (x), so the reviewer
is somewhat justified to point out that this incapacity is an 'anomaly'
(Rev. 1819: 75), adding that Brunton might have said more about the
matter. Taking together these three points: the excellence of the memoir, his role as mentor, her inability to master maths, it is inevitable that
one arrives at the conclusion that a clear gender and genre bias are at
work. Brunton could not teach her maths as that is not the province
of the female mind. Mary Brunton was certainly an admirable novelist,
but, the review implies, the status of the female genre of fiction is way
below that of Belles Lettres or maths.

The interpretative problem resides in determining to what extent
the Mary Brunton we encounter wears this monothematic straitjacket
that the memoir's unbending religiosity has woven for her. Clearly, the
answer must be in the negative, or else we might just as well pick up a
prayer book as a volume of her fiction. Perhaps the critical neglect she
has suffered since her death until very recently is an illustration that
Alexander Brunton's garment was certainly close-fitting. Yet, perhaps
an interesting clue is provided by her remarks that she is in the prime
of life, that she is happy. Here, the memoir implies that religiosity does
not necessarily mean life has to be devoid of pleasure, though at many
points it most certainly paints a very grey picture of a profoundly tedious life. In the 'Extracts from Journal' a far livelier figure emerges. For
example, when just south of the border, she records that 'the women
are prettier, the accent is perceptibly English, and hats and shoes are
universal' (Brunton 1819: 103). At the other end of the country, on the

Isle of Wight, we are likely to encounter 'the most ignorant brutes that ever were made' (136). Even from this brief extract, an inquiring, critical mind emerges; it is this spirit which informs the whole of the journal. Scottish Presbyterianism is not naturally associated with the public performance of music or with religious art: Mary Brunton is keenly enthusiastic about both, as she records in her 1812 visit to London:

> — called to take us to an oratorio at Covent-Garden. As we are *nobody*, he advised us to go to the pit, that we might have some chance of seeing and hearing. We were no sooner placed, than the adjoining seats were occupied by some very drunk sailors, and their own true loves, whose expressions of affection made it necessary to change our quarters. The music was far superior to any thing I had heard before. But in such a place, and in such a company, the praise of God seemed almost blasphemy. (106–7)

That such a respectable group actually goes to the pit is in itself a situation ripe for comedy; the presence of the sailors with, as she ironically describes them, 'their own true loves', confirms this. She is enthusiastic about the wonderful music while insisting that what makes the performance close to blasphemy is that the pit is just one stop above a brothel. We should not be too quick to see this as a condemnatory remark of a prude, as the following lines infer that it is more a case of blasphemy against great art and its location than blasphemy in a moral sense. Neither should we lose sight of how 'blasphemy' is tempered both by 'seemed' and 'almost'.

Mary Brunton visits Burghley:

> Cecil had as good a taste in houses as his mistress had in prime ministers. Admirable pictures! – A Magdalene, by Carlo Marrati; Domenchino's mistress, by himself – loveliness personified! Above all, the Salvator Mundi! [...] But the magical expression of the countenance! The inimitable execution of every part! Such benevolence – such sensibility – so divine – so touching – cannot be conceived without the soul of Carlo Dolce! How blest must the creatures have been whose fancy was peopled with such images! (105–6)

The admiration for this second painting extends for over a page. In her visit to Magdalene College, she again expresses her admiration for Carlo Dolce, as well as for Guido Reno's *Venus Attired by the Graces*. Bearing in mind, first, the dates of three artists: Guido Reni (1575–1642),

Carlo Dolci (1616–86) and Carlo Maratta (1625–1713), second, that the Baroque period is commonly dated as starting at the end of the sixteenth century and finishing at the beginning of the eighteenth, Brunton's three painters occupy the length and breadth of that movement. Particularly significant is her description of Mary Magdalene's 'loveliness personified' and the coupling of art and religion in describing 'the soul of Carlo Dolce'. Brunton's enthusiasm for Baroque masterpieces and their subject matter, especially the representation of Venus and Mary Magdalene, places her light years away from the much narrower views of life and morality expressed in the memoir. Indeed, Mary Brunton's admiration for Baroque art extends into an interjection which praises the salutary effects exercised on Catholic worshippers, thereby predicting Johnstone's creation of a similar situation for her character Flora in *Clan-Albin* (474–5). There can be no shadow of a doubt that Brunton enthusiastically admires the celebration of religion and beauty through their representation in public venues: the concert house, the picture gallery and chapel. Her enthusiasm for the public display therefore clashes with the widespread belief that Puritans and their descendants approved of art only within the sanctity of the home.

In this attempt to present a figure that differs from the dull figure of the memoir, two additional biographical pieces of information are required to complete the task: the first is her ancestry. The memoir states laconically that she 'was the only daughter of Colonel Thomas Balfour, a cadet of one of the most respectable families in the county of Orkney. Her mother was Frances Ligonier, only daughter of Colonel Ligonier of the 13th Dragoons' (Brunton 1819: vi). The most salient point is that her family is a military one; presumably Alexander Brunton, consciously or unconsciously, equates respectability with the military, an equation that she dismantles with great gusto in *Self-Control*. It must strike any reader that Ligonier does not sound Scottish at all. Mary McKerrow's *Mary Brunton the Forgotten Scottish Novelist* (2001) is an indispensable guide to unravelling a complex family history. What and when her husband learnt about her background is phrased in these terms: '[n]ot until many years later was Alexander Brunton to learn that his wife had a French grandfather who fought for the Hanoverians against the Jacobites, and an Orkney grandfather whose estates were wrenched from him because of Jacobite loyalties' (McKerrow 2001: 69). Due to simplified cultural mythology, it is perhaps normal to conflate Jacobitism with France, but in this case, the Ligoniers came to Britain as Huguenot refugees. John Ligionier (1680–1770),[2] Mary Brunton's great-uncle, was born in Castres (Tarn) and emigrated to Britain, having had an extremely successful military career in the Hanoverian army: he rose to the rank of Field-Marshal and in 1757 became Commander-in-Chief. This astonishing achievement indicates a lot about his own personal qualities and also something about social mobility in an institution that is generally seen as being somewhat resistant to outside influences. In short, McKerrow's point is that biographical information about Mary Brunton often begins by stating that she was born in Burra, Orkney Islands, a fact which linked to her religious views produces a writer who was out of touch with the world, remote in distance and intellectual concerns from the metropolis and worldly affairs. These few biographical details offer a different picture: her family history highlights both the conflicts of a war-torn Europe radically divided along religious boundaries a century after the Thirty Years War, and strife-riven, eighteenth-century Scotland.

As McKerrow goes on to explain, Mary was educated in Edinburgh, adding that '[s]o autobiographical do some of the early pages in *Discipline* seem, that Mary may have made Ellen her mouthpiece when she left school at the end of seven years of "laborious and expensive trifling" with only one real accomplishment – music' (2001: 53). Another thing that Alexander Brunton either did not know or purposefully ignored was that his mother-in-law, Frances, was illegitimate. Alexander and Mary's marriage also has an interesting story to tell. Alexander tutored Mary's brothers in preparation for their going to public school. McKerrow explains that Frances suspected that something was going on between the tutor and the boys' sister; she was definitely not keen on having her daughter marry a man 'with a ridiculously small stipend, and no social standing' (56). One way of stopping this liaison, Frances thought, was to pack Mary off to London to stay with her godmother, Lady Wentworth, in order to be introduced to London society. This would initially seem an enticing proposition as glamorous, cosmopolitan, social connections would provide the opportunity of meeting suitors with large stipends and considerable social standing. Mary preferred Alexander.

The story of their marriage is akin to that favourite theme of romance: elopement. The situation was as follows: Frances had sent Mary to Gairsay, whose population in 1798 was 33; McKerrow likens her situation to Rapunzel's (57). She goes on:

Somehow he [Alexander] managed to arrange for Mary to give him a pre-arranged signal from the island, and he then, as chivalrous as the proverbial knight in shining armour, would secretly row over in a small boat, probably from the mainland, and whisk her away. An operation, no less romantic for being undertaken in the sometimes fickle late autumn weather. But fortune favoured him and he rescued his girl. (58)

This reads like fantasy; it is open to debate whether, were we to turn their affair into a story or a film, we would be accused of stretching credibility beyond belief, for, out of this Mills and Boon setting, the two main characters go on to become the author and subject of the piously dull, passionless 1819 memoir.

By now, it should emerge that the biographical information authored by her husband gives a misleading picture of Mary Brunton. Much in the way that opponents of Presbyterianism would stereotype the object of their dislike along the lines that Knox equals Nox, Alexander Brunton has clipped his wife's creativity by reducing her whole life and ideas to one concept: humble piety. Yet, it is easy to show that she has a much wider range of interests and ideas than her husband would make us believe, or possibly had himself. This is why I have stressed that in the 1819 volume itself, her ideas about art and music extend far beyond her husband's limited horizons. Side by side with her favourite books, according to or selected by her husband, we must place her emotive enthusiasm for Baroque art, Mary Magdalene included. She shows herself to be a wry observer of humanity in the incident at Covent Garden, as well as even-handed in judgement: the north of England has something to show for itself while the Isle of Wight is best avoided. If we accepted Alexander Brunton's memoir as the whole truth, Mary Brunton would be an uninteresting author of some uninteresting novels, but luckily, the memoir uncovers a much more dynamic, worldly author.

Perhaps my emphasis on Mary Brunton's life and interests has moved too far away from some of her professed ideas and intentions. In order to counter the criticism that I am endeavouring to promote a subversive Brunton whose texts demonstrate how powerfully all traces of unorthodoxy must remain well hidden in a maze of complicated plots that inevitably resolve themselves along doctrinal solutions, let us recall that Brunton tells us in a no-nonsense fashion what her intentions are in the dedication of *Self-Control* to Joanna Baillie: 'The regulation of the passions is the province, it is the triumph of RELIGION. In the character of Laura Montreville the religious principle is exhibited as rejecting the bribes of ambition' (1811: 1:vi–vii). Brunton herself capitalizes the key word. There is no doubt in her mind as to how religion functions and what fiction is supposed to demonstrate and preach. If the argument stops here, then most of what has been expounded in the preceding pages looks decidedly shaky. However, that is not the case, I would propose, for two reasons at least. First, the triumph of religion is a subject she writes about in the same manner as the Baroque painters whom she so much admires illustrate virtue and saintliness on canvas. If we dismiss Mary Brunton's claim, then coherently we would have to dismiss not only Brunton but also Handel, her favourite painters and, in the interests of coherence, all religious art. What makes Brunton an innovative writer is that, consciously or unconsciously, she makes the subject of her inquiry not only the value of religious principles, but also how these are sustained when they enter into conflict with two powerful institutions: the military and the ruling classes.

Heroinism

Johnstone uses this apparent neologism in *Clan-Albin*: in the course of a conversation, a female character, with a slight note of surprise, ponders why this concept is not more widely recognized. This fictional character is suggesting that little attention is paid to female characters' actions and personalities in works of fiction. They undoubtedly have a presence, even a major presence, but presence is one thing and activity is another. The conversation occurs during a military campaign in which an attempted rape has taken place, thus incorporating the central Gothic plot, the pursuit of the vulnerable female, into a historical romance. It is a truism to say that participation in early nineteenth-century war – the context of Johnstone's novel – is a predominantly male domain, but perhaps there are additional implications. What Johnstone's character is expressing, and what Brunton's fiction often attempts to do, is bring about a change in our perception of language which apportions to resistance the same or similar value as military gallantry. It is therefore erroneous to see resistance and flight as merely forms of escape from a threatening world; self-control and discipline, the titles of Brunton's two finished novels, indicate this.

This approach to the subject is therefore unlike Ellen Moers's in her study *Literary Women* (1977), the second part of which is called 'Heroinism'. She argues that literature partly enables women to overcome the passive role patriarchy obliges them to play through providing a forum for relatively free expression. She adds that:

> More significant is the whole thrust in women's writings toward physical heroics, toward risk-taking and courage-proving as a gauge of heroinism, long after male writers had succumbed to the

prevailing antiheroic, quiescent temper of the bourgeois century, and admitted, with whatever degree of regret or despair, that adventure was no longer a possibility of modern life. (131)

Consequently, *Jane Eyre* functions as a blueprint: it opposes confinement and promotes the narrator's right to take control over her life, right down to the decision of choosing a partner. The differing timescales for male and female texts would add to the argument that Waverley is an extremely innovative figure. This emphasis on female assertion is perhaps best illustrated by Moers's parody of Carlyle's *On Heroes, Hero-Worship, and the Heroic in History*, which forms the epigraph to chapter 10. Moers's fascinating study gives little importance to religion in the work of Wollstonecraft and her followers, something which is, in my opinion, fundamental to their world-view.

The opening chapters of Brunton's first novel, *Self-Control*, take place in Glenalbert, near Perth, in a 'solitary village' (1:11), in the whereabouts of what Scott symbolically denotes the 'stupendous barrier' (Scott 1985: 73), the dividing line between Lowlands and Highlands. Laura Montreville's father is a relatively poor captain on half-pay, which he took when his regiment was about to go on a tour of duty to the West Indies. Right from the opening lines, the army and empire have made their presence felt; not going to the West Indies is presumably a decision to favour life over death. The greatest threat to Laura's integrity during her Wordsworthian 'solitary ramble' (1:5) or 'solitary walk'[3] (1:13) is the sudden appearance of another military figure, Colonel Hargrave, at this moment an attractive future husband. Her life depended on one military man and presumably will continue to do so. However, that recurrent literary trope of pastoral peace does not correspond to reality, even in this remote location.

In addition to a geographical or historical context, I would advocate that the most fruitful reading of Brunton results from the recognition of its debt or homage to Richardson's fiction. Previous critics have also noticed this. Julie Shaffer argues, for example, that *Self-Control* 'is in some ways so similar to *Clarissa* in plot and movement and in individual episodes that it virtually demands to be read as a revision of Richardson's novel, as though it means to restate that novel's critique of codes for judging female worth more clearly and emphatically' (1992: 111). My point of departure is that there are, of course, notable similarities but also important differences, of which the Scottish setting is the most obvious example. In addition, as Brunton favours life over death, marriage over rape, morality over passion, it is surely the plot and structure of *Pamela* that is at least as, if not more, influential in the novel's design. It would be easy to overburden this chapter by continually referring incidents in Brunton's fiction back to Richardson, commenting on whether the incident is more reminiscent of *Pamela* or *Clarissa*. However, as the basic hypothesis has been made, I will limit myself to pointing out the most important of the many similarities. It is hardly surprising that Alexander Brunton never mentions that his wife had read either, but their presence is felt right from the opening incident.

As this encounter is the trigger incident which determines the course of the novel, it is worth observing it in some detail as Laura's behaviour is predominantly a juggling act between conventional resistance, as the memoir would lead us to expect, and less conventional mental states, which the memoir would never have dreamt of mentioning. To start with, Mary Brunton stresses several points. First, that Laura is young (only 17), and that she does love Hargrave, which accounts for the weeks of his absence being 'tedious' (1:15). In other words, the pursued is not pursued by an enemy, as in a Gothic novel, but by the very person she desires. Brunton likewise stresses that her youth and innocence turn the dreams that occupy his absence into 'highly-coloured pictures of happy love, scenes of domestic peace and literary leisure; and, judging of his feelings by her own, dreamed not of ought that would have disgraced the loves of angels' (1:15). If this is a misguided view of bliss – 'loves of angels' reveals her ignorance of sexuality – then it is surely close to a caricature of that same religiosity that, according to the memoir, both Bruntons – and Pamela – fervently shared. If that is the case, then Mary Brunton is being ironic at the expense of both female innocence about male desire and the ideal bourgeois marriage, as commonly represented in didactic fiction, which has been subsequently endorsed as the centrepiece of her own life and beliefs. This is surely a bizarre way to write an opening chapter.

The long paragraph which describes the meeting emphasizes the intensity of her desire in such conventional phrases as 'the heart of Laura throbbed quick as he expressed his rapture' and particularly 'never had Laura felt such seducing tenderness as now stole upon her', so it is no wonder that 'his entreaties wrung from her a reluctant confession of her preference' (1:16). At this moment, she pleads that she cannot marry so soon after her mother's death; whereas Hamlet uses the image of funeral baked meats, Brunton uses dress: 'Laura threw a tearful glance on her mourning habit. "Is this like bridal attire?"' (1:17). We then read that marriage, after a respectable period of mourning, is not exactly what he has in mind: '[p]ressing her to his breast with all the vehemence of passion, he, in hurried half-articulate whispers, informed her of his real design. No words can express her feelings, when, the veil thus rudely torn from her eyes, she saw her pure, her magnanimous Hargrave – the god of her idolatry, degraded to a sensualist – a seducer' (1:17). She then faints. With the words of the dedication in mind, Hargrave has broken Brunton's golden rule by allowing his passions to take over from any religious or secular-based morality. The violent, hymeneal image of the torn veil suggests that on regaining consciousness she will now enter the adult world of earthly sexuality, a place unlike her dreams of social and literary pleasure. If her ideal marriage was a fantasy, an excess, the immediate reaction in which Hargrave is instantaneously the devil incarnate is likewise an excess, a case of demonization. What I am trying to put forward is that the radical switch of opinion takes place in Laura's mind because she has no words with which to articulate a halfway house between heaven and hell. This is why the phrase '[n]o words can express her feelings' applies not solely to the common connotation of being emotionally shocked but also back to the denotation of being literally speechless. The heroine lacks judgement and is hardly saintly.

On seeing Laura faint, Hargrave is presented with the ideal opportunity of lifting Laura up and taking her away to his equivalent of Bluebeard's castle. Indeed, a large proportion of the text consists of his elaborate plotting to create a situation in which he can kidnap her; in other words, do what he did not do in the first chapter. Yet here he refrains; we are told by the narrator that he did so because, '[s]eduction, he perceived, would with her be a work of time and difficulty; while, could he determine to make her his wife, he was secure of her utmost gratitude and tenderness' (1:19). He might have few scruples, but his ultimate goal is marriage and a sense of respectability is still intact. Like Lovelace, he is patient, but unlike Lovelace, in an initially confusing mixture of ideas: seduction and marriage still belong to the same process, as they eventually do for Pamela's pursuer-cum-suitor Mr B.

It is important to note that Laura's troubled nights are not solely caused by distress or fear, for part of the night was passed 'framing excuses for her lover' (1:24). Hargrave has made an indecent proposal, has aroused her desire, thereby causing her enormous turmoil; Martha Musgrove takes this one step further by insisting on her 'sexual infatuation' (2007–8: 237). She partially resolves the problem by telling Hargrave to steer clear of her for two years, telling him he will then be judged by sober, pious people to gauge his worthiness. However much emphasis is placed on sobriety and religion, all her actions in these early times have a simple explanation: the inability to understand the libido and the consequent expulsion of all feeling from her life. Sigmund Freud argues that our main source of suffering comes from 'our relations with others. The suffering that arises from that source perhaps causes us more pain than any other.' One solution which Freud identifies in human behaviour is the path she chooses: '[d]eliberate isolation, keeping others at arm's length, [which] affords the most obvious protection [...] the happiness that can be attained in this way is the happiness that comes from peace and quiet' (2002: 15).

Peace and quiet are not possible and Hargrave returns to pursue her in the London chapters, let it be stated again, in order to marry Laura. When Laura unexpectedly comes across Hargrave, 'this recognition was not made without extreme emotion. She trembled violently and a mist spread before her eyes' (1:286–7). 'Trembled' surely suggests mixed emotions; in addition, Isabelle Bour is right to contend that 'the body, ultimately, seems to be uncontrollable'. She adds that 'this is certainly not a conclusion that Mary Brunton intended her narrative to convey' (1997: 27). Does she manage to do so successfully?

There are certain indications that she does not. On the one hand, Laura has only seen him from behind; there has been no eye or verbal contact. The sight of the back unleashing erotic tension is a powerful reminder of how deliberate this isolation has been in terms of both time, the two-year moratorium, and place, from Perth to London, and therefore an infallible indication of how deep her desire is. In addition, her father expresses his wish that she marry Hargrave. This causes her to blush, adding, 'No, Sir, I have no wish to marry. I pretend not to lay open my whole heart to you' (1:262). Her reluctance might have materialized from, first, the most obvious source, that she is beginning to favour another pretender; second, that the overt sensuality of Hargrave is something that simultaneously attracts and repels her; third, this dual allegiance is the major cause for having purposefully decided to enter into sexual isolation. Awareness of desire for another has led to self-loathing.

Critics, such as Sarah Smith (1986), have commented on Brunton's insistence that in her first novel one major objective was 'to bear testimony against a maxim as immoral as indelicate, that a reformed rake makes the best husband' (1819: xlii). This is a strange remark, as, although it accounts for her dislike of the materialist Richardsonian universe of *Clarissa* – the maxim itself is from its preface – there is nothing 'reformed' about Hargrave at all, apart from some small details near the novel's beginning; arguably, Brunton is not aware of how clumsy the demonization is. If Brunton seems confusing or ambivalent, we should recall, first, that the reformed rake *par excellence* is Pamela's husband, Mr B, and second, Brunton's own words that '[i]t is alleged, that no virtuous woman could continue to love a man who makes such a début as Hargrave. All I say is, that I wish all the affections of virtuous persons were so *very* obedient to reason' (Brunton 1819: xlix). Desire is desire is desire.

Chapter 17 recounts Laura's confrontations with the two military men who strive to determine her life: first, Hargrave, and second, her father. In the space of a few pages, therefore, Laura encounters all the emotional crises which heroinism should overcome. Laura tries to calm her father down by using one of her favourite strategies: to insist, as if she were fulfilling Lear's idealization of Cordelia, how much she loves him and then embrace and/or kiss him. This time, he wants to speak. He admonishes her, 'Laura, you carry your scruples too far' (1:336). Her 'wan' (1:336) complexion is a symptom of her rigorous denial. The struggle enters a linguistic battle when she replies, 'How can my father urge his child to join to pollution this temple, (and she laid her hand emphatically on her breast) which my great master has offered to hallow as his own abode' (1:337). Her father replies that rather than being humble and pious, she is vain, consequently he upbraids her for having spoken offensively about an influential member of the aristocracy who is offering her marriage. This is not the only occasion on which her views are contested, but it is highly significant that in this case it is by her father, who, she repeatedly insists, is the most important person in her life. To conclude this side of the argument, a young girl who tries to extinguish her desires and refers to her heart as God's temple is coming close to solipsism through attributing such importance to her own personal feelings. What is curious is that such hyperbole is precisely that of the moralist Brunton purportedly was. It is language which is completely inappropriate to the situation in which it is uttered and for the person to whom it is addressed.

On the other hand, there are moments when Laura is fully in command of her emotions, and is, therefore, evidently capable of controlling her body. The same chapter demonstrates a particularly feisty young woman taking on the two most important men in her life and ends in her father's death. A similar seesaw emotional conflict takes place: the chapter ends with her father's gentle death in a moving moment of tenderness, despite the irony in his lament uttered a few paragraphs earlier that 'she is cold – cold as clay' (1:353), which turns out to be a premonition of his own fate.

As the story progresses, Hargrave rapidly becomes the devil incarnate, as opposed to the earlier, passionate but in the end attractive, Byronic figure. The source of his evil nature is partly due to a weak mother, a recurrent trope in the fiction of that time. He commits all the sins expected of his kind: he is impulsive and violent, he frequents the theatre, gambles and so on. On the rebound from Laura's rejection, he has an affair with Lady Bellamer, and therefore engages in two-timing. After she becomes pregnant, he fights a duel with the wronged husband. As the novel progresses, the extent of his wrongdoing reaches ludicrous proportions, above all in the case of the successful kidnapping.

There is an occasional moment when Laura's and Brunton's joint hatchet job of Hargrave temporarily lets up. For example, his duel with the cuckolded husband makes him reflect that:

> Laura, thus on the point of being lost, was more dear to him than ever; and often did he wish that he had fallen by Lord Bellamer's hand, rather than he should live to see himself the object of her indifference, perhaps adversion [...] he quitted Laura in the full conviction that she would never be his wife. (1:370–1)

Even at this late stage, he reasons in terms of marriage. The often baffling thoughts the pursuer and pursued have about each other are best explained by Toni Bowers's account of the late eighteenth-century seduction novel. She argues that a distinction has to be drawn between '*courtship*, supposedly a process of mutual consent, *seduction*, which involves the gradual achievement of female collusion with primary male desire, and *rape*, an act of force defined by female resistance or non-consent' (2009: 141). For Bowers, the major exponent of collusion is Pamela. The validity of this taxonomy hinges on what exactly is understood by 'collusion', or, in the case of Laura, to what extent the opening pages explore her misconceptions of what sexuality really consists. At certain moments, as when she sees his back, desire is still alive and courtship is therefore an option, but when it is repressed, collusion ceases to exist and courtship transforms itself into a preparation for rape – in Laura's case in the older sense of being forcefully abducted.

Such moments of doubt do not last long, as one of the reasons why Hargrave is so villainous is a result of a campaign against his social class, a similar pattern to that established in the first volume of *Pamela*. Here, Brunton's intentions are laid out in an unequivocal manner.

One essential element of heroism is resisting the advances of individuals like Hargrave, but another is resisting the assault of the aristocracy as a whole. This is where Brunton parts company with Richardson, whose aristocracy contains both the reformed and the unreformable. In *Self-Control*, Hargrave is assisted by Lady Pelham, Laura's aunt. What exactly Pelham would possibly gain from their marriage is hard if not impossible to imagine, yet the relentless way she plots matches Hargrave's persistence. Brunton admitted that she had 'always *felt* that Lady Pelham was a little tedious' (1819: xli), though she was presumably not tedious enough to prevent the creation of a similar aristocratic misfit – Lady St Edmunds – to accompany the heroine of *Discipline*. Lady St Edmunds is deeply involved in similar plotting with the same objective: to ensure that the bourgeois heroine marry an aristocrat, namely Lord Frederick. Plotting for both ladies is a way of life from which they derive great pleasure. The reason for this recurrent theme is possibly a simple one: plotting is seen as a component part of the genetic code of the upper class.

In *Self-Control*, Brunton narrates two stressful events in Laura's life in successive chapters. Their proximity highlights both Laura's danger and its source. In chapter 28, after many failed attempts at trying to bend her will towards a match with Hargrave, Lady Pelham resorts to her most dastardly strategy: to force the marriage through an elaborate web of debt. At this moment, Laura has a certain amount of money on which she can live comfortably, a situation which does not prevent her titled aunt, considerably higher up the social ladder, from borrowing money from her with no intention at all of ever paying it back. Laura is to be forced to gamble at cards and lose to Hargrave, therefore being in his debt in both a financial and an emotional way. Brunton refers to this strategy as if it is a lengthy campaign; this is only the first essay, which will take place in a large social gathering – Laura's shyness will therefore make a refusal to play a hand embarrassing if not impossible. It is important to note that the nexus of sex and money becomes a leitmotif in these pages in phrases such as '[y]ou need not mind what you stake with Hargrave' (2:282), 'stake' being a word that the villain also uses in this double sense. The clash in values is evidenced in comments about the half-a-guinea stake. For some, '[i]t is nothing. It would not buy a pocket handkerchief' (2:283), whereas Laura reminds herself, though she will not utter the thought publicly, that it would feed a poor family for a week. The pressure that Laura is put under is made evident by the voices that echo the belief that the affair is whimsical and her attitude unsociable. Eventually she is offered an escape route, which she takes, but not without Lady Pelham pinching her arm 'till the blood came' (2:287).

The second round takes place in the next chapter where an even more elaborate plot involves false documents that supposedly prove that Laura is in debt. To escape the debt-collectors, she locks herself in her room. This incident is also narrated in terms of physical assault; Hargrave is again the instigator, and Lady Pelham the accomplice. The phrase 'force the door' (2:316, 2:317) is repeated within a very short space, thus extending meaning from the door itself towards the intended violation of her body, which is now Hargrave's aim. The aristocracy is defined by its rapaciousness in the pursuit of both middle-class money and middle-class females; however ardent the pursuit of the female body may be in the classic Gothic trope, it is, by now, less an objective in itself than a means to obtain funds. It is not the case that the aristocracy are penniless, but with Laura at hand, there is a cashpoint close by. Laura is therefore involved in a struggle which oscillates between a war of the sexes and a class war.

A similar plot is developed in *Discipline*, where the nexus is given greater development without being taken to the melodramatic lengths we have seen here. The heroine, Ellen, is born into a very wealthy family which falls on bad times, so she experiences poverty, eventually recovering happiness and wealth at the novel's conclusion. Ellen is vivacious and wilful, and extremely attractive to Lord Frederick. In part, this is because she is beautiful, but of greater importance to him is her fortune. Trained in the ways of a young lady, Ellen is deeply concerned with her appearance and those graces which also personify Susan Ferrier's young marriageables. Her schooling in Edinburgh, which, as previously stated, McKerrow (2001: 53) believes might reflect Brunton's own experiences, has provided her with one skill, music, and instilled another, which she then develops, flirting. On several occasions, she repeats the same sentiment: 'I was supremely indifferent towards Lord Frederick, and never entertained one serious thought of becoming his wife' (1:97), and '[i]f I am in love with Lord Frederick, I am sure I don't wish to marry him' (2:63). The difference between the two cases is that in the first, she is still just playing, and unaware that most of her contemporaries have already paired them off, and in the second, she is just about to elope, aware that her father has forbidden the liaison and that she does not love him (Frederick) at all, despite being told the contrary by Lady St Edmunds and others. Ellen eventually assimilates Lady St Edmunds derogatory views – shared by Lady Pelham – on moral, upright people. Lady Pelham calls them 'narrow-minded bigots' (2:162) whereas Ellen uses the term 'waspish bigots' (1:157). Why then does Ellen agree to elope if she does not love her future spouse? Basically, because her father has continually forbidden the match. At first, Ellen received great pleasure from the fact that Lord Frederick was so summarily dispatched from her home by her father. But a hundred or so pages on, the situation has changed; Lady St Edmunds has planted doubts in her mind, and displeasing her father becomes an attractive proposition. Her father explodes into anger, warning her, 'Did I not tell you, I wouldn't have this puppy of a lord coming here a fortune hunting? [...] you shall marry no proud, saucy, aristocratical beggar' (2:69). Ellen is aware that her father's description of the situation is correct, which just adds to the cachet of parental disobedience.

The escapade fails because that very day her father's business crashes; Lord Frederick does not turn up to meet his lover at the appointed inn. While waiting, Ellen looks at two pictures, one of the Durham Ox and the other of the Godophin Arabian. Brunton's irony seems to be impenetrable here, as side by side hang pictures of a giant castrated ox and a thoroughbred stallion, without any indication as to what they signify to Ellen or the readership. Musgrove (2007–8: 241) asserts that this reinforces Ellen's belief that she is to be a trophy wife, but that is surely rather tentative. Eventually a letter from Lord Frederick arrives which Ellen snatches from Lady St Edmunds's hand; it reads, '[t]he old one has failed for near a million [...] See what a narrow escape I have had from blowing out my own brains' (2:88). This is no revelation, as Ellen has known his real motives all along, but the letter proves something else. The childish, slangish tone of the letter indicates a mental state bordering on the infantile, reinforcing the weight of 'puppy' in her father's phrase 'puppy of a lord'. I would propose that even though, as we shall see, there is clear promotion of the values of a distinctly austere cast of mind which emphasizes saving, frugality and other waspish virtues, the plot of the second novel is quite different. Old money seems to be an inappropriate term as money now seems to be mainly in the hands of the middle class throughout Britain. Presbyterianism, or Scottish moderation or canniness are parts of what form a much larger picture – the evangelical impulse of an affluent and militant middle class.

Fredric Jameson, in his discussion of the Gothic, argues that what is under siege is not so much the female body as property, thus 'Gothics are indeed ultimately a class fantasy' (1991: 289): that is precisely what Brunton's fiction illustrates. Both the female body and middle-class prosperity are continuously assailed by their supposed social superiors who have a certain interest in the former and a larger interest in the latter. In short, love and money conflate in the figure of the middle-class heroine, engaged in what looks to all intents and purposes as a class war based on the ideological foundation that the aristocracy is incapable of managing money and, therefore, it has forfeited its right to govern. The radical nature of Brunton's critique comes to the fore when attached to Egenolf's statement that in *The Cottagers of Glenburnie* 'Hamilton thus indicates that the cottagers in the area cannot hope for any benevolence from the person most financially suited to aid them' (2009: 132), that is, the landlord. Lady Pelham's action of borrowing and not returning is therefore a representative example of a much larger phenomenon. Consequently the distinction between good and bad, uncharitable or generous landowners no longer holds, as mismanagement is the rule rather than the exception.

The fate of Brunton's heroines also casts an interesting slant on what Nancy Armstrong labels hypergamy, in brief, marrying up. A heroine might temporarily have to sever the roots with her current social position, but this 'enables the family to achieve higher status through her [...] should she marry into a higher social position' (1987: 131). Although this seems a convincing argument to bring to the fiction of her contemporary, Jane Austen, Brunton's fiction confidently demonstrates that in marrying up, the heroine would, in fact, be marrying down, into a class with diminishing funds whose major occupation is therefore to track down new sources of money to finance age-old vices.

Parents and education

In what seems to be very much a perennial motif in fiction, Brunton's heroines lack mothers; for example, in *Self-Control*, Laura's mother, Lady Harriet, disappears without trace in the opening chapter. Consequently, surrogate mothers take their place, either of the religious sort, Mrs Douglas in this case, or from the conniving aristocracy, like Lady Pelham, a situation which sets up a female equivalent of Jekyll and Hyde, of a double set of values, which runs close to a distinction between virtue and vice. In *Discipline*, the mother is dispatched with similar haste; nurturing is more extensively developed, as concerns both the spiritual guidance of Miss Mortimer and the education in fashion and courtship given by Lady St Edmunds. In the second text, in the pre-elopement chapters, Ellen is confused because she feels attracted by the power that coquetry so easily gives her while she is fully aware of the need for moral values that question it. In fact, it is reasonable to argue that Ellen is aware that coquetry, a word commonly associated with falseness, the superficial and the trivial, is the only power a girl of her station and status can exercise in society. It is a much more effective and presumably realistic term than other vaguer ones like charm or beauty. At the same time, Brunton does portray fathers in some detail.

Initially, it would seem that the two father figures have a position of authority which might, in part, make up for the absent mother in her role as primary instructor, following the dictates of the female reformers of the final two decades of the eighteenth century. However, it should be stated immediately that this does not happen. The need for a spiritual guide, Mrs Douglas (*Self-Control*) or Miss Mortimer (*Discipline*), derives from the fathers' ineffectiveness to act as responsible parents. That might seem like a comment from a waspish bigot, but the evidence is there in the novels themselves. I have already mentioned the rather weak figure of Laura's father. His resignation from the army and his inability to run a farm show that he is unable to make a going concern of anything he turns his hand to, which extends to his incompetence in managing the annuity he himself has laid out for his daughter. The trip to London, which worsens his health and causes his death, is brought about by 'some informality in the deed' (1:50). We have no hard information about the nature of the informality, so nothing contradicts the assumption that when it comes to managing his financial affairs, he is a complete dunce. He will not allow his daughter to paint, which, at that moment, is their only source of income. If that reminds us of Tansley's taunt in Virginia Woolf's *To the Lighthouse* (1927), 'women can't paint, women can't write' (67), then his role as a despot eliminates the positive aspects that his rank in the army and his role as a laird, in short, the perfect Scottish gentleman, should provide. It would certainly explain that his preference for Hargrave responds to his desire that his daughter marry one of his own kind, a display of *esprit de corps* which would lead to the worst of all possible fates, given his own shortcomings and those that Hargrave later displays. Two officers do not make an army, but in this case there is little positive to be said about either of these two major personages, who – as the father sees Hargrave as an ideal projection of himself when young: romantic, good-looking and rich – have a lot more in common than is first apparent.

In the second novel, *Discipline*, a similar pattern emerges. Ellen has no real education for life. Unlike Laura, she would have no qualms in spending half a guinea on a handkerchief. In a lengthy episode in chapter 6, a modern angle on the widow's mite, she is made aware that true charity is to be distinguished from a celebrity display of giving away money. Unlike the first novel, initially we see a father who is keenly aware of ins and outs of the financial world; his attempt to ward off hungry aristocratic gold-diggers reflects his desire that his daughter should lack nothing. One day he receives a letter which unnerves him completely: it is the announcement of his ruin – his daughter will be left penniless. What is interesting about Mr Percy is that rather than simply waste away, he commits suicide. All we are told is that on entering his room Ellen sees the bloodstained 'form that seemed my father' (2:95). In this godless world, even a corpse in the room is not enough to put off a creditor, who arrives shortly after. After Ellen abandons her home, it is very much a case of out of sight, out of mind. Brunton sets up the possibility of a tragic event, but the speed with which it happens, added to the comment that it was too horrible a sight to describe, apparently justifies the lack of inches dedicated to this newsworthy event: leading industrialist slits his wrists and leaves his daughter destitute. But we receive hardly any indication of Ellen's thoughts on the subject in a three-decker which expounds her change in personality from spoiled brat to responsible woman at great length in practically all other circumstances. The reason why the suicide is barely attended to might lie in the fact that it is inherently a criminal act, the ultimate sin. That in itself diminishes or even excludes any lengthy disquisition on her emotions; in short, it becomes a prediction of the cul-de-sac more elaborately articulated in *Emmeline*. The circumstances are different but in both cases there is a reluctance to emotionally involve the reader in an arguably immoral situation. One fact stands out: weak fathers, whatever their rank or success in life, cannot provide for their daughters either spiritually or materially.

With mothers absent from the stage and fathers present but of little use, the family has, to all extents and purposes, ceased to exist, so heroines turn to the Bible and religious figures for guidance: the latter is the logical consequence of the former. Phrased in such terms and left like that, Brunton's fiction would be extremely moral, predictable and not very interesting. But the parentless child – whether biologically or morally – is a device that the Great Unknown uses extensively too, as I shall show in Chapter 4. Waverley will feed on Jacobitism in the figure of Fergus and Hanoverianism in the figure of Talbot. The first major difference is that Brunton's tutors are religious, Scott's are not; the Highlands are placed in contrast to and therefore separate from Waverley's home, whereas in Brunton, the threat is narrated in terms of pursuit and proximity. The traditional Gothic plot locates its pursuit in a Mediterranean, Catholic context, but in Brunton's fiction, similar threats come from much closer at hand – in fact, as Katherine Green (1991: 128) points out, from Lady St Edmunds's boudoir. To conclude, we return to where we began, to Perthshire, where even a solitary ramble can be a dangerous occupation, especially without the protection of a family or the Bible. Ironically or pointedly, heroines are intent on forming solid families as a result of their dance with death, which has been precipitated by their exposure to danger that itself is the result of the lack of parental guidance.

Locations

However accurate Garside's dating of the early chapters of *Waverley* is, it does not detract from the validity of John Sutherland's affable comment that it is 'one of the hoarier creation myths of nineteenth-century literature [... but one] [t]he reading public have always loved' (1995: 169), or, put simply, it has been a very successful piece of fiction. All three female novelists under discussion have similar stories whose truth or falsity is difficult to judge, but it would surely leave an objective observer with the belief that predating the origins of a novel was a party game in which all novelists felt obliged to participate. The genre question is vital; as Hogg wittily noted in the 1 June 1811 number of *The Spy*, epic verse had already provided the right tools for a distinctive literary location:

> Whoever goes to survey the Trossacks, let him have the 11th, 12th, and 13th divisions of the first canto of the *Lady of the Lake* in his heart; a little Highland whisky in his head; and then he shall see the most wonderful scene that nature ever produced. If he goes without any of these necessary ingredients, without one verse of poetry in his mind, and 'Without a drappie in his noddle'; he may as well stay at home; he will see little, that shall either astonish or delight him, or if it even do the one, shall fail of accomplishing the other. (2000: 401)

One only has to go back half a century to Boswell's account of Corsica (1768) to notice the gulf that separates Boswell from Scott and his contemporaries. Apart from the perfunctory details commonly identified with Mediterranean countries – rocks, olive trees, calm sea and so on – Boswell describes this mountainous country with scant attention to the landscape. He insists that he 'had full leisure and the best opportunities to observe every thing in my progress through the island' (1955: 163). That 'every thing' refers effectively to people and customs – the powerful figure of Paoli, the hangman, the fate of criminals – which invite more general or abstract debate on marriage, the state, Catholicism and so on.

Brunton's geography is different from Scott's. The journey common to the Jacobite novels is basically northwards, conceptually from the metropolis to the periphery, historically from modernity to the past, and geographically from Lowlands to Highlands. In *Self-Control*, the novel opens in Scotland where it also concludes; consequently the exotic flora and fauna it examines are not those of the Highlands but those of London and its corrupt aristocracy. They, like stereotypical Highlanders, are shown to be potentially dangerous, as the presence of Hargrave in the opening chapter augurs; no corner of Britain is free from their undesirable presence. Although it is worth reminding ourselves that Brunton's first novel was published in 1811, I doubt whether it can ever be seen as a predecessor to *Waverley* as the descriptions of Scotland are not distinctive at all. Glenalbert, once Hargrave has died, is an oasis of peace. Scotland is certainly 'Blessed [...] among nations!' (2:450) but there is little description other than vague props such as '[t]he blue mountains in the distance, – the scattered woods, – the fields yellow with the harvest' (2:449–50). Brunton ensures that her heroine returns on a Sunday so that Scotland is seen at its very best, hence the focus on Sabbath customs. To Brunton, the best of Scotland is not the Trossachs but its pious people and their sober attire, therefore she has no need of whisky or Scott's verse to evaluate the landscape. We are thrown back on the same conventions employed in Boswell's time: a country is primarily defined by its people and their customs, not by its raging torrents, misty glens and sublime landscape.

Consequently, while reading through the following extract from the memoir, from Alexander Brunton's pen, we should note how crucial 'manners' is to defining locality:

> A part of the book [*Discipline*] from which she herself received very great pleasure in the composition, and from which anticipated with most confidence its popularity, was the sketch of Highland manners in the third volume. She had been delighted with the pictures of Irish character which Miss Edgeworth had drawn so skilfully. (Brunton 1819: lix)

Brunton's religious outlook and didactic fiction give these words a ring of truth. Bearing in mind that the memoir was written in 1819, ten years before Scott's celebrated praise of Edgeworth in the 'General Preface' to the Waverley Novels, it is curious to note the similarity to Scott's laudatory remarks on Edgeworth's exemplariness.

In this next extract from the memoir, Brunton explains the effect the publication of *Waverley* had on his wife's second novel; the final lines display an awareness of a major difference between Mary Brunton's and Scott's agenda:

> When this part of the book was nearly completed, *Waverley* was published. It came into her hands while she was in the country, ignorant of its plan, or of its claim to regard; she was so fascinated by it, that she sat up till she had finished the reading of the whole. Her anticipations of its success were, from the first, confident and unhesitating. With the honest buoyancy of a kindred spirit, she exulted in the prospect of its author's fame; and, in rejoicing that a favourite object had been accomplished so admirably, forgot at first how much the plan interfered with her own.
>
> When this view of the subject struck her, with all the native openness of her mind she felt and acknowledged her own inferiority. Not from disappointment of ill-humour, but from pure and unaffected humility, she resolved at first to cancel the Highland part of her own story altogether. I could not agree to the sacrifice. I endeavoured to convince her that the bias which Waverley might give to the public taste, might prove more favourable to her plan; that public curiosity would be roused by what that great master had done; that the sketches of a different observer, finished in a different style, and taken from entirely a different point of view, would only be the more attractive, because attention had previously been directed to their subject. She allowed herself to be persuaded. (lxiv–lxv)

Brunton tries to please everyone by acknowledging Scott's greatness, while placing equal if not greater emphasis on his wife's virtues: her national honesty and her Christian humility. His business sense persuades her not to ditch the third volume; perhaps 'She allowed herself to be persuaded' shows condescension towards his wife, or perhaps she did not really need all that much persuasion in the first place. The fact that her novel was published in December 1814 – *Waverley* had come out in July – gives weight to the importance of the second suggestion.

The memoir alternates the husband's narrative with his wife's correspondence. In a letter to her good friend Mrs Izett, dated 15 August 1814, she states:

> Have you finished Waverley? And what do you think of the scenes at Carlisle? Are they not admirable? I assure you, that, in my opinion, they are absolutely matchless, for nature, character, originality, and pathos. Flora's 'scam,' and the 'paper-coronet,' are themselves

worth whole volumes of common inventions. And what think you of Evan's speech? It delights my soul! (lxxiv)

There is a world of difference between the ponderous words of Alexander Brunton and the lively words of his wife both here and throughout the memoir. There is no reason why these two accounts of what is basically the same event should be similar, but not the slightest note of preoccupation is manifest in her words: the letter shows no concern at all about the Highland chapters. Therefore, if there is one person who was 'mortified to find he [Scott] had published a work on the Highlands shortly before her novel was released' (Alker 2000: 200), it is the husband, not, as is often claimed, Mary Brunton.

I have included these two extracts from the memoir in preparation for the hypothesis that the Scottish chapters of *Discipline* share few characteristics with *Waverley*. 'Scottish chapters' is a more accurate description than Alexander Brunton's 'Highland part', as the focus is first on Edinburgh.

That it is not going to be a pretty picture and one that lends itself to a simple contrast between north and south is predicted by what Ellen believes to be her most favourable asset: 'my skill in playing on the harp, had recommended me as a teacher in a country which pays for her fruitfulness in poetry by a singular sterility in the other fine arts' (2:229). This acid remark shows little patience with the belief that Edinburgh is the Athens of the North. Brunton's remarks on the beauties of Baroque art therefore take on even greater importance as a remarkable contrast to her – admittedly – fictional Edinburgh, a city with few social and cultural assets. Her Edinburgh is close to the most important contemporary critique, *Peter's Letters to his Kinsfolk* (1819), where Lockhart draws a picture of a dull, uncultured bourgeoisie unable to recognize the value of, for example, the poetry of Wordsworth or Coleridge. Their cultural landscape is defined by what the (wrong) review has instructed them to admire or detest. It is striking that Ellen will instruct the Scots in the harp, that most powerful symbol of resistant nationalism, to follow the arguments of that all-important scholarship that emanates from Trumpener (1997). If the harp is so vital to bardic nationalism, it is certainly peculiar that the instructor is going to be a Southron fallen on hard times. It is easy to say that this is done without any deliberate intention, but this is surely not satisfactory. First, because the harp, as stated, is not simply any old instrument, perhaps only the bagpipes have an equal or greater link to popular representations of Scotland. Even that is questionable, as the harp, furthermore, extends its symbolic

reach to Ireland, crosses genders (Glorvina and the harp), and is arguably a much more potent symbol of resistance. Second, the presence of
Ellen as harpist disqualifies the contrastive readings which have become
so important to interpretations of national tales and which have therefore to be put temporarily on hold.

Ellen's initial impression of the city is negative. Originally, she was
going to stay with Mrs Murray, who is away. Her bachelor son, however,
who is struck by her beauty, has no qualms in letting her stay in their
home. A plea for help to an acquaintance of the Murrays is met by 'the
repulse of frozen reserve' (2:256). Eventually, she obtains a post with
the Boswell family. Ellen's dislike of Mrs Boswell is patent: after calling
her 'poor woman', she continues, 'Her uniform selfishness, her pitiful
cunning, her feeble stratagems to compass baby ends, filled me with
unconquerable contempt: – a contempt which, indeed, I scarcely strove
to repress' (3:9). This character assassination is strongly worded if not
downright vicious; it would be difficult to think of a crueller phrase
than 'to compass baby ends'. These stratagems are simply attempts
to get more money out of her husband. There seem to be no limits to
Mrs Boswell's evil: when Ellen leaves, she receives no pay; Mrs Boswell
poisons Ellen's dog in an act of revenge, then has her confined to an asylum.[4] In a palimpsest of Ellen's own experience of her mother's death,
Ellen plays the role of mother in caring for Mrs Boswell's daughter
while she is critically ill. On her recovery, Mr Boswell undiplomatically
states that the child's biological mother has forsaken her and that Ellen
has taken over her duties. So he thanks her, clasps her hand, and in an
open display of affection, kisses her on the forehead (3:58). Ellen knows
the gesture is wrong, not least because it will confirm Mrs Boswell's
suspicions that the two are having an affair. We consequently have a
situation in which none of the characters is guiltless: Ellen's venom is
uncharitable; Mrs Boswell is dominated by sexual jealousy; Mr Boswell's
kiss naturally provides his wife with the proof she needed. The greater
importance of nurture over nature is yet another example of the dys-
functional nature of Edinburgh family life. That said, we should not lose
sight of the fact that Mrs Boswell's suspicions are well founded and that
her husband is deeply attracted by Ellen, hence her reaction to what is
certainly not an innocent gesture. There is little doubt that his feelings
are reciprocated, hence the blush results from her recognition of her
own desire to return his kiss. As in her first novel, the pivotal moment
is again a deeply sexual one: just as was the case of Laura, sexual desire
determines the outcome of the plot within the admittedly 'famously
[sexually] muted' (Parrinder 2006: 31) English novel. Furthermore, in

this novel, desire is located in its traditional setting, in adultery. Again, we are thrown back to Bour's phrase that 'the body, ultimately, seems to be uncontrollable' (1997: 27), whether male or female. Edinburgh life, at this level, has no saving graces, it has no redeeming features. There is no Christian charity on display; both young bachelor and husband are predatory.

Therefore, at this point, a contrastive view of North and South is impossible, as there is simply nothing, or nothing positive, that distinguishes Edinburgh's emerging middle classes. In addition, apart from the lesser presence of aristocrats, Edinburgh does not seem all that different from the London depicted in *Self-Control*. In both places, we simply encounter that predictable combination of sex and money.

Like her London, Brunton's Edinburgh has an underside which Ellen visits, and it is precisely there that the Boswells' daughter is infected. It is unhealthy in many other ways: for example, there is no sense of community among the poor. Although such ideas are topical features of cityscapes, Brunton focuses her attention almost exclusively on one subject: the fate of Highland soldiers. Sharon Alker (2002) offers us a timely reminder that the novel is set in the time of the Clearances, mentioning specifically the Sutherland estates, but Brunton's vision corresponds more to the general plight of the Highlands than one particular instance. This marks the beginning of an educational process by which Ellen is instructed simultaneously with the reader. Gaelic, for example, changes its status and becomes mellifluous. The text is accompanied by that recurrent device of footnotes which explain lore and customs. That education begins in Edinburgh – rather than in the Highland chapters – foregrounds the fact that the city is full of displaced Highlanders, whose ruin has been brought about by a lethal combination of war and lairds. In short, the wives of Highlander soldiers are driven to poverty and have had to leave their holdings, despite their hard work and 'frugality' (2:261), a virtue that Johnstone also assigns to them; they have been stripped of their belongings. That this is not an uncommon occurrence is made clear through a bystander's words, 'Many a one has been rouped out before now' (2:262). Brunton places blame on unscrupulous lairds for the plight of the destitute; the reasons for joining a Highland regiment are not questioned at all.

Evidence accumulates that Edinburgh is a tainted metropolis, but perhaps, if a North–South axis cannot provide a pattern for her fiction, the emphasis on the inhospitable city might suggest that, following the lines of the first novel, *Discipline* is proposing an opposition between Highland and Lowland, along the lines of Scott's *Rob Roy*. That is not to imply that

Scott was conscious of Brunton's novel at that juncture, but it is clear that the Edinburgh of *Waverley* has very little – if anything – in common with Brunton's vision of a city divided between those who have and those who have not. Musgrove argues that however dangerous the city is, in exchange for 'a diminished sensibility' women receive 'the conditions that prompt their moral and spiritual growth' (2007–8: 234), yet that is possibly far too optimistic a reading of Brunton. If the city was able, to a lesser or greater extent, to empower, this would make it difficult to explain why the voluntary movement is always away from the city, whereas the compulsory movement, to London to settle the annuity, to Edinburgh to find work, is always in the opposite direction. The common argument that Scottish fiction rarely deals with the urban poor and that there is no real equivalent to the two nations debate which is so fundamental to the mid-century English novel is difficult to counter, but it can be adjusted. For Brunton, there is a two-nation Scotland in two senses: there are Highlands and Lowlands, and the Highlanders are always poor, whether they live in the town or the country.

Expectations that the Highland chapters might depict a paradisiacal location have several reasonable foundations. First, the ecstatic words and pleasurable scenes that occupy the final pages of *Self-Control*. Second, the preparatory comments in *Discipline* which are stretched over 100 pages from the introduction of the first Highlander to Ellen's arrival in the Highlands. These take the form of the footnotes and descriptions of Highland life that I have previously mentioned. Third, and as a consequence of the former, the promotion of Gaelic language and culture as positive values, following the line taken by the major male figure Maitland, who combines the roles of mentor, lover, husband and spiritual guide, so often encountered in the fiction of Jane Austen. Fourth, after squalid, featureless Edinburgh, surely nothing could be worse.

Three words of warning are required. First, as mentioned previously, although the memoir talks about the possible cancellation of the Highland part of the book, this comment is misleading. For, if it is true that the Edinburgh section occupies the best part of nine chapters, chapters 19 to 27, the Highland part occupies less than half of this: from chapter 28 to 30. In other words, the fact that the Highland chapters conclude the story has to be set against the fact that there are only three of them! In short, in terms of length Edinburgh occupies double the space. Second, the joyful welcome to the Highlands 'the land where never friend found a traitor, nor enemy a coward!' (3:198) make for fine sentiments yet they are empty ones, incompatible with the fate of the destitute soldiers in Edinburgh, suffering the consequences of their lairds' incompetence. Exploitation, if that is a more fitting term than betrayal, has been shown to be home-grown. Third, at several key points, Brunton has made reference to the fictional status of her work, for example in this comment on the inadequacy of fiction: 'How little do they know of a death-bed who have seen it only in the graceful pictures of fiction!' (3:168). Another occurs precisely in the Highland chapters when Ellen comments on the loyalty shown to the absent laird: 'It is strange! I never saw any thing like affection in servants, except in a novel!' (3:209). Such a puzzling intertextuality at such a strategic moment is certainly thought-provoking. Truth is, we assume, stranger than fiction, but as we are reading this comment in a work of fiction its veracity is inevitably questioned by that fictional location. Like Hogg's comment on the Trossachs, we are invited to doubt a Romantic or escapist portrait of the Highlands.

What are Brunton's Highlands really like? Features that strike Ellen are courtesy, familiarity among social classes, loyalty, beautiful nature, the Scotch breakfast (though she finds totemic oatcakes repellent) and other topical features. Of greater interest is that contrary to her expectations of uncovered legs and feet, children wore 'attire that was rather ludicrous than mean' (3:220). The feudal home itself has 'many elegant conveniences of modern life' (3:217). Ludicrous is a word that smacks of disparagement, yet I would uphold that Brunton's aim is to set up her Highlanders as anything but noble savages, as the emphasis on modern conveniences distances them farther from primitivism. Even though many of these features are part of the common stock of descriptions of the Highlands, Brunton intervenes to make the following point after some remarks on hospitality:

Feudal habits were extinct; and the days were long since gone, when bands of kinsmen, united in one great family, repaid hospitality and protection with more than venial veneration and love. (3:223)

Bour is right to point out that here there is 'no Romantic idealization of the Highlands' and that 'the Highlands do not embody a timeless past, but are presented as post-feudal, as having suffered from the Forty-Five' (1997: 31). In fact, we are told that one son has been exiled for 30 years and another has just died in the West Indies, a place associated with death right from the opening chapter of *Self-Control*: there is certainly little enthusiasm shown for imperial expansion. However logical, rational and straightforward this all is, it leaves with the beguiling question of what the marriage, the union at the novel's conclusion, implies.

Unlike *Waverley*, we are not provided with a postscript to start sketching out a map of symbolic national fulfilment, but we are given four paragraphs of what life has been like since marriage. We are informed that sexual desire is still alive: her husband is 'still a lover; and [...] I retain a little of the coquettish sauciness of Ellen Percy' (3:275). 'Coquettish sauciness' comprises two elements that are almost identical in meaning, therefore the arguable redundancy of one or the other term is a timely reminder that fiction does not have to limit sexual pleasure to the first year of marriage or the birth of the first child. Ellen is also a happy mother and after a few more perfunctory remarks, the novel ends with similar sentiments to those expressed at the end of *Self-Control*: Ellen concludes that the Lowland tongue is insufficient for the task of expressing her views on her changed life. If Scott presents a heavily politicized union, Brunton goes down another path: namely, the joys of family life, and all that the bourgeois respectability of Edinburgh life might have promised but never delivered. Is Brunton simply opting out of committing herself to a cause, old or new? Is this simply the highly moral union that has more to do with Edgeworth than Scott? These are all possibilities; there is an impression that Brunton is reneging on her own fictional device, as she has dedicated considerable time and effort to descriptions of Highland life, starting a long way before the novel reaches its Highland destination. Bour (1997: 31) points out that contemporary reviewers found the Highland wedding a fascinating episode.

Three possible answers present themselves, which I would position halfway between an explanation and a justification. One is that if we admit that Brunton decides in favour of the family, this in itself is not evidence that she is turning a blind eye to the political world of *Waverley*; instead, she is turning some very open eyes to the family as the one essential union which deserves to be spelled with a capital letter because it belongs to the female sphere of activity and because it is in need of a drastic overhaul. Her Highland retreat comprises many idyllic features, but it has to have them in order to accentuate the shortcomings of modern Edinburgh. Consequently, there can be no national platform for a writer like Mary Brunton without a radical change in the role the family and education play. This explains, partially or fully, why the Boswells represent everything a family should not be. Second, Ellen's remark about her sauciness indicates that desire can be contained within marriage, rather than marriage being simply for bearing children for the future. In other words, it is difficult to direct the novel towards yielding a political reading after the fashion of *Waverley*. The third possibility comes from Smith (1986), namely that 'Brunton's Highlands picture a society more familiar to historians of other cultures torn by war, in which women hold considerable political, social, and economic power, often by proxy' (54). Her Highlands correspond to the formulation of the post-conflict situation being a cultural category, in which peace does not break out; instead, the paradigms and conditions of war spill over into peacetime for a much longer period than is usually perceived (Usandizaga and Monnickendam 2007: 1–16).

Exotic locations

Self-Control contains a much-commented episode: Hargrave eventually manages to kidnap Laura – the novel's final three chapters narrate her adventures. She is taken to Canada, imprisoned and finally escapes. Mary Brunton herself expresses her views in a frank letter to Mrs Izett. The book is described as 'patch work', but, she goes on:

> The American expedition, too, – though in the author's opinion, the best written part of the book, – is more conspicuously a *patch*, than anything else which it contains. Though I do not see the outrageous improbability with which it has been charged, I confess that it does not harmonize with the sober colouring of the rest. We have all heard of a 'peacock with a fiery tail;' but my American jaunt is this same monstrous appendage tacked to a poor little grey linnet. (1819: xlviii)

Brunton is sometimes difficult to gauge. Although there is not a necessary contradiction between the patch being well written, a reference to its style rather than content, her focus on structure, to judge by the bird images, does not extend beyond patches. To change metaphors, Brunton is aware that the American chapters stick out like a sore thumb. In the second sentence, she switches from a third-person identification of the 'the author', to a more direct first-person address, after 'I do not see'. Yet, if we asked a simple question about her opinion of this episode, it would surely contain elements that contradict each other. Jane Austen, in a letter to Cassandra of 11–12 October 1813, says, 'I declare I do not know whether Laura's passage down the American River, is not the most natural, possible, every-day thing she ever does' (Le Faye 1997: 234), while in a letter to her niece Anna Lefroy of November 1814, she comments that 'my Heroine shall not merely be wafted down an American river in a boat by herself, she shall cross the Atlantic in the same way, & never stop till she reaches Gravesent' (282). In addition, Gonda (1996) points out that in a satirical 'Plan of a Novel', the need for a family to hide out in Kamschatka and the '20 narrow escapes from falling into the hands of the Anti-hero' (Austen 1926: 11) are allusions to Brunton, though it is more probable that they could be equally apt for many other works of fiction.

If the idea of Laura paddling a canoe wrecks the suspension of disbelief, then we are likely to find her struggling against the power of nature as she nears a waterfall absurd rather than tragic. Brunton, in a letter to her brother written in 1818, humorously remarks about *Discipline*, 'No fear of the falls of Niagara! Ellen is too common-place a person for such achievements' (1819: lxx). Similarly, if Hargrave's guilt after the supposed death of Laura leads him to suicide, we should not lose sight of Brunton's remarks about patches, but, more significantly, her views on fiction in general. They cannot justify an absurdity, but they certainly clarify why the absurdity is written. Quite directly, she tells Mrs Izett in a letter dated 10 April 1810 that she dislikes a recent publication – which is not identified – because it is a '"Historical Romance" – a sort of composition to which I have a strong dislike' (xxxii). This aversion has two components: first, the episode is 'as known as that of the deluge' (xxxii) which no amount of dramatizing can make interesting; second, Brunton believes that fiction detracts from history, and 'true history deprives me of all interest in fiction' (xxxii). This is a remarkable comment, given the current application of the category of historical romance to much of the fiction of the early part of the nineteenth century. Her remarks clash, for example, with the admiration for Scott that she manifested in her concern for the fate of her second novel. If we knew for certain what the term 'historical romance' meant to her, we would have a clearer answer. Is it stretching the imagination that however conscious she is of Scott's commercial success and power in the literary market, she would not approve of a story about the Forty-Five as an example of an event as known as that of the deluge? As any evidence is going to be circumstantial, I would only put forward the proposal that in this instance Brunton dislikes the historical romance in question because all fiction must have a clear moral direction; we return to the dedication to Baillie (see p. 32 above). The problematic nature of the American chapters – for Brunton at least – resides less in a question of geography and more in the question of the role of fiction. It is precisely the conflict between art and morality which makes her final publication so fascinating.

Cul-de-sac

Smith (1986) states that '[t]hrough her Calvinist heritage, Mrs. Brunton is able to make a thoroughgoing critique of the novels of her contemporaries and immediate predecessors' (53). This is evident in both the content and the form. Brunton herself states in a letter to Joanna Baillie on *Self-Control* and the character of Hargrave that 'I merely intended to shew the power of the religious principle in bestowing self-command; and to bear testimony against a maxim as immoral as indelicate, that a reformed rake makes the best husband' (1819: xlii). As stated previously, it was Richardson who warned against this. I have also argued that the way in which she turns Hargrave from an attractive proposition into a heinous criminal is heavy-handed. Smith pointedly remarks that Brunton's choice of name, Hargrave, harks back to Sir Hargrave Pollexfen from Richardson's *The History of Sir Charles Grandison* (1753). Brunton's use of several plot devices – kidnapping, imprisonment, a duel and so on – are also reminiscent of Richardson, but it is difficult to determine whether these are direct allusions to one novel or novelist or whether they are simply very common fictional devices; if that were the case, she would be casting her critical net far wider. I will argue that the question of the love-plot is her target and later her nemesis. The location of her final unfinished work is not moral Scotland but pastoral England.

Emmeline begins as if it were a pastiche of romance, decorated with the 'tinsel of the bad romantic novel' (Smith 1986: 56):

> The dews were sparkling in the summer sun, the birds sang in full chorus, the antic sports of animals testified activity and joy, and gladness seemed the nature of every living thing, when the loveliest bride that ever England saw was preparing for her nuptial hour. Affluence waited her, and to her rank belonged all the advantages of respectability, without the fetters of state. That hour was to see her united to the gallant Sir Sidney de Clifford, – a soldier high in fame, – a gentleman. (1819: 3)

Not only do we have the loveliest bride, in addition she is shortly going to marry that embodiment of romance, an officer and a gentleman, a hero of the Peninsular War; in other words, he seems to be all that Hargrave was not. Brunton goes farther: '[t]he shadow of gigantic oak and knotted elm dappled a verdure bright as a poet's dream of the lawns of Eden' (5). It is easy to believe that Brunton is lurching towards the territory of the first decade of the nineteenth century's equivalent to Barbara Cartland, nevertheless her intention is to burst this romantic bubble. For, in this case, even though this is a marriage born of love, a slippery concept in Brunton's universe, it is Emmeline's second marriage. What appears as a dream will rapidly become 'a sketch for a nightmare' (Smith 1986: 53).

If the couple are presented as perfect, it is because, save the question of the second marriage, they are the perfect couple as envisaged in historical romances, and therefore what is being called into question are the tropes that subgenre relies on. What makes *Emmeline* unusual is that the lovely, beloved heroine is not only a beautiful bride but a mother, and in marrying for love has given up her children and, to all intents and purposes, a person who seems to have been a decent husband: he gives her a substantial gift of money, £10,000, with no strings attached. However, following strictly moral lines, Emmeline deserves to suffer and be punished and should not attract sympathy.

This is illustrated during the episode when her husband, against her wishes, looks at her drawing book:

> Two infant figures were repeated in every attitude of sport and of repose. Many of them were blotted with tears. Upon some the names were written again and again, as if the very names were dear; and sometimes they were joined with a short and melancholy sentence that sued for pity or forgiveness.
>
> While De Clifford hurried over his comfortless survey, Emmeline unresisting stood by and wept. (83)

Emmeline's emotions are displaced onto her drawings, and the tears she is reluctant to weep in the presence of her husband are wept when he is not looking on. 'Comfortless survey' is certainly an evocative phrase, and Emmeline's passivity poignant, partly because the text lacks at this point those strident moral comments which interpolate Brunton's fiction in her two completed novels. The highlighting of empathy might be explained by the sense of impending doom that is present in the characters' minds right from the beginning of the story (the wedding ceremony), when we are told that Emmeline's bosom heaved not from happiness but from sadness, and when she momentarily doubts that the slightly stooping figure approaching is in fact her husband. The couple know what will eventually transpire but profess love in conventional terms, which only enforces their sense of alienation.

Gonda suggests, with *Discipline* in hand, that perhaps Brunton is less feminist a writer than Elizabeth Inchbald (1996: 202). Rather than engage in debates as to what feminist in these circumstances may or may not mean, I would stress that *Emmeline* is primarily concerned in representing episodes and attitudes rarely attempted in fiction of this period: a detailed study of the aftermath of a second marriage contracted between two mature adults. In other words, Brunton, by not using a template of youth, impetuosity and redemption is opening up a completely new field of female fiction and is arguably writing against her own beliefs, as expressed in her previous novels.

There is no doubt that the marriage will disintegrate; the interest lies in the way the subject is handled through the narration of external and internal causes. To envisage this in the form of a table, we could say that there are two characters, husband and wife, and four voices, the narrative, the interpolations (the couple's and those of outsiders), making a total of eight points of view. If this were simply a moral story, along the lines of the previous texts, then the play or friction between the variables would be minor. Bour argues that '[t]he emptiness of their life is made worse by the superficiality of their religious feeling, and their irritability increases with the length of their exclusion from social life [...] very few external circumstances are mentioned' (1997: 32). My reading will not totally concur, as while religiosity in the two completed novels and in the memoir is the key to salvation, in *Emmeline* this is not the case. It is not because religious principles are no longer the answer, but that the question requires a different set of parameters. Yet, although the novel does certainly indicate 'emptiness', religion no longer plays that crucial role it did before. In other words, Bour is possibly reading the third novel as if it were a continuation of the previous, almost monothematic novels, whereas I will argue that it is radically different, which, although it is very much a minority view, was hinted at by a few of the contemporary reviews, such as the *British Critic* (Rev. 1820: 166–74). Some moral strictures are shown to be so uncharitable that the narrative, the interpolations and the outsiders' voices do not speak in unison.

Emmeline's declaration to her husband that 'with you I cannot but be happy' (11) is made early on in the book. In the words of an innocent young thing, like the characters of the earlier novels, these words would be shown up to be ingenuous by the harshness of life that follows their declaration. But here, the couple complicitly lie to each other right from the beginning, as they know the language of romance could never faithfully express their experience. Soon after, she feels 'the deadly pangs of remorse' (17); if remorse is, as Adam Smith says, such a powerful emotion, then they presumably entered their marriage knowing that happiness would be the one thing it would never produce.

Emmeline rarely leaves their home, but her husband has a little more freedom:

> Then he would ride out without an object, or wander in his grounds till he was tired; then he would return to the society of his beautiful wife, till he was tired of that too. (55)

Boredom dominates their lives. The difference between men and women's freedom is evident on many occasions: he can attend meetings of the gentry, he can address the epitome of virtue, Mrs Villiers, and, most importantly, as we learn from the sketch in the memoir, the novel would conclude with his return to the army (Brunton 1819: lxxxvi). Mrs Villiers is pictured as she 'walked out of church, attended by her numerous and blooming family, and a train of decent domestics' (66). She is the picture of perfection; she represents everything that Emmeline has knowingly forsaken. The 'train of decent domestics' strikes an odd note, but presumably corresponds to the mother's role both as educator of her children and manager of her household. At this juncture, there can be no doubt that Emmeline's abandonment of her children – more than the marriage itself – represents the most anti-natural crime, for which she receives the severest punishment. The virtuous Mrs Villiers, it must be noted, snubs Emmeline by moving to another part of a shop to avoid contact with her (72). As Musgrove so rightly argues, '[i]n Brunton's novels, shops are less places of consumption [...] than transformative places of agency' (2007–8: 231). Here, Mrs Villiers is empowered to humiliate someone of the same sex and similar social standing. In fact, Mrs Villiers is the last of a long line of Brunton's female characters who show little sympathy to other women. It is as if the schoolgirl rivalry of the early chapters of *Discipline* extends into adulthood irrespective of whether the perpetrator is vicious, like Mrs Boswell, or virtuous, like Mrs Villiers. There is little forgiveness on display.

It is precisely the most virtuous people who make the most condemnatory remarks about Emmeline, remarks which are repeated in *Blackwood's* strong dislike for the fragment (Rev. 1819: 183–92). In the early pages of the novel, on the newly weds' arrival at the manor,

> Among all the gazers, one heart only was touched with gentler feeling towards poor Emmeline. The old curate, as he bowed his gray head to De Clifford, glanced compassionately on the bride. 'God help thee! poor thing,' thought he; – 'so young and yet so wicked! God help thee!' (27)

Similar beliefs are echoed by the virtuous Mrs Villiers near the fragment's conclusion. Her child has been ill and is cared for at the De Cliffords' manor. Mrs Villiers recognizes that her son evokes feelings of pain and lack in Emmeline:

> Mrs Villiers gazed on her with a compassion that rose even to pain. 'Lovely, miserable thing!' she thought, 'must thou, so formed to adorn virtue, charm only to disguise the deformity of vice!' (93)

A few pages on, Emmeline says to herself 'Oh De Clifford! What have I not sacrificed for you!' (95). These examples show that Emmeline is suffering tremendously and therefore the possible consequence is that empathy or even deep sympathy is aroused. The likelihood of this occurring is raised as a result of the treatment meted out to men in these situations being less draconian than that meted out to women. Furthermore, she believes that her husband will abandon her – 'What am I but his toy?' (80) – for a fuller life and a younger woman. In brief, Brunton seems to have steered herself into a cul-de-sac by illustrating the effects of a despicable act but in so doing causes her heroine to suffer so much from the consequences of desire that the reader acknowledges the depth of her pain. As a result, this leads to questioning whether the punishment – complete social ostracism and deep unhappiness – fits the crime.

The Edinburgh Monthly Review states that Brunton 'does not intend to render Emmeline and De Clifford objects even of our compassion' (Rev. 1819: 84). While it is fruitless to enter into arguments about intentionality, the journal implicitly acknowledges that something is wrong: sympathy for Emmeline could bring into question the story's moral purpose, hence the assertion that

> these characters, as delineated, never, we apprehend, did nor could exist [...] Their disposition, sensibilities, and virtues, are incompatible with their guilt, in the first place; with their abhorrent marriage, in the next; and, in the last place, with their attempt, or even wish, to mingle with honourable society, whose most sacred bonds they have daringly set at nought. (85)

The Edinburgh Monthly Review is adamant that the characters should either have appeared in fiction in which they had not committed sinful acts or else other, more obviously evil characters should have taken their place; in other words, Brunton should have written a different book. The journal is, therefore, fully conscious that the fragment might arouse its readers' sympathy and therefore cast into doubt that fundamental tenet of Edgeworth that 'a maxim is illustrated through the plot, or an episode is rounded off with a moral conclusion' (Bour 1997: 30). Again, it is not the case that the moral is not there, that abandoning one's children is a punishable offence, but that the depth of feeling in the mind of both main characters has become too prominent.

Of course, it has to be stated that Emmeline and De Clifford can never be religious in more than name, as no one who practises religion in the active way Brunton's virtuous characters do could ever contemplate Emmeline's abandonment of her children. There is a sense that the second marriage is an act of hypocrisy, when, for example, 'the words, "forsaking all other, keep thee *only* to him," seemed to her ear-marked with an almost reproachful emphasis' (13). Neither should we forget that the *égoïsme à deux* is compounded with enforced social isolation from their peers and even from the most virtuous and religious of people. It is significant that Mrs Villiers, as a mother whose child has recovered, refuses to communicate with Emmeline, as a mother grieving for the absence, and therefore total loss, of her own children. In addition, and at the risk of repetition, Brunton makes it abundantly clear that De Clifford leads an almost satisfactory life, with a minor degree of socialization, whereas as his wife, Lady De Clifford is just an outcast.

What I am proposing is that *The Edinburgh Monthly Review* intuits the existence of this cul-de-sac, which is why it goes to enormous lengths and labyrinthine arguments to convince its readers that the main characters could never have existed. However revealing this is of the reviewer's perplexity, its mere existence testifies to Brunton's bringing her fiction to an impasse within the agenda of moralizing fiction that she associates with Edgeworth and which she so earnestly practised in her first two novels. Perhaps my conclusions to this chapter will become more significant if we approach Emmeline's dilemma from the opposite angle, from a simply secular one. What *The Review* is shying away from is the possibility that readers may identify Emmeline not from the perspective of Mrs Villiers or the old curate but as a person with a tragic flaw whose downfall is the result not simply of that one weakness but also of the discriminatory treatment so often dispensed to women by both men and other women. If this is the case, then Emmeline is very close to being a woman who shares many of the virtues of heroinism, and *Emmeline*, closer to tragedy than to a moral tale. This could be phrased in another way: the comments by Mrs Villiers and the old curate no longer ring true.

After reading the memoir, it might seem odd that my principal finding is that Brunton is keenly aware of the nature of sexual desire and that her characters' fortunes will be determined by the degree of that awareness. In the cause of Laura, her inability to shake off Hargrave, whether as pursuer or as a presence until well into the novel when she enters into a more conventional relationship with Montague, demonstrates that the second relationship is a deliberate attempt to avoid the troublesome nature of her initial, powerful sexual desires. Ellen's encounter with Mr Boswell takes her perilously close to the standard locus of passion in Western art: adultery. Unlike Laura, she tells us clearly that her marriage still gives her physical satisfaction. Emmeline's fate is more complex, simply because desire is the fragment's underlying motif. Conceptually, desire enters into conflict with religiosity, but as *Emmeline* is a much more secular text, the female character has literally nothing to mitigate her depression. In her three texts, we can identify how Brunton pits desire against convention: two of her heroines overcome the problem, the third does not. This explains how Brunton has steered herself into a cul-de-sac, which the lengthy review article senses. Contrasting Emmeline's misfortune to the other heroines underscores not only Brunton's religiosity, which no reader can ever doubt, but the awareness of how desire will not always be contained by a conventional marriage or by a conventional happy ending or union.

It is customary to give an enormous importance to final or posthumous works of authors who die young or tragically. For example, it is a cliché to wonder what Burns or Keats might have gone on to write, or where Mozart's final symphony was pointing. However, this is often hagiography or speculation, as what we have on the page alone constitutes the evidence. In this case, it is a fragment which is sufficient in itself to demonstrate that Mary Brunton's final work lays bare the ideological paradoxes of the fiction she had endorsed in her two previous novels. Whether she was conscious of the fact or not is open to question, but the lengthy article in *The Edinburgh Monthly Review* indicates that it firmly believed that *Emmeline* had escaped from its author's hands and that its language and plot were in the process of taking a different tack. Or, to use another metaphor, *Emmeline* was beginning to subvert the conventions of respectability within which it supposedly should be located, and to which the straitjacket of her husband's memoir had so successfully restricted it for the best part of two centuries.

2

Susan Ferrier and the Lucre-banished Clans

Master. But Jacques, I don't observe this fondness for pets only among poor people. I know titled ladies who surround themselves with a whole pack of dogs, to say nothing of cats, parrots, and chirruping birds.

Jacques. A menagerie that makes them and all their friends look ridiculous. They don't love anybody, nobody loves them, and they throw all the feelings they don't know what else to do with to their dogs.

Marquis de Arcis. To love animals or to throw your heart to the dogs – that's a peculiar way of looking at things. (Diderot 1999: 148)

Literary persona

John Doyle, Susan Ferrier's great-nephew and editor of *The Memoir and Correspondence of Susan Ferrier* (1898), tells us in the opening sentence of the introduction that she 'lived a life so quiet and uneventful as to afford little scope for a memoir'. Although he immediately qualifies this by stating that her correspondence might be of interest to readers of her 'clever and *still* popular novels' (7), Alexander Brunton seems to have cast his shadow here. Both relatives play the role of protector while exposing the humdrum life, almost devoid of interest, of women involved in the unedifying occupation of writing fiction. If becoming Professor of Oriental Languages, in the case of Brunton, and Fellow of All Souls College, Oxford, in the case of Doyle, count as great events, then Ferrier's life might seem dull, yet Doyle's statement is difficult to judge as anything but deceptive unless we share the very strict criterion that only public office is of any merit. If that were the case, either the gender–genre division, low against high culture, becomes irrefutable or else Scott's life, and his dedication to literature rather than the law, would also rank him among the nondescript.

It is conceivable that Doyle is just using a formulaic phrase: Ferrier's time spent in Inveraray, her literary success, her acquaintance with the Scotts, among other things, do make for a memoir, and it is precisely Doyle himself who weaves it together: the first and final fifth chapter deal with her youth and old age, and the three central chapters are so closely linked to her fiction that they are structured around the events leading up to the publication of *Marriage* (1818), *The Inheritance* (1824) and *Destiny* (1831). Again, Doyle's denigration of fiction strikes a discordant note in that it is predictable at the beginning of the century but rather peculiar for 1898 – Knut Hamsun, Joseph Conrad, Leo Tolstoy are all active at this time – yet it is tempered by his insistence on the fact that she wrote 'popular novels'. Nevertheless, it would be ingenuous to suggest that Doyle is assuming a distinction between high and low art, as he would presumably also look down on Scott as someone whose anonymity as a novelist locates him within the authorship conventions of 'by a Lady'.

Whatever the truth of the matter, it is undeniable that Doyle's opening words are representative of what I would call that 'retiring spinster syndrome' which has determined the reception of her fiction. However, as I will propose a rather different Ferrier, it is necessary to consider the biographical evidence which has produced this. My point of departure is that it is based on certain contradictions; to begin with, the retiring spinster lived life right at the heart of Edinburgh, which shares little in common with the cultural desert portrayed in Brunton's second novel. Her elder sister Jane was the muse in 'On the Death of John Hunter Blair' and the same 1787 edition of Robert Burns's verse contains the poem 'To Miss Ferrier' with its jocular praise, 'Jove's tunefu' Dochters three times three / Made Homer deep their debtor; / But gien the body half an e'e, / Nine FERRIERS wad done better.' One of her brothers married into the Wilson household, which, in part, may account for a lengthy review of *Marriage* in *Blackwood's* soon after its publication. A second appearance in *Blackwood's* occurred in 1831 in 'Noctes Ambrosianae'; North comments that 'Miss Ferrier appears habitually in the light of a hard satirist' who has a very specific agenda:

> Sir Walter Scott had fixed the enamel of genius over the last fitful gleams of their half savage chivalry; but a humbler and sadder scene – the age

of lucre-banished clans – of chieftains dwindled into imitation-squires
[...] the euthanasia of kilted aldermen and steam-boat *pibrochs* was
reserved for Miss Ferrier. (533)

Ferrier's father was law agent to the Duke of Argyll, and she spent long
periods at Inveraray. If it really is from her stay here that she took her
portraits of incompetent aristocrats, this leads to various, rather reiter-
ated interpretations: either we censure her because 'her earliest work
was disfigured by direct and unsparing portraitures of living people
among her acquaintance' (Douglas 1897: 112), or else we claim that her
work was not disfigured at all; instead, we enjoy it, '[r]eaders were in
such gales of laughter over the book that its rambling plot was scarcely
noted' (Grant 1957: 100). In either case, the basis for disapproval of
approbation rests, in this particular instance, on the closeness of her
characters to real-life equivalents. Furthermore, even though Inveraray
might now still be accessible only by the narrowest of the roads, its
geographical marginality has to be contrasted to its centrality to court
life. The Duke's eldest daughter 'was at one time backed to marry the
Prince Regent' (Fletcher 1989: 63); in the end, '[s]he eloped with the
impecunious Henry Clavering, who, in early 1809, became involved in
the Mary Anne Clarke affair, one of those recurrent meteoric sex scan-
dals in which the British public delights' (63–4). If we wanted to argue
that Susan Ferrier was a correspondent for *Hello!* or *OK* who used inside
information from her contacts with the aristocracy as a basis for scurril-
ous satires of the well-to-do, evidence is certainly not hard to find.

The chief culprit for portraying the submissive female writer is Ferrier
herself; in a letter which Doyle states was probably addressed to Lady
Charlotte Bury, dated winter 1829, she reflects:

My chief happiness is enjoying the privilege of seeing a good deal of
the Great Unknown, Sir Walter Scott. He is so kind and condescend-
ing that he deigns to let me and my *trash* take shelter under the protection of his mighty branches, and I have the gratification of being
often in that great and good man's society. (Doyle 1898: 245)

If we wanted to find confirmation of Scott's domination of the literary
scene from the mouth of a successful contemporary novelist, it would
be hard to find a more explicit example than this, built on the metaphor
of the mighty regal tree of knowledge contrasted to a straightforward,
unequivocal, description of her own work which is simply, in marked
contrast, (italicized) trash, and therefore only fit for pulping. Bearing in

mind that this is winter 1829, Ferrier can only be referring to *Destiny*, if this is a reference to something that was to be published. It seems that Ferrier has confirmed her great-nephew's opening sentiment. The only possible counterarguments would be that either she is being ironic or that the self-effacement here does not correspond to the pattern of the rest of the material that describes their relationship.

This is undeniably the case. It is interesting to note that the next letter in her collected correspondence is from Anne Scott, who comments that 'Papa was *so delighted with* "Destiny," – *really and truly so.* I need not say what I thought of it! My dear Miss Ferrier, I wish so much papa would review it in the "Quarterly," or Lockhart' (248). This fully illustrates the incestuous relationship between novelists and reviewers as well as suggesting that the admiration that Scott had for Susan Ferrier was genuine and reciprocal rather than being based on subservience. Neither in Scott's journal nor in his biography is there any suggestion of anything other than mutual respect and warmth. For example, his journal entry for 19 January 1827 comments on the death of her father, nicknamed Uncle Adam because of his longevity; Scott refers to her as 'his accomplished daughter' (1891: 342). The entry for 12 May 1831 simply states:

> Miss Ferrier comes out us. This gifted personage, besides having great talents, has conversation the least *exigeante* of any author, female least, who I have ever seen among the long list I have encountered, – simple, full of humour, and exceedingly read at repartee; and all this without the least affectation of the blue stocking. (820)

In the light of his knowledge of her humour and repartee, we can perhaps read her self-effacing use of 'trash' as self-deprecatory. In addition, chapter 23 of the third volume of *Marriage* contains one of the most extraordinary spoofs of the bluestockings in which Byron's and Scott's literary personae play a prominent part. This lampoon, it could be argued, shows little or no respect for the Great Unknown. It is also revealing to read Scott's own description of Ferrier alongside Lockhart's description of the same visit:

> his [Scott's] daughters had invited his friend the authoress of *Marriage* to come out to Abbotsford; and her coming was serviceable. For she knew and loved him well, and she had seen enough of affliction akin to his, to be well skilled in dealing with it. She could not be an hour in his company without observing what filled his children with more

sorrow than all the rest of the case. He would begin a story as gaily as ever, and go on, in spite of the hesitation of his speech, to tell it with picturesque effect – but before he reached the point, it would seem as if some internal spring had given way – he paused and gazed around with the blank anxiety of look that a blind man has when he dropped his staff. Unthinking friends sometimes pained him sadly by giving him the catch-word abruptly. I noticed the delicacy of Miss Ferrier on such occasions. Her sight was bad, and she took care not to use her glasses when he was speaking; and she affected to be also troubled with deafness, and would say – 'Well, I am getting as dull as a post; I have not heard a word since you said so and so' – and being sure to mention a circumstance behind that at which he had already halted. He then took up the thread with his habitual smile of courtesy – as if forgetting his case entirely in the consideration of the lady's infirmity. (5:331)

As we live in a society naturally concerned with ageing and dementia, it is easy to identify the cohabitation of pathos and humour in this almost theatrical piece. We know that Scott was struggling with *Count Robert of Paris* at this time, a circumstance which contributes to making this scene one of the most moving in the biography, doubly moving by the knowledge of Ferrier's own malady. But here, even though both people are old and infirm, it is Ferrier, rather than Scott, who is in control and is thus able to hoodwink, in a graceful way, the tree she shelters under. A year previously, an ophthalmologist in London had confirmed that there was no cure for her failing eyesight, which, as Kathryn Kirkpatrick explains in the introduction to *Marriage*, is the reason why no novel followed *Destiny*. She continues, '[t]he fact was so well known to her last publisher, Richard Bentley, that in 1850 he suggested a personal secretary and scribe as "literary aid" to lighten her "labours in the more mechanical part"' (xxii). In conclusion, there is simply no evidence to support the retiring spinster syndrome, but plenty more to suggest the opposite, that despite her illness, rather than retire to her drawing-room, Ferrier got out and about.

The critic George Saintsbury is probably best remembered for his *History of English Prose Rhythm* (1912) which Joyce used as the basis for the 'Oxen in the Sun' section of *Ulysses*. His other influential works include *A History of Criticism and Literary Taste in Europe from the Earliest Texts to the Present Day* (1900–4) and *A History of English Prosody from the Twelfth Century to the Present Day* (1906–10). Saintsbury also wrote an introductory essay on Ferrier which accompanies the 1882 Bentley edition of her three novels; it also can be found in *The Collected Essays and Papers of George Saintsbury 1875–1920*. He rates Ferrier very highly, laying down many of the accepted views of her fiction. He highlights the power of her humour; for example, of *Marriage*, he is complementary about the 'capital' (1923: 314) figure of the Rev. Redgill and praises Lady MacLaughlan as 'one of the strongest and most original characters who had yet found a home in English fiction. Her defects are two only, that she is admitted to be very nearly a photograph from the life, and that, like too many of the characters of *Marriage*, she has but very little to do with the story' (309). Critical response is based on a limited number of parameters: laughter, real-life characters and no plot. That said, even though two defects stand against one virtue, we should not lose sight of Saintsbury's agenda. He is not analysing Ferrier as part of the history of the Scottish novel but as an integral part of a much wider field, 'English fiction'. Saintsbury also believes that *The Inheritance* 'deserves a great deal of praise' (320); *Destiny*, he argues, has a much better structure than either of its predecessors.

Although there is no simple answer as to why Ferrier cannot find her true home in English fiction, Saintsbury is trying both to stake a claim for her and to explain why others have not been able to do so convincingly. This leads him to a very deft description of why her humour is unsatisfactory, as initially it would seem odd that a writer who is humorous and skilful is homeless. Saintsbury's explanation stems from a comparison with the writer whose house has the strongest foundations in English fiction, Jane Austen:

> On the other hand, it is interesting enough to conceive what Miss Ferrier would have made of Lady Catherine, of Mr Collins, of the Meryton vulgarities. The satire would be as sharp, but it would be rougher, the instrument would be rather a saw than a razor, and the executioner would linger over her task with a certain affectionate forgetfulness that she had other things to do than to vivisect. (327)

The two metaphors for satire, the razor and the saw, are certainly explicit enough, as are their implications. Ferrier's style is devoid of subtlety; in the end, her satire lacks polish, which in turn diminishes its effectiveness. The image of Ferrier eagerly sawing away in a state of forgetfulness predicts his final conclusions that of the four requirements for a novelist – plot, character, description and dialogue – Ferrier is only weak in the first department.

Due to Austen's current undisputed canonical status and Ferrier's very low standing, it is perhaps curious to see how Saintsbury talks about them as novelists who are more or less on the same level, distinguished by the style of their humour as well as by the former's ability to construct plot and the latter's inability or unwillingness to do so, except at certain points of *Destiny*. Saintsbury's analysis shows two things: first, the slings and arrows of literary fortunes, and second, a geographical design for English fiction which he uses in this essay and which is developed at greater length by his near contemporary, Margaret Oliphant.

In the third volume of Oliphant's *The Literary History of England in the End of the Eighteenth and Beginning of the Nineteenth Century*, published in the same year as the Bentley edition of the Ferrier novels, she writes extensively on Edgeworth, Austen and Ferrier. Oliphant starts with a reflection:

> There is a curious symbolism in the names which stand at head of this page – three women representing with great fitness the three countries that form Great Britain, all writing the same language, and embodying to a great extent the same ideal, yet revealing each the characteristics of her race in a manner as amusing as instructive. (3:202)

What the three inhabitants – Austen, Edgeworth and Ferrier – of the house share is their interest in the life of relatively ordinary people whose lives are 'disturbed by no volcanic events' (3:205), as would occur to characters enmeshed in a historical novel. This might express disapproval of certain facets of the historical romance, similar to those expressed by Mary Brunton and analysed in the previous chapter, but volcanoes do not necessarily refer to cataclysmic public events; cataclysmic passion could also form part of the excluded topics. What exactly is Oliphant implying in the oblique phrase 'a curious symbolism'? Why 'curious'? Obviously the three novelists write in the same language, follow a certain allegiance to the 'instructive' mode, but it is difficult to know how important the question of 'race' is, except that, on Oliphant's scale, it lies far below language and didacticism. In fact, 'race' serves, it would seem, only to highlight the relevance of the other two variables: language and didacticism. As a result, the situation she presents us with is the desire to discuss the merits of her three representative authors whose origin is of some importance, but not as crucial as the word 'race' would suggest to us today in our postcolonial world.

Oliphant, like Saintsbury, emphasizes Ferrier's humour: '[i]t is not generally supposed that mirth is characteristic of Scotland, but certainly there is more laughter to be got out of Miss Ferrier's three books than out of the voluminous series produced by Miss Edgeworth. It is on this ground that she is strong' (3:238). It is immediately evident that Oliphant moves between comment on the individual authors and their 'race'. This remark about the dour Scot is hardly original, but it serves as yet another example of a critical commonplace, whilst it shows Oliphant distancing herself from Edgeworth and 'the voluminous series', a position also taken by Ferrier herself, in such comments as to be found in a letter to Charlotte Clavering, 'Have you read Edg[e]worth's "Fashionable Tales"? I like the two first, but none of the others' (Doyle 1898: 65). Her acerbic comments filter into a much stronger dismissal of Edgeworth's *Patronage* for being 'the greatest lump of cold lead I ever attempted to swallow' (Bury 1908: 2:176). Oliphant takes great pains to pinpoint that Ferrier does have a specific field of interest that distinguishes her from Scott:

> Sir Walter depicted the last chapter of real power and greatness, the tragic and splendid ending of the reign of Highland chiefs and devotion of clans, it was Miss Ferrier's part to show the more melancholy downfall, the contempt of the modern world for what had become a mere romantic fiction, and breaking up of all reality in the obsolete position itself. There is some truth in the criticism as applied to *Destiny*. It is the reverse of that more dignified conclusion which made an end of the race of Vich Ian Vohr. (3:244)

Oliphant is staking a major claim for Ferrier's fiction along the lines articulated in 'Noctes Ambrosianae': she is the chronicler of the day after. She is making a fundamental distinction between the two novelists' timescale and hence subject matter: Scott depicting the end of the chiefs, and Ferrier the bleak aftermath. If the distinction is not immediately clear, it is worth reminding ourselves that the 'last chapter', the dramatic fall, is the subject of the epic, whereas the mundane events of everyday life, when chieftains are no longer chieftains, is not. Ferrier, according to Oliphant, has chosen a distinctly unromantic world as her subject. Oliphant goes much farther than simply pointing out that each novelist has a separate agenda: she stresses that it is precisely modernity that has transformed history into 'a mere romantic fiction'. As such, that is a generalization about nineteenth-century fiction, but it is difficult not to reach the conclusion that if there is one literary document that has contributed to this situation it must surely be the postscript to *Waverley*; if there has been one event responsible for this happening, it must be the king's jaunt, and therefore if there is one person 'almost single-handedly responsible for the modern mythology of the Highlands' (Buzard 2005: 41), it must be Scott himself. Oliphant is inscrutable in this particular part of her study, but has praised Ferrier over Scott in her depiction of 'the commonplace of Scottish gentry' (3:239). The second volume's lengthy analysis of Scott likewise criticizes certain aspects of his fiction but is on the whole deeply favourable; it includes a refutation of Carlyle's thesis that Scott was a genius *in extenso*. Ferrier is also compared to Austen; for example, 'there are points in which Miss Ferrier is almost superior to Miss Austen, having a touch more tender and a deeper poetic insight' (3:247). At this point, Oliphant returns to questions of race: 'Jane Austen was lost in the mediocrity of that featureless English life in which the good people, with a proper pride, hold themselves aloof from all doubtful classes' (3:248).

The detailed analysis carried out by Saintsbury and Oliphant in itself demonstrates that both considered Ferrier to be a writer of some stature. I use the word 'some' in a conceivably vague fashion, in preference to contradictory terms as a major minor writer or a secondary writer of importance, labels attached to Oliphant herself. Both critics share a vision of the three female authors which is light years away from our contemporary views. Not only do Austen and Edgeworth seem now to belong to another galaxy, but few if any scholars would propose that in certain aspects Ferrier has the edge. Rather than put forward impressionistic claims about the relative value of Ferrier over her contemporaries, I am affirming two things. First, Ferrier was once considered an important writer both within and outside Scotland, which has not been the case since, I would argue, 1898. Second, both critics share a belief in the uniqueness of her humour. Oliphant states that her connections with Scott should not be reduced to homage or replication; on the contrary, Oliphant shows a critical stance towards romanticizing Scottish history and turns her attention towards the unsavoury aspects of life that Scott, in her view, ignores. I would also propose that one of the consequences of the comparison with Jane Austen is to reinforce, perhaps unwittingly, the image that successful female writers live in seclusion. In sum, Doyle's picture of a dull life and insignificant fiction is a completely false one.

Heroinism

Given the emphasis on Ferrier's humour and her lack of ability or willingness to create a sustained plot, it might seem risky to attempt to argue that Ferrier could or wanted to create female characters with sufficient interest for them to be considered beyond the limits of types, humours or caricatures. However, picking up on Saintsbury's remark that *Destiny* represents an improvement of structure over the earlier two works, I will put forward the idea that it reveals a more committed Ferrier than the generally recognized one, but in order for that to be a sustainable argument, several claims have to be staked. The first concerns the opening chapter of *Marriage*; the second would be the limited nature of the critical terms associated with Ferrier, and the third would be the nature of comedy itself.

The chapter in question represents one of the most dramatically effective openings in fiction. We jump *in medias res* into the travails of a young lady. There is no preliminary description of the background or circumstances at all; the novel opens with the Earl of Courtland's threatening words to his 17-year-old daughter, Juliana, 'Come hither, child' (1), as he summons her to his study to talk of marriage. Many of the Ferrier motifs are present; vanity, lapdogs with daft names, wit, irony in company with the use of free indirect style. Vanity is present in both the narrowness of Juliana's outlook on life: dogs, clothes, fashion, love and so on, and, more subtly, in the father's belief that his words carry unquestionable patriarchal authority. He tells Juliana that '[s]he shall marry for the purpose for which matrimony was ordained amongst people of birth – that is, for the aggrandisement of her family, the extending of their political influence – for becoming, in short, the depository of their mutual interest' (2). The mercenary reasons for marriage are heavily underlined in that closing phrase – 'the depository of their mutual interest' – which looks as if it were taken from a bank leaflet. Marriage for love, the Earl insists, is 'confined to the *canaille* [...] for ploughmen and dairy-maids' (4). Humour is present when Juliana informs her father that she objects to his – very rich – proposed future husband because 'he's red-haired and squints, and he's as old as you' (3). Irony, or perhaps some attempt at psychology, is present when Juliana is initially seduced more by the gifts of the rich suitor than by the promises of the poorer one. The father foolishly believes that his word is final, whereas the truth is that he interprets her initial reluctance in that way, mistakenly equating the thunderous sound of his voice with absolute power over his chattel. However, in the end, elopement is chosen, followed by life in the Highlands. In a wonderful example of free indirect style, which corresponds to an ironic glance at Scotland-in-romance, Juliana 'had heard the Duchess of M. declare nothing could be so delightful as the style of living in Scotland: the people were so frank and gay, and the manners so easy and engaging: Oh! it was delightful!'

(6). As we find out, in a novel which, as can be appreciated from this description, shows a keen awareness of social class, there are many different styles of living in Scotland. However, what also deserves notice is Ferrier's comment that the couple therefore 'bade a hasty adieu to the now fading beauties of Windermere' (7). They are fading simply because of the short-sightedness of the viewers; in other words, we are made aware that for Juliana the interest in Scotland derives primarily from its top ranking in the list of fashionable places to be: it has now overtaken the Lake District; Wordsworthian sites will be replaced by Scottish ones.

I have talked about this chapter in some detail for three reasons. The first is that such an intense, suggestive chapter seemingly bodes well for a novel. We have the dominant female relationships: father/daughter, daughter/lover, played out in a limited and therefore manageable scenario. However, Ferrier does not write for long in this way; *Marriage*, after its opening chapters, spreads out into a novel about many marriages and many relationships. This does not necessarily mean, as many critics have stated, that the fiction is flawed for its episodic nature, as one device which Ferrier uses, and which I believe has not yet been more than tangentially discussed, is that of repetition, be it of motifs or situations. These echoes usually occur within the same book but sometimes across them. Juliana will repeat the gist of her own father's words to her own daughter, 'I am determined to have no disgraceful love-marriages in the family' (347) without realizing it. The book opens with an elopement, and the third volume will narrate one towards the end. *Marriage* describes the experiences not only of Juliana's two daughters but the experiences of their relatives and friends down two generations; the episodes are therefore connected, or at least the attempt has been made to do so. There is, I would suggest, a clear intent to reveal that each generation faces similar problems but not necessarily with any more success than its predecessor. Both Mary Cullinan (47) and Anne Mellor (50) are conscious of this. Juliana's trip to Scotland is paralleled by Lady Elizabeth and Florinda's in *Destiny*; just as Juliana has Venus, Plato and Cupid, Lady Elizabeth also has three lapdogs. Whether this repetition represents a lackadaisical approach to previously used material or is something more sophisticated and therefore closer to a palimpsest is arguable; I incline more towards the palimpsest. As the novel's title suggests, the parallels primarily concern the way that courtship and marriage are played out in different places and in different circumstances. Juliet Shields's heavily political reading of national tales puts forward a very convincing case: 'its multiple marriages refract the Anglo-Scottish

Union in various distorted forms – those made to further the parties' political and economic interests, those made in the heat of passion, and those founded in rational affection' (2010: 130).

One consequence of this dynamic opening chapter, in with a bang rather than a whimper, is that the rest of the novel, or if that is not an exaggeration, certainly the second and third volumes, do not live up to the expectations the first chapter creates. A lengthy article in the *Scottish Review* (Rev. 1899) epitomizes this belief. In short, the opening scene is a difficult act to follow. This second reason is compounded by a third one: both Juliana's fate and Ferrier's critical status are largely determined by the opening chapter of *Marriage*. Likewise, as I shall illustrate in a moment, most of the interpretations of Ferrier are heavily influenced by the extent to which the text in question successfully or unsuccessfully matches the impact of this opening chapter: most critics have seen subsequent writing as inferior. This has far-reaching consequences, as it pigeonholes Ferrier as a patently flawed comic writer. The so-called failures therefore indicate that the text in question does not live up to the intense comedy of the opening chapter of *Marriage*, a presupposition that such comedy was Ferrier's exclusive interest. As I shall try to argue, heroinism was central to her fictional world.

Ferrier's critics tend to repeat themselves by going over three basic ideas: realism, cruelty and religiosity. William Blackwood wrote that 'any one who has ever associated with the English of a certain class will at once recognise in Dr. Redgill the living portrait of hundreds, though never hit off so well' (Doyle 1898: 139). The *Edinburgh Review* mentions her 'power of literal delineation' (Rev. 1842: 500). Saintsbury says that one of the characters from *Marriage* is 'very nearly a photograph' (1923: 309). Such comments point to certain limitations, suggesting that she cannot create; she can only be a recorder. Perhaps it is more unexpected to find many remarks about her cruelty. This begins in 'Noctes Ambrosianae' when North suggests, rather patronizingly, that she is a 'hard satirist; but there is always a fund of romance at the bottom of every true woman's heart' (1831: 533). Saintsbury not only transforms her pen into a saw, but extends his metaphors of aggression when he tells us that she occasionally 'lets her acid bite a little too deeply' and that 'the sharp strokes which Miss Ferrier constantly dealt to the vices and follies of society – strokes sharper perhaps than other lady novelist has cared or know how to aim' (1923: 324). She certainly has a large arsenal! John Millar also called her 'cruel' (1903: 544). Moving closer to the present day, Cullinan stresses that the predominant voice in *Marriage* is 'rather cruel and wickedly funny' (1984: 56). In a telling contrast to Lockhart's *Peter's Letters to His Kinsfolk*, she argues that '[h]er depiction of Mrs. Bluemits's literary circle is even more critical than Lockhart's comments. Her satire allows for no middle course: these women are all absurd and vulgar' (23). A final example is provided by Alice Meynell (1905), who places derision at the heart of Ferrier's comic effects. That said, it is important to fully comprehend how far Ferrier's characters can go, reaching almost surreal degrees of political incorrectness, as in this example, a comment by Miss Pratt in *The Inheritance*: 'Poor Miss Mary! What a pretty creature she was once; and as merry as a grig; but she has taken rather a religious turn now; – to be sure, when people have not the use of their legs, what can they do?' (1:117). And so on. These comments have to be contrasted with those which emphasize her religiosity, which are simply so numerous that there is little point in highlighting one rather than another. Ferrier is therefore a writer who seemingly punishes more frequently than she pardons, or, as Francis Russell Hart puts it, she is 'severely religious' (1978b: 57). This is not the only account of Ferrier as a paradox, but I believe that the paradox, if it is such, has another explanation.

These critiques extend the remarks I was making two paragraphs back, namely, there is a certain reluctance to allow Ferrier to move outside a very narrow set of parameters. She apes her contemporaries, but when she tries to become moral, she flops. Talking about *The Inheritance*, Saintsbury claims that 'there is a considerable fall off in *verve* and spontaneity' (1923: 321). This common belief is echoed by Herbert Foltinek, himself an editor of *Marriage*, who says in similar fashion that '[t]he other two novels have long ceased to appeal' (1985: 131). These statements, however valid we judge them to be, all obey the same logic: the magic of *Marriage*, and particularly the first volume, is lost and replaced by something far less interesting. This mindset prevents any consideration of her work which deviates from this path and, necessarily, excludes the possibility of looking at her later work on its own terms rather than as a dissatisfactory continuation of an earlier comedy.

Such views presuppose a notion of comedy which is incomplete. Let us pick up on Oliver Elton's remark (1912: 1:367) that Ferrier follows the tradition of Jonson and Molière, that is to say, comedy can be serious and moral. I would extend this to a more ambitious level, namely that of Shakespeare's problem plays, such as *Measure for Measure*. A comedy is classically a struggle between old age and authority pitted against youth and rebellion, which is both generally humorous and always ends in marriage. This would seem initially to be close to the pattern of Ferrier's fiction, right from the opening chapter of *Marriage*. However, although

Shakespeare's problem plays end in marriage, the shadow of cruelty and hardship darkens or questions the conclusion. A fine example is that sexually charged comedy in which a novice nun is given the choice of sparing her brother's life by surrendering her virginity to the figure of authority, or keeping to her principles and consequently watch her brother die. We should note two points: first that the play does end in marriage, and second, that the play is humorous, replete with scabrous sexual puns, notably in its second scene, set in Mistress Overdone's London brothel. Carnivalesque bawdiness is not to be found in Ferrier, but the darkness that covers the final scene is definitely there. If a tragedy, through its cathartic power, suggests a new life, renewal and the future, a problem play suggests something rather different, namely by forcing a return to reality through marriage; life goes on, however terrible it may turn out to be. In *Measure for Measure*, the concluding marriage scene is such a terrifying enactment of power that, despite being conducive to marriage, it is certainly not conducive to happiness. Therein lies the problem: a comedy can be far more sinister than a tragedy. Something of this realization and something of this pattern is evident, I propose, particularly in *Destiny*. Once we shake off, if only temporarily, remarks about her comic arsenal and her religiosity, replacing them with ideas closer to those of the problem plays, a more challenging Ferrier emerges.

The novels' titles themselves provide a slight indication of change. The first two novels refer to two closely linked material phenomena which, following Courtland's ethics, are vehicles for consolidating the wealth of the aristocracy. *Destiny: or, the Chief's Daughter* starts with an abstraction before proceeding to highlight the person the novel focuses on. If not immediately apparent, as the novel progresses, the heroine's main objective is to try and establish an identity which is her own rather than one which reifies her as the chief's property, an attitude displayed by many of the characters. Below the title on the title-page is a Shakespearean quotation, 'What's in a name?', which refers to the traditions of family and honour that the novel will go on to describe and criticize. These words come from the most romantic part of Shakespeare's most romantic play: the balcony scene of *Romeo and Juliet*. Furthermore, in the opening exchange between the lovers the word itself is used six times to separate name from allegiance. Juliet asks Romeo to refute his name; he tells her his name is hateful to himself, and so on. Juliet's exact words are: 'What's in a name? That which we call a rose / By any other name would smell as sweet' (2.2.41–2). What have star-crossed lovers to do with lucre-banished clans? Two points suggest themselves – the clan system with its attendant rivalry, and the subservience of the individual to the clan; Juliet is, from this point of view, another chief's daughter. Juliet's belief that names can be doffed – her own term – is completely mistaken, hence the tragedy. Nothing so dramatic will happen here, as this is a romance not a tragedy, but the heroine's name also deserves attention. The etymology of Edith comprises two ideas: the first is riches, blessedness and prosperity, the second, war. This is an odd combination outside the world of pirates and mercenaries.

The radical change in Ferrier's approach to fiction is patent in the opening chapter; instead of the humour and parody of the first two novels, we are given a curt, hyperbolic generalization: 'All the world knows that there is nothing on earth to be compared to Highland Chief.' The opening chapters are marked by two formal devices. One is the use of lists; the second sentence reads:

> He has his loch and his islands, his mountains and his castle, his piper and his tartan, his forest and his deer, his thousands of acres of untrodden heath, and his tens of thousand of black-faced sheep, and his bands of bonneted clansmen, with claymores and Gaelic, and hot blood, and dirks. (1831: 1:3)

Another example is the laird's vision of religion:

> He had a vague, confused apprehension, that an Evangelical pastor was a sort of compound of a Popish priest, a stiff-necked Presbyterian, a sour-faced Covenanter, a lank-haired Seceder, a meddling Jesuit, a foul-tongued John Knox, a what-not, that had evil in its composition. (1:44)

Such harsh judgements highlight the chief's ignorance through displaying a whole list of prejudices located in representations of Scottish religious life; in other words, we would not have to open too many books to find 'a sour faced-Covenanter' or 'a foul-tongued John Knox'. But what exactly is the point of this almost postmodern collage? It draws attention to the items themselves. Nature might be glorious, but what purpose do thousands of acres of untrodden heath serve? Very little, would be the point. What do tens of thousands of black-faced sheep signify? Possibly prosperity, but more to the point they indicate the effect of the Clearances. So, to use a much abused turn of phrase, these lists certainly deconstruct their head-words, in this instance questioning the chief's outdated view of his magnificence and his world-view of religion.

As seen above, alliteration is used widely; a good example is provided by this description of the chief as 'proud, prejudiced, and profuse; he piqued himself upon the antiquity of his family' (1:5). Ferrier is attempting to describe the chief in some depth: we are also informed of his good looks and his generosity. Even the hanger-on, Benbowie, is subjected to similar analysis. Whether we find these changes in style successful or not is basically a matter of interpretation; even so, it is important to note the marked difference between the Ferrier of verve (*Marriage*) and the Ferrier of seriousness (*Destiny*).

No better example is provided than by this morose description of Edith's birth:

> At the end of two years a daughter was born, but far otherwise was her birth commemorated. A lifeless mother, – a widowed father – a funeral procession – tears, regrets, lamentations, and woe – these were the symbols that marked her entrance into life, and cast a gloom upon her infant days. The child was christened Edith, after its mother. And so ended Glenroy's first attempt at connubial happiness. (1:7)

Again, a list is used to form an impression, in this instance of relentless suffering. The many symbols of death have no antidote as new life brings no happiness, and no prospect of renewal is visible on the most distant horizon. It would be difficult to find a more depressing sentence than the final one, where the everyday 'And' belies its function as a conjunction to place an end – or at least a break – in the chain of sadness depicted by the definitely unfunny Ferrier. I would propose the melancholy of these lines is enhanced by the absence of that second feature of her style which supposedly wrecks her comic side: her religiosity. In this wasteland, there is no indication of redemption or solace, a fact doubly surprising in a writer who gives such importance to birth and motherhood, as we shall soon see.

However convincing this line of discussion might be, it has not cleared one obstacle in Ferrier's path, namely that after dynamic openings her fiction rambles about. To what extent this dropping-off occurs or not depends, to a great degree, on how she develops heroinism in Edith. I will concentrate on two of the recurrent themes: the father/daughter relationship and the love-plot.

Brunton drew two frank pictures of paternal failure, but such a project would initially seem to be unlikely in *Destiny* if it is sketchy, structurally weak like *Marriage*, or if we accept Cullinan's hypothesis that '[m]ales do not feature prominently in Ferrier's fiction except in mandatory roles of lover (good or bad) or father-figure (usually negligent). They are there specifically either to help the heroine or to impede her progress toward happiness' (1984: 51). This does need some modification, for surely if they either help or impede, they are arguably important. Whether their low profile is a question of degree is an open one, but in *Destiny* males certainly do feature prominently. In fact they are a seedy lot: nasty, hypocritical, mean and misogynous, as the following incident illustrates. During an extended visit, in which social obligations have led to boredom, the saintly Mrs Malcolm suggests that a game of goose would be a suitable way of passing the time:

> 'Most men find it enough to have played the fool with a wife, without having to play the goose with her next,' said Inch Orran, with one of his bitter smiles.
>
> A burst of laughter from the unmarried part of the company testified their approbation of this sentiment. (1:175)

Inch Orran is particularly vile, a possible forerunner to Uncle Ebenezer in Stevenson's *Kidnapped*. It is noticeable that the bachelors found his words funny; we do not know the reaction of the married section. To a certain extent, his remark is a reflection on his own experience of his wife being a shopaholic, an idea reinforced by his riposte to the remark that he is being too harsh: 'A man may learn a useful lesson even from a goose, sir, if he can take the hint in time' (1:175). This is ample proof of his nastiness, yet it is uncertain whether it implies that he or other husbands find out in time or not. Whatever the case, he has purposefully brought about the public humiliation of his wife.

The Chief's Daughter is a title which highlights parentage but also property: Edith is his daughter, to be disposed of at will. After the death of her brother, the estate will pass on to her cousin Reginald; everyone believes they will marry. Endogamy, marriage within the same social group, is a common polemic in fiction of this time, when it looks back to *Pamela* as its major *mise en scène*. However, if Ferrier shares similar concerns, the proposed marriage demonstrates not solely thematic affinity but also reveals a much closer-knit social group: this is not simply a matter of social class but the in-breeding of a dying caste, the lucre-banished clans. It would be stretching the point to say that the fact this marriage does not take place is evidence of Ferrier's disapproval of their narrow interests, but the suspicion certainly remains.

Glenroy treats his daughter as both a servant and a burden. The fact that her birth was not commemorated, as we saw, is a result of her mother's death, but is also the consequence of the new arrival being female. Gender is heavily marked by education. For the boys the chief is willing to pay 'an Englishman, a first-rate scholar, a man of elegant, refined manners, fond of study' (1:36). Edith attends their classes to learn 'the solid branches of education' whilst a female, 'the fag-end'[1] of his clan (1:37), will teach her the feminine skills. The main advantage of employing Molly Macauley is that 'she costs nothing' (1:41). In other words, her education is provided at no extra cost. However, in the end Macauley's home-grown values, 'a good, stout, sound, warm heart [...] a compound of the simplest articles of belief' (1:38) and her knowledge of Scottish songs will turn out a more humane product, in short, the heroine.

The chief's treatment of his daughter is best illustrated by his obsession that Edith marry Reginald, though this is never going to be a marriage between equals, as for the chief, Edith as a daughter, as kin, hardly exists, whereas the new heir is everything to him. The chief rejects another suitor, Lord Allonby, because '[t]he king can make a lord any day, but I defy him to make the Chief of Glenroy, and that's what you'll be, Reginald, when I'm gone' (2:26).[2] In one short sentence extreme vanity, misogyny and endogamy unite. In a domestic scene a little later on, Edith's role as servant is forcefully communicated in that typical set piece, the Scottish breakfast. Reginald's melancholy has taken away his appetite, but this does not satisfy the chief. He says two extremely hurtful things – first: 'What's reason there's nothing at the table Reginald can eat, Edith?' As a statement this is totally untrue, as it places the blame entirely on Edith's shoulders. Second, he adds: 'We never have a proper meal, now that your brother's gone [...] He would never have set you down to such a breakfast' (2:55). The silliness of the claim is immediately evident, but the use of the present simple in 'We never have' is especially spiteful, suggesting that this is always the case, or, in other words, that Edith is incapable of fulfilling the female role assigned to her, that of house manager. Such absurdity parallels the narrow-mindedness of the claimant.

Worse is to follow after the chief's death:

Glenroy's estate was strictly entailed upon the male heirs, and his personal property was found not equal to the amount of his debts. His marriage had been made without the formality of settlements; and his natural indolence that related to matters of business, together with his habits of reckless profusion and ostentation, had ever prevented him from taking any steps towards securing a provision for his daughter. (3:28–9)

The truth of the matter is that at one blow Edith is both an orphan and penniless. This again points to the common motif of male financial incompetence, coupled here with the chief's feudal habits, inappropriate for the age he lives in. This is perhaps a play on the themes of *Castle Rackrent* in a minor key, minor, because a Scottish context seemingly prevents such a carnivalesque combination of drink, excess and death. Although the chapter relating these events begins with the sentence 'And now Edith felt as though her destiny were sealed' (3:21), the very word 'destiny' is deceptive, in that it can never be attributed to cruel fate, which is an abstraction, but only to the financial incompetence of her father and the 'deceitfulness and the inconstancy' (3:20) of her first lover's heart, both material phenomena.

That these two events – financial and emotional bankruptcy – coincide obeys a logic that operates in Ferrier's scheme of things. What they clearly demonstrate is that her life has been ruined by two males of different generations, or, perhaps it would be more accurate to say, by the two men who meant most to her and who had the possibility, each in his own way, to help her either through actions, in the case of the father, or by honesty, in the case of Reginald. The love-plot and the family die almost simultaneously. Consequently, in this instance the whole question of heroinism is brought to the fore through this ironic use of the word 'destiny'. To survive, Edith has to edge her way through an obstacle course designed by the people closest to her, precisely those who could easily protect her, as happened to Laura in Brunton's *Self-Control*. This is most obvious in the case of her father, where attitudes are shown as rooted in an outmoded belief system, but can we say the same about the lover?

Ferrier closes the chapter describing Edith's 'destiny' with a brief citation from canto one, stanza sixteen of Byron's *Child Harolde*, 'Ye who have known that 'tis to dote upon / A few dear objects, will in sadness feel / Such partings break the heart!' This is the sadness that leaving home produces in Edith; that said, many parts of Reginald's make-up seem Byronic, above all his melancholy. There are others, sometimes in vague aphorisms such as 'love, perhaps, is peculiar to Italy' (2:227). The emotional epicentre of the novel is the moment when Reginald, Florinda and Edith are in a boat, caught in the sublimity of an unforeseen mountain storm. Reginald blurts out that his desire is not for his cousin Edith but for the more glamorous Florinda. Ferrier, instead of transcribing his words, narrates the scene in free indirect style: 'Florinda lay dying – dead – before him, he threw his arms around her, called upon her in broken accents of the most impassioned tenderness to revive, and be his – his life – his love!' (2:316–17). Of course, Reginald has never spoken to or acted towards Edith so passionately. Yet the reason why the truth has taken so long to surface has nothing to do with Byronic torment at all. Both Reginald and Edith, betrothed while very young, feel unable to break their commitment, in fact they are unable to speak their own thoughts. This exculpates Reginald to a certain degree, as neither of them feels free to act.

This leaves us with a conundrum, which will not be totally clarified at this point: how are passive heroines to be understood? Its importance cannot be overstated. Madame Latour, a French travelling companion who accompanies Florinda and her mother, in comparing the two young women, wonders whether Edith is 'insipid', a thought that must have occurred to all readers of historical romances when faced with ethical heroines, from Glorvina or Rose downwards. Interestingly enough, even though this suggestion predictably outrages her mentor, Mrs Macauley, the comment is summarily brushed under the carpet rather than addressed satisfactorily at this point. The fact that it is Madame Latour, an outsider, who asks the question, intensifies its power through estrangement; readers of romance are so accustomed to this type of character that they have possibly laid aside such doubts about what suffering and sufferance imply, as the perfunctory resolution of the love-plot has probably inured readers to its significance, thus never permitting an in-depth debate about the nature of heroism. There is never any doubt that the saintly heroine will marry the saintly hero; in actual fact the set-up is even more anaesthetizing than what happens, say, in Scott's lay-novels, as sanctity reduces the possibilities of desire being subverted. In addition, if Maria Warren's claim that there are about 80 references to religion in *Destiny* is true (1942: 222), we should remind ourselves that a large number of these comprise critical remarks of religious practices and practitioners. Such criticism predicts the reasons for the Disruption,[3] particularly the grotesque caricatures of the ministers themselves. Ferrier's famous Rev. Redgill, who makes an appearance in Meg Dod's (Johnstone's) *The Cook and Housewife's Manual* (1826), has a Scottish successor in M'Dow who, without going so far as to reach the hypocrisy of Burns's 'Holy Willie', seems to suffer from at least three of the cardinal sins: lechery, avarice and gluttony. Part of heroism, in this case for the saintly Lucy (a secondary heroine in *Destiny*), is to deflect his advances. Again, this points to a centrifugal impulse, painting a larger canvas of Scottish males and churchmen, but it farther reduces the number of eligible males. So vindictive is Ferrier in this instance, that M'Dow will marry an equally vile wife and have children even uglier than they are. To use a Biblical analogy, in Genesis 18, God promised that he would not destroy Sodom if there were ten just men there; but in Ferrier's Scotland, there do not seem to be ten just men eligible to be husbands of their 'insipid' heroines.

To conclude, it is clear that 'insipid' is a vital word in that its estrangement disguises, wittingly or unwittingly, partially or completely, what in radical terms could otherwise be denominated as the deletion of the female from social life. But what gives it a more specific location is the fact that this process is not simply determined by gender difference but by a specific location – Scotland – in an identifiable historical moment – the end of the clans. Reginald and Edith might seem incompatible or mismatched, which would reinforce the material nature of these forces. Reginald's melancholy is simply another symptom of the same predicament. Finally, if we just briefly think back to Brunton's heroines, even though their origin and journeys are similar to Ferrier's, there is no sense or inkling that freedom of movement or any form of independence is ever likely to appear. This can be illustrated by recovering Musgrove's proposal that commerce and shops become places in which Brunton's heroines can operate. Whether we agree or disagree with her intriguing hypothesis, its innovatory direction is highlighted if we try to apply similar ideas to Edith and her world. It just would not work, as even the modest amount of movement Brunton concedes to her characters is inconceivable for Ferrier's. A similar conundrum, of precisely the same nature, the interchangeability of insipidness and heroinism, lies at the heart of union in the Waverley Novels, a subject for the latter part of Chapter 4.

Parents and education

It is not difficult to identify similar patterns in Brunton's and Ferrier's fiction. The latter's heroines lack biological mothers to give them guidance and therefore adopt or are adopted by spiritual ones who will guide them along the straight and narrow. In fact it would be a simple matter to accumulate a long list of critics' dissatisfaction with surrogate religious mothers. As stated previously, Doyle's marked antipathy towards Mrs Douglas (*Marriage*) could arguably be interpreted as a reaction against a type – Brunton's Miss Mortimer is doubly saintly – as much as a reaction against one particular character in one particular book. That may be the truth, but not the whole truth.

In order to focus with more precision on this, I would like to underline two important concepts; the first is open to discussion, the second is simpler to apply. The first is the fact that mother–daughter relation-ships do not figure prominently in Western literature, whereas the Oedipal ones, son–mother, or the Electra ones, daughter–father, most certainly do; *Hamlet's* pivotal role in our culture would simply con-firm this. Two further examples from English classics, whose influence extends far beyond the British Isles, cast an interesting light on this. Maggie Tulliver in George Eliot's *The Mill on the Floss* (1860) has a bio-logical mother whose obsession with household goods is a symptom of her narrow materialism; she has not been educated to educate her child. Woolf's Scottish novel, *To the Lighthouse*, shows distrust of masculine rationality and of the Waverley Novels while at the same time express-ing doubts about the role of motherhood both conceptually, in the case of Mrs Ramsay, and physically, in the death of her own daughter at childbirth. Both mother and daughter are eliminated from the text. Daughters, it would seem, do not want to or should not follow their mother into motherhood. Therefore, if this problematic relationship is also given scant attention in these novels, they are simply adapting to a long-established literary convention. Second, many critics have remarked on Mary Wollstonecraft's influence on Ferrier; it is this factor that gives the novels their specificity.

Mellor writes that '*Marriage* can be read as a fictional translation of Wollstonecraft's [*A*] *Vindication* [*of the Rights of Woman*]' (1993: 49). I will argue that this is certainly true, while at the same time insist-ing that it is necessary to understand that many of the ideas in Wollstonecraft are not exclusively hers, but could be found in the work of Hannah More, Maria Edgeworth or in a legion of their con-temporaries. For example, Mellor states that Lady Juliana is 'seduced by sentimental romances' (49). Reading romances is a major weakness: Lady Juliana reads them well into adulthood. To judge by the evidence of chapter 12 of volume two, she is not particularly bothered in which order she reads the volumes, as it does not make any difference whether you start with the third or the first, an unequivocal comment on her own and the genre's vacuity. In *The Inheritance*, the narrative voice is particularly critical of the maiden aunt Betty, who 'read all the novels and romances which it is presumed are published for the exclusive benefit of superannuated old women and silly young ones, such as the Enchanted Head; – the Invisible Hand; – the Miraculous Nuptials, etc. etc. etc.' (1:26). If reading romance is not a hallmark of stupidity, it is at the very least described as a pernicious habit as hard to give up as smoking. However, in this particular instance, it is difficult to pinpoint the source as exclusively Wollstonecraft, who in this instance is far more adamant than Ferrier, stating that they 'tend to corrupt the taste, and draw the heart aside from its daily duties' (1993: 283); their authors are branded 'stupid' (283).

At the same time, there are instances where the connection is easier to make. One example would be the presence of Fordyce's *Sermons to Young Women* (1765), seen as compulsory reading and therefore the alternative to romance by the three pious aunts in *Marriage*. One aunt gifts Mary 'a flaming copy' (194) on her departure for England, as a preparation for the world of vice which lies south of the border. Ferrier is clearly mocking both the book and its readers here. Wollstonecraft comments that for Fordyce 'all women are to be levelled, by meekness and docility, into one character of yielding softness and gentle compliance' (1993: 177), before going on to add that the model female 'ought to be an angel – or she is an ass' (178), and presumably insipid. If there are doubts as to the direct allusion here, fewer can be found in one of Ferrier's motifs, the lapdog, which appears in all three novels. Aunt Betty (*The Inheritance*) has an old, epileptic lapdog which she spoils with a breakfast 'mess of hot rolls, cream, and sugar' (1:43–4).

As stated earlier, Lady Elizabeth in *Destiny* has three of these fashion accessories. That in itself is not enough for a translation, to use Mellor's terms, but *Marriage* is rather different. Like their owner, these town dogs are ill-adapted to life in the country, hence they chase the sheep when taken out for exercise. However, a certainly more unsettling situation arises when Lady Juliana has just given birth to her twin girls. The situation revolves around the father's exclamation that they are 'nice little creatures' (117); nevertheless, this apparently innocent remark becomes more disturbing as Juliana believes girls are worthless, so she asks for Psyche 'quite wretched at being so long away from me' (118) to be put on the bed instead. She lavishes more attention on her other creatures – her dogs – than on her children, whom she refuses to breastfeed, something which she considers 'so odious an office' (118). I am claiming two things here: the first is that this passage certainly is a translation, as the next three citations from Wollstonecraft's *Vindication* (1993) show:

> Besides there are many husbands so devoid of sense and parental affection, that during the first effervescence of voluptuous fondness they refuse to let their wives suckle their children. They are only to dress and live to please them: and love – even innocent love, soon sinks into lasciviousness when the exercise of a duty is sacrificed to its indulgence. (151–2)

And she who takes her dogs to bed, and nurses them with a parade of sensibility, when sick, will suffer her babes to grow up crooked in a nursery. (269)

I do not like to make a distinction without a difference, and I own that I have been as much disgusted by the fine lady who took her lap-dog to her bosom instead of her child; as by the ferocity of a man, who, beating his horse, declared, that he knew as well when he did wrong, as a Christian. (270)

There is a slight difference in that it is Juliana and not her husband who dislikes the idea, but that is a minor point in that it simply highlights the fact that Juliana is the epitome of a fashionable – a word Wollstonecraft herself uses – woman. For, suckling should be, she argues, something which fills the husband's heart with delight; it is not simply a thankless duty but a pleasure for husband and wife. Furthermore, Wollstonecraft sees suckling and the education of children as two inseparable acts, therefore Juliana, by refusing one will naturally refuse the other, hence her thoughts in response to being reunited with her daughter, '"Mother! What a hideous vulgar appellation!" thought the fashionable parent to herself' (Ferrier 1997: 223). Not only is the thought made explicit, but that keyword 'fashionable' is present. She does not require a husband to renege her womanhood. The remarks about dogs need less comment, as 'a parade of sensibility' is precisely what we witness throughout the text. Particularly evocative is the image of 'the fine lady who took her lap-dog to her bosom instead of her child', which highlights impropriety through a thoroughly bestial association. This brings me to the conclusion that what is translated from Wollstonecraft into Ferrier is a relentless picture of human folly. Therefore, what critics considered her cruelty may be part of her personality, may be the wit employed in her circle, but surely has its origins in Wollstonecraft's critical portrayal of her affluent contemporaries.

The final remark about 'as a Christian' leads to another important conclusion. Wollstonecraft is wary about passion, describing the early stages of marriage as 'voluptuous fondness' and suspecting desire to be 'lasciviousness', as the quotation above describes. Other parts of Wollstonecraft's *Vindication* make this even more apparent:

Friendship is a serious affection; the most sublime of all affections, because it is founded on principle, and cemented by time. The very reverse may be said of love. In a great degree, love and friendship cannot subsist in the same bosom; even when inspired by different objects they weaken or destroy each other, and for the same object can only be felt in succession. The vain fears and fond jealousies, the winds that fan the flames of love, when judiciously or artfully tempered, are both incompatible with the tender confidence and sincere respect of friendship. (1993: 152)

Wollstonecraft often uses the flame as a metaphor for love; it not only burns but, by its very nature, is ephemeral: it will soon go out. Ideally, it can be replaced by friendship. Ferrier is aware of the distinction. Happy marriages, except those which conclude the novels and therefore remain an unknown quantity, are short-lived, as husband and wife are rarely intelligent enough to be friends. All Ferrier's heroines look for friends only to find that they are more illusive than lovers, hence Nancy Paxton's perspicacious comment on Mary and Lady Emily (*Marriage*) that 'the growth of their friendship is presented in a thoroughly believable and well-dramatized way – also a rarity in nineteenth-century fiction' (1976: 24); it is precisely because it is so uncommon that Wollstonecraft attaches so much value to it; it is far more durable than passion.

Many aspects of the educational programme, so important to Wollstonecraft, appear in Ferrier's work. As this has been thoroughly analysed by Mellor (1993: 49–52) in some detail, there is nothing substantial I could add. But it is worthwhile taking up a point made by Paxton. Clearly, education defines womanhood for both writers. Consequently, Mellor's chapter which discusses Ferrier is pointedly entitled 'The Rational Woman', as rationality is what education has brought about for some men and should do so for women. Likewise, Ferrier's heroines, like many of their fictional contemporaries, visit the poor and their cottages – witness the case of Hamilton's *The Cottagers of Glenburnie* (1808). Ferrier is not exempt from this activity nor from poking fun at patronizing attitudes, as evident in the fourth chapter of *The Inheritance*. Gertrude suggests that a seriously ill cottager could do with a bit of carpet on his clay floor: this idiotic suggestion is replaced by the wife's macabre request for '[a] suit o' gude bein comfortable dead claise, Tammes, [...] would set ye better' (1:42). But in the end Ferrier joins her contemporaries in their insistence that women be rational, with the accompanying belief that mothers or surrogate mothers should be the illustrative role-models.

Hence Paxton makes some original claims for the much maligned Mrs Douglas, Mary's educational mother. Paxton's hypothesis is that 'she dares to be most unconventional in her education of Mary, a fact disguised by her piety' (1976: 23). Mary is educated following Rousseau's model for Émile, 'she has been taught modern languages, and has been encouraged to think for herself' (23). Paxton argues that both Mary and Mrs Douglas appear conventional, but that is simply appearance; indeed, she says that her education 'is notably similar to the very radical one Mary Wollstonecraft describes as the birthright for every women' (24). Paxton goes on to say that the Christian morality, which has made Ferrier so difficult for many readers, is a disguise. I beg to differ. What is more likely is that piety, morality or Christianity lies at the very base of Wollstonecraft's thinking, especially in her distrust of passion.

Let us consider this proposal from *Vindication*:

> Yet, if love be the supreme good, let women be only educated to inspire it, and let every charm be polished to intoxicate the senses; but, if they be moral beings, let them have a chance to become intelligent; and let love to man be only part of that glowing flame of universal love, which, after encircling humanity, mounts in grateful incense to God. (Wollstonecraft 1993: 145)

Although remarkably similar to the moral language of *Destiny*, this is Wollstonecraft's own voice. The human flame of passion is described as vastly inferior to 'that glowing flame of universal love', which, it is worth insisting, comes from God. I am therefore proposing that if we accept that *Marriage*, as representative of Ferrier's fiction, is a translation of Wollstonecraft, then there is no disguise, no subversion at play. The more Ferrier insists on the importance of education, rationality and religion rather than physical love, the closer she is to Wollstonecraft. To put this another way, the presence of Wollstonecraft is most evident in those moments in Ferrier's fiction which show that supposed lack of verve. Of course, Ferrier has adopted and adapted Wollstonecraft for her own use and devices, so it is undeniable that the pious Ferrier is a product of the pious Wollstonecraft. Doyle's dislike of Mrs Douglas's doctrinaire views is in the end therefore a reaction against the religiosity of *A Vindication of the Rights of Woman*.

This conclusion goes against practically all of the published criticism of Ferrier, but I think the evidence is convincing. In addition, an increased emphasis on the religiosity of Wollstonecraft is central to Janet Todd's study *Mary Wollstonecraft: A Revolutionary Life* (2000). It could be argued that the tedium caused by great lumps of moralizing stems not from the fact that Wollstonecraft is the source text but that Ferrier's translation is at times a bad one. Although that is a perfectly feasible argument, so far, I have yet to see it spelled out in print.

Locations

Leah Price (2000) argues that Ferrier's fiction is difficult for modern readers for a completely different reason. The latter's 'glib derivativeness' (76) results in the inclusion of an enormous amount of quotation and borrowing; consequently, '[n]othing but narrative padding differentiates the structure of Ferrier's fiction from the form of contemporary anthologies' (76). In other words, rather than fiction defined by the author function, we encounter arguably the consummate literary collage. This might initially seem a rather extreme reaction to both Ferrier and the common practice of epigraphs, the incorporation of snippets from other works to illustrate a point, and the all-pervading obeisance to Shakespeare as the ultimate authority on the human condition. Price's argument stands in contrast to that upheld by Kate Flint, who states that 'to employ a literary reference is to assert one's place within the cultural assumptions of that society. Quotations could thus be a means for women to claim, even if not consciously, their right to be considered on equal terms with other, male writers' (1993: 257). This is particularly important in the case of the romance, whose traditionally low status requires such strategies to justify its reading as other than merely escapism (258). The radical difference in stance is accountable to several factors. One is that Flint's frame of reference comprises a later period, 1837–1914, when the practice was less abusive though still pervasive than in Ferrier's work and time; a fine example would be Elizabeth Gaskell's *Mary Barton* (1848), where lines, stanzas and whole poems infiltrate the text. Second, Ferrier's own usage is excessive in contrast to her own contemporaries. Such deep intertextuality is most frequently employed in descriptions of landscape; Price surely has a strong case.

Let us consider, for example, the pivotal incident in *Destiny* when Reginald, under considerable emotional stress, reveals that his true feelings are for the glamorous Florinda not for the patient Edith. The setting is Scotland, the storm is Burkean, inspiring 'awe' (2:316), but, one wonders, is this really a rewriting of a more extended storm scene which was played out in a more direct translation of *A Vindication of the Rights of Woman*, namely Wollstonecraft's own fictional translation *Mary* (1788)? The heroine's religious views and the narrative's religiosity in chapter 20 are uncannily similar to Ferrier and Brunton. Perhaps Reginald's ambivalent remark about admiring Scotland but loving Italy (2:227), added to the words about de Staël on the previous page, indicate that Ferrier is trying to redesign the fate of the Scottish hero Lord

Nelvil of *Corinne* (1807) along the lines set by Wollstonecraft's distrust of passion. Moers (1977) argues insistently that women writers were fascinated by this novel.

It has to be acknowledged that however fascinating any inquiry into intertextuality might be, it is virtually impossible to come up with watertight evidence. Price (2000: 75) emphasizes rightly that Mary, before reciting Thomas Moore's poem 'Careless and Faithful Love', admits that, 'my sentiments are therefore all at second hand, but I shall repeat to you what I think is *not* love' (Ferrier 1997: 321). However, that does not necessarily mean that *Weltanschauung* is exclusively textual. That said, it is easy to draw out a design of the early chapters of *Marriage* in which Lady Juliana's view of Scotland, taken from romance, is tested against reality. This would initially seem to be the case once we accept that Price's focus on 'at second hand' extends to a whole series of icons and ideas far beyond the textual. Juliana's enthusiasm stems from the fact that 'she had heard the Duchess of M. declare nothing could be so delightful as the style of living Scotland' (6); these anthological ideas, such as Gretna Green marriages, are common currency.

As stated earlier on, Juliana's experience of Scotland is anything but delightful. This is pointedly illustrated when the couple arrive at Glenfern Castle. Juliana exclaims: 'Good God, what a scene! how I pity the unhappy wretches who are doomed to dwell in such a place! and yonder hideous grim house; it makes me sick to look at it' (9). The grim house is of course the castle she had fantasized about. Nature is likewise firmly unresponsive to her expectations. Rather than wear a duffle coat and sensible footwear, she dons a 'lilac satin pelisse, and silk shoes' (35). Aware of the obvious consequences of wearing this ill-suited attire outdoors, the aunts even argue that her ladyship 'will frighten our stirks and stots with your finery. I assure you they are not accustomed to such fine figures' (36). Even this astute appeal to her vanity is of no avail. Simultaneous to this process of matching dreams with reality is the gradual falling out of love with her husband, whose presence was never very appreciable but now simply peters out. Therefore two essential ingredients of a romance – romantic scenery and the love-plot – rise and fall together.

As far as it goes, this argument is convincing, but it is incomplete. For if the fantasy Scotland has sources which are common currency and literary – Thomson and Ossian are both mentioned in the country-walk chapter – it would not be true, I will propose, to see Juliana's confrontation with Scotland as a confrontation with reality. For, if we extend Price's hypothesis one step farther, it is feasible to argue that what

Juliana encounters is not real Scotland but the grotesque Scotland of gloom and despair that is also such common currency that it leads to the superstition that *Macbeth* should never be referred to by its name but only by the disparaging term 'the Scotch play'. That is to say that Juliana, on finding the castle not to her liking, switches from one extreme to the other: if the castle cannot be Disney World, it can only be that of the Thane of Cawdor. This has not been so easy to identify because of the insistence that much of Ferrier's fiction is based on the observation of real life, and therefore grotesque fictional characters must necessarily be drawn from grotesque real-life characters. For example, the more we insist on the fact that the three maiden aunts (*Marriage*) were portraits of the Edmonstone sisters and that the grumpy figure of Uncle Adam (*The Inheritance*) was a good likeness of her own father, the less we can detect that their origins are also to be found in folklore.

A similar incident from *The Inheritance* provides further evidence. The tyrannical Lord Rossville forces the heroine's mother to take a walk up the aptly named Pinnacle Hill to admire the magnificent view. Of course, she is not aptly dressed for the occasion. Gertrude tells her mother that she looks cold, '"Cold!" repeated Lord Rossville, in a tone of surprise and displeasure; "impossible – cold in the month of May! the day would be too hot, were it not for this cooling breeze"' (1:47). Whether or not the Scottish climate is capable of freezing our bones in May is beside the point, which is that Lord Rossville is both a character in a work of fiction and an instantly recognizable caricature of Scottish dourness.

Consequently, we could ask the pertinent question whether Ferrier ever tries to describe a landscape which is real, in the sense that it is neither a parody nor an intertextual ensemble. The juxtaposition of these two comments in *Destiny* highlights the problem: one character remarks, 'It seemed as if Scott's beautiful description of the Trossachs had started into life' while the other replies, 'Nonsense [...] it is a frightful, a *dangerous* road' (2:141). Perhaps the answer lies not so much in the description of nature itself but, to use Raymond Williams's argument in *The Country and the City* (1973), to what extent, how and why the landscape is managed and populated. *Destiny* again throws up some interesting arguments. The dourest figure of all, Inch Orran, is asked whether he has noted any improvements in Scotland on his return after 40 years' absence. This might possibly be a refutation of the progress attributed to Scott's 60 years, but in any case, Inch Orran's laconic reply, 'I do see a change, sir; but that is not wonderful' (1:73), is developed as the novel progresses into an exposé of why the Highlands are not wonderful. The lairds are set in their own ways and have no economic know-how at all. In this particular case his idea of improvement is limited to increasing the number of trees (2:25). There is no forward-looking optimism along the lines of the postscript of *Waverley*. Occasionally there are moments where intertextuality is pushed aside, for example:

> Lochdhu was as ugly as any Highland place *can* be; but there was a wild grandeur in its dark mountains, and roaring streams and track-less heaths, and a varying interest in the lights and shadows of its stormy frith, which atoned for the want of more florid beauties. There was perfect neatness, and even some embellishment, around the house; but the shrubs were yet in their infancy, and the flowers were not so luxuriant as in brighter climes, and beneath more costly culture. (1831: 1:140)

There is clearly an attempt to be balanced, contrasting ugliness and grandeur with an explanation of what the house is lacking. This description shares with the laird's plantation policy the same common feature: it is as empty of people as it was 40 years since. Consequently, as Ferrier so pithily puts it, 'the Highlands may be said to open for the season as the King's Theatre shuts' (1831: 1:14). In other words, out of season, the landscape is almost as empty of local inhabitants as it is of visitors.

When not being overtly intertextual or analytical as in the above example, Ferrier points to two important instances of subjectively determined landscape. The first case is youth or naivety, as is the case of Gertrude at the beginning of *The Inheritance*. There, landscape is described in the following terms: 'The dark, lead-coloured ocean lay stretched before them, its dreary expanse concealed by lowering clouds, while the sea-fowl clamouring in crowds to the shore announced the coming storm' (1824: 1:14). This is possibly the most neutral and real-istic of Ferrier's descriptions, though, in deference to Price, it is highly conscious of its literariness, exemplified by the heavy alliteration. Ferrier allows Gertrude – but not her mother – to ignore this unwelcoming wel-come to Scotland for some time while she enthuses about nature. But this is solely because she is young: the illusion will not last long.

The more important example of subjectivism is caused by absence. As if they were living in a developing country, exile is almost a require-ment for any adult male save the laird and his handful of unexportable male retainers. Accordingly, large numbers of women remain behind, which is why there are so many spinsters populating her fiction. The final chapter of *Destiny* provides some striking accounts of nature. Edith returns after a short exile in 'stifling' (1831: 3:384) London; she looks forward to 'the silent glens and the free mountain air' (3:384). Again, we should note that there is emptiness because of improvement or the Clearances. The party arrives in spring, but Ferrier brushes that aside by stating that 'far beyond all the loveliness of nature were the glad faces, the fond tones, and the warm embrace of long-severed friends' (3:386). In other words, the solitariness that Wordsworth so desired in the company of nature is not something that Ferrier approves of or promotes. Natural beauty is of little value, whereas friendship, that all-important term for Wollstonecraft, is greatly cherished.

Does nature, landscape or whatever we may call it, have any real significance to Ferrier? Two answers present themselves. One is to promote the validity of Price's hypothesis. If intertexuality is everything, then Ferrier's Scotland is well and truly just text, and consequently its specificity is determined not by its national or local colours but by being represented at second hand. The other answer would be that Ferrier is deeply sceptical of those who aestheticize nature, as such appreciation presupposes a solitary state, itself a result of a creaky economic structure which, in the case of the Highlands, is at least 40 years behind the times. To conclude, there is very little evidence that Ferrier was at all interested in describing a landscape, Scottish or otherwise. Such an activity seems to her a distraction from the everyday questions that humanity has to encounter in the battle for survival.

Cul-de-sac

Although Susan Ferrier lived until she was 72, she published only three novels. In an 1837 letter, that is to say written six years after the publication of *Destiny*, Miss Hope MacKenzie informs Ferrier that she is authorized to offer her £1000 for anything she would care to write (Doyle 1898: 268). Doyle states that '[o]n the back of this note Miss Ferrier wrote, "I made two attempts to write *something*, but could not please myself, and would not publish '*anything*'"' (269). Richard Bentley, in a letter dated 26 May 1852, affirms, 'I sincerely trust you may be able to contribute another work to those you have already given to the world, and which have become classics' (315). Bentley, who had bought the copyright of her fiction, can hardly be considered a disinterested correspondent, and in place of the word 'classics' maybe 'financially successful' would be closer to his thoughts. Nevertheless, even over the age of 70, Ferrier is seen as a valid business proposition. She never wrote the fourth novel. The material reason given is her failing eyesight; the more speculative ones have to do with lack of verve and the increased moralizing tone of her fiction. I will put forward others which respond to certain unresolved problems evident in her own writing, namely four: the love-plot, cruelty, Miss Pratt and Walter Scott.

Whatever our views about the use of the term 'union', it is undeniable that two central features are the conflation of the public and the private spheres; it is necessarily optimistic. Scott looks forward to a more prosperous Scotland while Manzoni hopes for a united, thriving Italy. Initially, Ferrier's novels would seem to follow this well-trodden path, but on closer inspection, not all of the features of union are present, while others appear in a twisted and deformed nature. At the end of *Marriage*, Mary marries Colonel Lennox, but it requires a quite prodigious feat of memory to be able to remember much about him, as he appears very late in the novel and has no idiosyncrasy at all. When asked whether a picture on the wall is really a portrait of her son, Mrs Lennox replies, '"He was only eighteen," continued she, "when that was done; and many a hot sun has burned on the fair brow; and many a fearful sight has met these sweet eyes since then; and sadly that face may be changed; but I shall never see it more!"' (266). One reason for delaying the great man's appearance is that Lennox is no young puppy, as his rank would confirm; he has been busy on active service in the time corresponding to the previous chapters. He has already had a long career, based, according to his mother, on suffering. Mrs Lennox's two references to sight forecast her blindness which is lifted temporarily – either miraculously or metaphorically – on her deathbed when she will at last see her son again. The deathbed is the site of the betrothal, an event so incredible that '[i]t was long before Mary could believe in the reality of what had passed. It appeared to her as a beautiful, yet awful dream. Could it be, that she had plighted her faith by the bed of death [...]?' (401). This is a rhetorical question. Rather than the stuff of romance, this is macabre; life continues only after much suffering, and resolution; happiness is therefore an inappropriate term as, even in the love-plot, it is never far removed from the proximity of death. Moers makes a similar point, 'I sense a specially female melancholy and weariness toward the close of the books that women writers have structured around the heroinism of travel and adventure' (1977: 140), but in this case, for the heroine, horrors are at, or near, home, and do not require much travelling. Similarly, in *Destiny*, the couple have made the passage through the valley of the shadow of death, and pick up sufficient experience and knowledge in order to survive, but the novels lack the optimism of union or the Glorvina solution. Devoid of the happy romance solution, fiction comes to a dead-end rather than indicate a promise of change. To push Saintsbury's comments on the weak plots a little farther, we could add that Ferrier's inability or unwillingness to provide a plot structure which could sustain a conclusion-cum-resolution is evidence of her inherent pessimism.

In making such an assertion, I am clearly distancing myself from the school of scholarship which promotes the centrality of union by allowing scarce if any divergence between the personal and political implications of that term. For example, Juliet Shields's excellent reading of Ferrier – and Johnstone – comes to a radically different conclusion from mine about the nature of the love-plot. Rather than stressing age and experience, she highlights the hybrid genetics of the couple: '[i]t is left to those characters whose mixed Anglo-Celtic ancestry links them to two cultures to perform the work of mediation and nation forma- tion. Regardless of their gender, these culturally racially liminal char- acters play the role of "wife" in a national union' (134). Along similar lines, Jina Kim argues that '[t]he marriage of the Anglo-Scottish hero, raised in England, and the Anglo-Scottish heroine, reared in Scotland, symbolically endorses and naturalizes the union' (2002: 191). I do not believe that mediation is meant to be read as successful and therefore neither can I agree that Ferrier intends to naturalize the union, whether political or sentimental. In fact, in Ferrier's fiction, I would propose, all human relationships are rendered somewhat suspicious, even, in certain cases, anti-natural.

A second trait which endangers her fiction is her cruelty. As stated previously, many readers have remarked that Ferrier is pitiless towards her characters, thereby making Douglas's comment that 'tolerance is not her strong point' (1897: 119) into a huge understatement. Cruelty is usually connected to her humour; we might recall that in 'Noctes Ambrosianae' she is called a hard satirist. However, my contention is that that assessment falls short; in her fiction, Ferrier is simply hard on everyone. This is evident from the early chapters of *The Inheritance*, which provide some of her most quirky creations, her funniest charac- ters and some of her most appalling puns. Outside the circle of humour, darker thoughts are present. A courting couple have to talk 'in the usual style of some such silly pair' (1:213). The bride-to-be is pretty but 'dif- fused with an intolerable air of folly, affectation, and conceit' (1:117). Married women get similar treatment, 'like many other excellent wives, she thought her husband's opinion carried the greatest possible weight with it' (1:289); in other words the opinion has no weight and the wife no brain. Maiden aunt Betty 'asked a great many useless questions, which few people thought of answering' (1:26). Men come in for equal treatment; they are either silly or vulgar, whatever their social class. The Laird is incredibly pompous, long-winded: he is one of the 'weak important people' (1.266). Here, cruelty is direct rather than comic. Gertrude's parents are simply an 'unfortunate pair, thus doomed to unwilling exile' (1:3). Of her father, Ferrier adds, 'three of his brothers had fallen victims to war or pestilence, and there now only remained the present Earl and himself, both alike, childless' (1:4). Their pointless existence makes them little different from the old maids Ferrier continually mauls with her unforgiving descriptions and commentary. In other words, the world is an extremely hostile place. Danger is lurking just round the corner and humanity is marked by its vulgarity and class distinctions. To put it another way, Ferrier has such a gloomy view of the world that humour alone is not enough to cover up this profound and unmovable pessimism. Hart, in *The Scottish Novel from Smollett to Spark*, likens Ferrier to her contemporary John Galt, which contextualizes her humour, but goes on to propose that Ferrier is 'a forerunner of Muriel Spark' (1978b: 62), a truly novel idea which allows to envisage how humour, cruelty and despair can all occupy the same text.

The third reason is the hypothesis that there is a certain similarity between Susan Ferrier and her most famous comic creation, Miss Pratt. As her name suggests, she prattles endlessly in the fashion associated with Austen's Miss Bates (*Emma* (1815)). Miss Pratt annoys her listeners so much that when she leaves, her 'departure was hailed as a joyful release' (1:274), for guests would no longer have to put up with her awful puns and ceaseless chatter. There is yet another reason for such joy: Miss Pratt is not simply a comic character but a wise fool whose remarks tend to call our attention to those pet-hates of Miss Ferrier, vulgarity and affectation. Men talk incessantly about politics, as there is a forthcoming election, yet the subject generally bores the females. Miss Pratt punctures their pomposity with a firm candidate for the worst ever, when she reports that the mysterious Anthony Whyte was told by Lord Punmedown that, 'if you wish to sit [in parliament] you've only to stand' (1:153). One can well understand the sentiment expressed by the narrative voice that 'to restrain the volubility of the female tongue is a task that has hitherto defied the power of man' (1:104). However uncomfortable her presence is, nothing escapes her gaze and subsequent comment. The total picture is of a society where people continuously talk at each other rather than to each other, making the possibility of any human communication or relationship somewhat remote. The problem resides in the fact that Ferrier has an excellent ear which she uses to illustrate human folly. Elton states that '[h]er genius was for transcription' (1912: 1:366), which is presumably positive, while he dislikes the portrayal of the three aunts of *Marriage*, stating that their 'talk [...] sounds like that of voices through a phonograph; reproducing every error and inflexion, but with most of the human quality gone out of it; and, mercilessly, taking as long as the actual talk copied' (1:368). This astute comment synthesizes the ambivalent attitude critics often experience: recognition of the accuracy of transcription, but a simultaneous sense of dissatisfaction. Ferrier does not curb her tongue at all, making a comic character's voice funny the first time its eccentricities are recorded, but after several exposures to uncut lengthy monologues, the text falters. As the extended length adds nothing that a more pruned passage could supply, in the end uncut transcriptions become detrimental. Ferrier does not mould the material she has so excellently taken possession of; in short, she has assumed the form of her literary creation, Miss Pratt.

The final reason why Ferrier possibly found it difficult to write again comes from what must initially be an unforeseen source: her distrust of Scott's personality or literary persona which spills over into his fiction. This is odd, if we keep in sight her remarks about his monumental works of fiction, which she contrasts to her own 'trash'. In her 'Recollections of Visits to Ashistiel and Abbotsford' (1874), Ferrier expressed two qualms about the Great Unknown's bonhomie. Every day guests assemble for a drive or a walk during which Scott expounds 'the same inexhaustible flow of legendary lore, romantic incident, apt quotation, curious or diverting story; and sometimes old ballads were recited, commemorative of some of the localities through which he passed' (331). Rather than being drawn into the circle of admirers, she goes on to say that 'I must confess this was an enthusiasm I found as little infectious as that of his antiquarianism. On the contrary, I often wished his noble faculties had been exercised on loftier themes than those which seemed to stir his very soul' (332). In other words, Scott's talents have been wasted on writing literature that does not ennoble either himself or his readers. After dinner, music and song follow, but Ferrier finds this vulgar: 'the glee seemed forced and unnatural. It touched no sympathetic chord; it only jarred the feelings' (332). As she feels fiction is a let down for a man of Scott's capacity, it is logical to assume that she cannot think highly of her own work. Hers she once judged as trash; Scott's might be great popular fiction, but for Ferrier, it is not art. Whereas it is difficult to judge whether Brunton's criticism of historical romance is a comment on Scott, Ferrier's is much more straightforward. The distinctive Scott persona receives no note of approval either. At this moment, if we asked Ferrier what is the point of writing a specifically Scottish novel, she would have probably answered that there was none at all; it is simply not lofty enough, which ironically returns us to Doyle's dismissive remarks about Ferrier's own popular novels with which this chapter began.

3
Christian Isobel Johnstone: From Centrifugal to Centripetal

Mrs Johnstone's *Tales of the Irish Peasantry* bring her honourably to our mind. Pray offer the good brave-hearted lady my hearty remembrances, good-wishes and applauses. – Radicalism, I grieve to say, has but few such practical adherents! Radicalism, when one looks at it here, is – a thing one had rather not give a name to! (Thomas Carlyle, in Carlyle and Carlyle 1985: 11:234)

Literary persona

Christian Isobel Johnstone's life could not be more different from that of Susan Ferrier and Mary Brunton. Whereas Brunton's and Ferrier's mediators write about their relatives in a peculiar game of biographical hide-and-seek when describing the two writers' lives and personalities, Johnstone was a professional writer, or, to put it as forcefully as possible, she was an active public figure who lived in Scotland's capital city, working right at the heart of its flourishing publishing industry. James Barron provides the following information about the founding of the *Inverness Courier* in 1817:

> The first editor was Mrs. Johnstone, the author of several novels, such as 'Elizabeth de Bruce,' 'Clan Alpin,' [sic] 'Meg Dods' Cookery Book,' &c. This lady afterwards edited Tait's magazine. Mrs. Johnstone was assisted in her labours by her husband, an old schoolmaster and good grammarian. (1903: 1:133)

Rather than an unintentional slip which moves her Highland novel to the Alps, Barron is surely thinking of Clan-Alpine from Scott's epic poem *The Lady of the Lake*, which accounts for the typo. Minor quibbles apart, her position as a prominent figure, novelist and editor is unquestionable. *Tait's Magazine*, in its obituary, tells a slightly different story:

> More than forty years ago she married Mr. John Johnstone, who, having been originally engaged in educational pursuits, was then Editor of the *Inverness Courier*, and the assistance of Mrs. Johnstone aided materially in giving to the *Courier* a character and tone not often attained by a provincial journal. ('Obituary Notices' 1857: 574)

The couple moved to Edinburgh, where the Johnstones continued their career, first with *The Schoolmaster and Edinburgh Weekly Magazine* (1832–33), which then became the monthly *Johnstone's Magazine*, which then fused with *Tait's*.

Odile Boucher (1983) makes two important statements about *Tait's*, which turn out also to be the pillars of Johnstone's literary output. The first is that the 'magazine was destined to counterbalance [...] the extreme conservatism of *Blackwood's*' (75). All the great subjects of reform, such as franchise, slavery, Ireland, to name but a few, are treated here from a distinctly liberal angle. Second, the important literary side of the journal was primarily the work of Johnstone (76). This is corroborated in various other sources, and probably lies behind the opaque remark about 'a character and tone not often attained by a provincial journal'.

Johnstone had therefore been able to surmount the obstacle that being someone's wife necessarily excluded the possibility of being someone in one's own right. In her case, having wealth and therefore being the proprietor facilitates the process; nonetheless, as we will shortly see, their finances can only be vaguely surmised. James Bertram, who had started as an apprentice at *Tait's* and worked his way up to become 'manager' or 'head-clerk' (Bertram 1893: 46) – this confusing terminology is of his own making – gives us a few glimpses of Christian Johnstone which are not to be found elsewhere, that is, neither in the obituary nor in the biographical dictionary entries. He claims that John Johnstone was a schoolmaster and that Christian had been one of his pupils (31). He states that she spent a month every year in 'the [Ettrick] shepherd's country' (49); both Johnstone and Tait 'resented' (49) the boorish picture of James Hogg that Lockhart had drawn. Extending the remarks made in the obituary, Bertram tell us that

> The politics of his [*Tait's*] magazine naturally reflected – and sometimes strongly – his own opinions as a philosophical radical, but, on

the whole, it was more of a literary than a political organ. Its working genius was Mrs. Johnstone, a novelist and critic of some ability, who was also that author of the well-known cookery-book familiarly known as 'Meg Dods'; while Mr. Tait conducted the necessary correspondence with the actual and would-be contributors. It was Mrs. Johnstone, however, who generally passed judgment on the articles offered, and she was herself a large contributor, both in fiction and criticism; many of the long and admirable reviews of important new books, for which the magazine was famous, coming from her pen. She also contributed every month the entire 'Literary Register' – concise notices of current literature – which added considerably to her labours.

Mr. Johnstone, it was good-naturedly said, helped his wife – by handing her books of reference, and mending her pens; but this report was probably unfair to him, for he was a clever man, and ably edited an abridgment of Dr. Jamieson's 'Scottish Dictionary.' (30–1)

The closing words refer to an abridged, 775-page version published by Tait in 1847. Bertram claims that if the journal was more literary than political, and that if the literary contribution was basically Johnstone's, then it was more Johnstone's journal than Tait's; in other words she was its guiding light. Bertram spends some time describing her championing of the 'ardent radical' (43) poet Robert Nicoll (1814–37). Not only did Tait publish Nicoll's poetry in a posthumous collection, but Christian Johnstone wrote a memoir of his life for the second edition, published in 1842; a centenary edition was also published in 1914. Bertram admits that perhaps she was too kind in her enthusiasm for young writers. Although this might have led to errors of judgement, it should not lead automatically to the stereotyping of her as a nice, kind old lady who offers aspiring writers cups of tea and encouragement. Generous she may have been in her thought and actions, but we should never lose sight of the fact that the journal's, the poet's and her own political thinking were always of a strong, committed liberal stance, or what more conservative voices would label stigmatically as radical.

The fact is that we know a lot less of Johnstone than the public nature of her life would lead us to assume. There are two reasons for this. The first is simple to explain but hard to understand. Most entries in the current *Oxford Dictionary of National Biography* of reasonably affluent citizens finalize their entry with details of their death, followed by details of their will and/or inventory. Such is the case of Susan Ferrier, as one would expect. But this is not the case of Johnstone, who left no will after her death in August 1857. Her husband died in November of the same year, but was also intestate.[1] In short, however well known Johnstone might have been among literary and liberal circles of her time, there are no Johnstone holdings or collected papers as such. All we have are very brief glimpses from contemporaries and collaborators, which very often turn out to contain almost no information of any substance. A good example is provided by Thomas De Quincey (2003: 11:107–8); an illustrious name sounds promising, but expectations are dashed when we are served a couple of platitudes. It is an odd situation, because we are dealing with two very literary people. In her exhaustive and vastly illuminating chapter on Johnstone, Perkins (2010: 207–80) has gone a long way towards remedying the situation, providing the most detailed picture available of some of the missing years (especially as concerns the divorce) of the Johnstones at work (based on research in the Oliver and Boyd archive) and of their dealings with Blackwood. Perkins is well aware of the difficulties involved when she states that the 'years Johnstone spend in Inverness have almost vanished from literary history' (214). However, although new material goes some way towards clarification, at the same time it occasionally increases the elusiveness.

Whatever the reasons for this situation, it confirms, in very real terms, the completeness of the erasure which was applied to the lives of Brunton and Ferrier, both of whom write about the horrors of being recognized as a writer. It is worth recalling how extreme this fear, whether real or feigned, becomes, leading Brunton to place the female writer on a par with a circus performer:

> I would rather, as you well know, glide through the world unknown, than have (I will not call it *enjoy*) fame, however brilliant. To be pointed at – to be noticed and commented upon – to be suspected of literary airs – to be shunned, as literary women are, by the more unpretending of my own sex; and abhorred, as literary women are, by the more pretending of the other! – My dear, I would sooner exhibit as a rope-dancer. (1819: xxxvi)

Perhaps the equation of being a known female writer with a bluestocking is in evidence here: both are conspicuous for their eccentric lifestyles. Ferrier, in her satire of the bluestockings, shares a similar dislike based on the idea that exposure primarily underlines the ridiculous part of human nature. Ironically enough, the only person in this study who has the ability to be female, public and serious, that is to say, as distant from the rope-dancer as possible, has left no correspondence worth consideration, or any other private record of her thoughts.

This process of suppression is compounded by another, which has Orwellian overtones. Connolly's *Biographical Dictionary of Eminent Men of Fife* (1866) tells us that '[v]ery early in life she married a Mr M'Leish, whom she was compelled to devorce [sic]. About 1812, she married, a second time, Mr John Johnstone' (244). The third edition of Chambers's *A Biographical Dictionary of Eminent Scotsmen* (1875) recounts, in almost identical words, that '[w]hen she was very young she married a Mr. M'Leish, who she was afterwards compelled to divorce. Her second and last husband was Mr. John Johnstone' (II:405). Needless to say, the *Dictionary of National Biography* (1892) repeats the same formula of Johnstone having no life till she married for a second time. These remarks about M'Leish, it has to be emphasized, are the opening words of the biographical sketch. It is also strange that even though her place of birth is identified, her maiden name, Todd, is not. Consequently, the obituary in *Tait's*, which basically talks about her literary career and her involvement in the journal, is, save for brief notice of the compulsory divorce, identical to the other biographical entries which supposedly cover the whole of her life. Whatever the reason may be, it seems that Johnstone was a non-person who came into existence at the moment she divorced her first husband. Even her birth is mysterious. Early accounts assume her place of birth to be Fife, hence her inclusion in the above-mentioned *Biographical Dictionary of Eminent Men of Fife*, though why this should be so is unclear, as there is a record of baptism at St Cuthbert's, Edinburgh, for a Christian Todd dated 12 June 1781. Either a piece of information we no longer have access to has been lost or perhaps one erroneous item, which no one checked, was passed on from one compiler to another.

Alexis Easley's *First-Person Anonymous: Women Writers and Victorian Print Media, 1830–1870* (2004) gives the fullest description of Johnstone's journalistic career. She states that her achievement is enormous; '[w]hen she assumed the editorship of *Tait's Edinburgh Magazine* in 1834, she became the first woman to serve as a paid editor of a major Victorian periodical'. She adds that her identity was like that of the Great Unknown, namely 'an open secret' (62). Easley provides a fascinating picture of the guises and disguises used to hide her identity. The most obvious of these was the fact that her name and credentials are never publicized (67). As for the explanatory causes, Easley proposes a mixture of *Zeitgeist* and personal concerns; the gendered world of journalism requires that anonymity. Johnstone's case shows that success is more likely to come with change from within: she consciously fostered the presence of women writers in *Tait's* both through direct contributions and through reviewing their books herself, '[u]nder her editorship, the number of female contributors increased from about 19% to 37%' (69). Easley insists that Johnstone 'was a divorcée and consequently had good reason to avoid public attention' (62). That might sound like an easy way round the problem, but that is definitely not the case. Easley points out that this semi-clandestine stance stands in marked contrast to Harriet Martineau's; in other words, it was Johnstone's conscious decision to be anonymous, one which she resolutely carried out. That is not to say that open recognition and public appearances as editor were necessarily options, but that Johnstone could have been less invisible if she had so wished. The fact that her name did not accompany her publications till the 1840s (Perkins 2010: 221) indicates the personal nature of her decision-taking. As stated previously, in stark contrast, her articles are easily traceable through *The Wellesley Index to Victorian Periodicals*. Johnstone's contribution of 400 articles represents '20% of the magazine as a whole' (Easley 2005: 272).

This protean identity, this darkness visible, explains, I believe, the tone of several of the reviews of *Elizabeth de Bruce* (1827). The very brief three-sentence notice in *National Magazine, and General Review* informs that:

> We have been given to understand that the authoress is a Mrs. Johnstone, a Scotch lady, who some ten or twelve years ago published a novel called Clan Albin. For some years Mrs. Johnstone had the conduct and editorship of a newspaper published in Inverness, which, however, she lately resigned, and has now taken up her residence at Edinburgh. (Rev. 1827: 315)

The pompous tone of the opening phrase – a passive construction with no agent – sets up the review as a repository of important information. Her name did not appear on the title-page of this novel; she is identified only as the author of *Clan-Albin* (1815). In this instance, her identity as a novelist is known, but what she is doing in Edinburgh is not. This is odd, to say the least, as, first, her highly successful *The Cook and Housewife's Manual* had been published the year before, and second, she was editor of the *Edinburgh Weekly Chronicle* from 1824 until 1832. Although her political ideas were a world apart from *Blackwood's*, it was Blackwood who published *Elizabeth de Bruce*, as this excerpt from 'Noctes Ambrosianae' points out:

> Shepherd. Do you ken onything about Elisabeth De Bruce, a novelle, in three volumes, announced by Mr Blackwood?

North. Nothing – but that it is the production of a lady who, a dozen years ago, wrote Clan Albin, a novel of great merit, full of incident and character, and presenting many fine and bold pictures of external nature.

Shepherd. Is that the way o't? I ken her gran'ly – and she's little, if at a' inferior in my opinion, to the author o'the Inheritance, which I aye thought was written by Sir Walter, as weel's Marriage, till it spunked out that it was written by a Leddy. But gud or bad, ye'll praise't, because it's a byuck o' Blackwood's.

North. That speech, James, is unworthy of you. With good-will do I praise all good books published by Ebony – and know well that Elizabeth de Bruce will be of that class. (1826: 781)

That this exchange takes place before the novel's publication in the following year demonstrates how much of a covert advertisement it is. The emphasis on its quality, as good as Ferrier, in the line of Scott, enhanced by North's assertion that he will praise it on its merits alone, are fine examples of competent, pre-publication marketing. For a second time, we can see that there is supposedly some communication between Hogg and Johnstone, 'I ken her gran'ly', a lead I have been unable to follow. His apparent ignorance of the real authors of the text greatly justifies the need for this and similar studies of Edinburgh fiction. She is therefore someone about whom something is known, but her persona is shadowy, to say the least. As we shall see, the question of anonymity has to be set alongside novels which express, either in the authorial or in their characters' voices, forthright opinions about current, polemical issues. As one review of *Clan-Albin* succinctly put it, '[t]he author has formed rather strong opinions [...] on many of those subjects which have agitated the public mind for these last thirty years' (Rev. 1816: 91). Presumably the forceful, muscular opinions could never be traced back to the pen of a lady.

Heroinism

That this word could derive as much as from heroin as from heroine might explain why it has never really caught on. Even in Johnstone's time, as in any other, it was rare. The *Oxford English Dictionary* cites it as an alternative to the equally scarcely used heroineship. Only one use of heroinism is recorded, that which occurs in the anonymous novel *The History of Eliza Warwick* (1778): 'you must therefore owe the preservation of your life to a calm and cheerful patience – dissipate your ideas they grow too interesting; and, by a noble effort of heroinism, recover at once your peace and health' (1778: 2:28–9). Being such a strange word, it is hard not to believe that Johnstone wants to call our attention to it when placing it in the mouth of one of her characters in chapter 35 of *Clan-Albin*. This is part of the third volume, when the stage moves from Scotland to Ireland. The hero, Norman, has volunteered and is there on service. His clan is irreparably lucre-banished; there is no money to pay for a career; in the post-Clearance glens, there is virtually nothing else for an aspiring young male to do. Joining the army demonstrates patriotism – which is probably applauded within the context of the novel – and hopelessness at the same time: it is the last resort. Norman's enlistment is unique for one fundamental reason. Whereas there are plenty of undesirables who choose the army rather than a life of crime, Norman is practically the only healthy, sane, patriotic recruit. Although that reflects upon his own personal circumstances, it simultaneously suggests that the future for the bright young man is the same as for proto-criminals, which, in turn, further highlights the futureless destiny of the Highlands. As we saw in Chapter 1, the cohabitation of devastation and the Highland regiments played an important role in Brunton's *Discipline*, where rural poverty was transported to the city. At the same time, twinning two epistemologically contrasting tendencies – patriotism and hopelessness – estranges the value of patriotism, which is so entrenched in the iconography and history of the Highland regiments.

Norman is going to be court-martialled for striking a superior officer, the despicable Sir Archibald Gordon, who plays the role of Norman's *doppelgänger*. Whereas Norman is all love, gentleness and generosity, Gordon displays hate, violence and cruelty. The fact that these two male characters follow each other around might appear as a forced series of coincidences which often plagues fiction of the time, but it is clearly a formal device which highlights this duality. Norman is walking along the shore with his faithful dog Luath, which Gordon had previously stolen. Luath is a particularly Scottish literary name, appearing both in Burns's 'The Twa Dogs' and as Cuchullin's dog in Ossian's *Fingal*. Norman hears a maiden in distress and rushes to rescue her from the violent clutches of his drunk superior. That this is an attempted rape is made clear by the woman's immediate flight, so aware is she of 'the strong sense of danger' (Johnstone 2003: 197). Gordon has an additional motive for singling out this particular female: she desires Norman's other double, Phelim Bourke, whose quick wit has made Gordon look ridiculous in front of his subordinates. Rape would also be a way of exacting revenge on Bourke. Luckily, Norman steps in in the nick of time. The brandishing of Gordon's threatening sword and the fact that it eventually penetrates Norman's arm, rather than the female body, gives additional force to the nexus of soldiery, sex and violence.

Despite his innocence, Norman is imprisoned and his future career is endangered. This is due not simply to the power of the caste system in the army but to the arbitrary nature of court martials, set up ad hoc yet possessing the power to pardon, punish or even impose the death sentence. Their arbitrary powers are incompatible with the rule of law and this anomaly was a pet subject for liberal reformers. In this instance, in what seems to be the exception to the rule, Norman is acquitted. But during the process, the females will have to sit at home, twiddling their thumbs, powerless to do anything that might compensate their inactivity. In the small-talk that precedes the officers' departure to court, we hear the casual comment 'Nobody thinks of *heroinism*' (336, italics in the original). Initially, it would seem that this term would fit very easily within the gendered reading of Johnstone's life and work, so cogently argued by Easley, as I have already indicated. If Norman is the victim here, at least justice is done, but the threat of rape and the pointless lifestyle women lead remain.

Four further points increase the importance of heroinism. One of the most famous opening lines in poetry is in Byron's *Don Juan*, 'I want a hero.' This lack is self-evident in the military if officers are anything like Gordon, but Johnstone seems to suggest that heroinism, although possible linguistically, as an abstraction, is impossible in any other sphere. The second would be if violence is both institutionalized within the army and legalized during warfare, which is of little comfort to half of the population, as the intended rape would prove. What marks heroinism in *Clan-Albin*, I would argue, is precisely this awareness of violence. To a certain extent, the novel predicts, and would possibly confirm, the analysis made by Sandra M. Gilbert in 'Soldier's Heart: Literary Men, Literary Women, and the Great War' (1983), where she argues that in addition to the front-line battle, on the home front there is an intense battle of the sexes. The two forms of warfare overlap, complement and reflect on each other as each acts as a metaphor of the other.

The third factor stems from the heroine's uncommon name, Monimia, one associated with female orphans. Contemporary Monimias can be found in Smollett's *Ferdinand, Count Fathom* (1753) and in Charlotte Smith's *The Old Manor House* (1793). However, Johnstone is far more likely to have in mind Thomas Otway's play *The Orphan, or, the Unhappy Marriage* (1680). This play was performed at this period, and Scott, in his 'Essay on the Drama', assures us that '[m]ore tears have been shed, probably, for the sorrows of [...] Monimia, than for those of Juliet and Desdemona' (1834: 356). In other words, her name became associated primarily with sentiment. The epigraph to chapter 16, in which Monimia's story is told, is taken from Otway's play (with a variation in the pronouns). Otway's exact wording is:

> There long she flourished,
> Grew sweet to sense, and lovely to the eye,
> Till at the last a cruel spoiler came,
> Cropped this fair rose, and rifled all its sweetness,
> Then cast it like a loathsome weed away. (4.1.294–8)

The flower language highlights fragility over beauty and consequently Thanatos over Eros. Gordon's behaviour represents a failed enactment to spoil and rifle, which forms the essence of this pessimistic take on how female beauty is used and abused. Although there are few Richardsonian echoes in Johnstone, this is surely a significant one, which, unfortunately, is not developed very successfully as Gordon's caricature-like villainy prevents the possibility of his having any redeeming or attractive qualities.

The fourth factor comes within the text itself. Norman is the young, principled hero who will eventually marry Monimia. Norman has, as I have indicated, two doubles whose lives form subplots, mirroring each other. He turns out fine, but Archibald Gordon and Phelim Bourke do not; the implications of Phelim's life and death will be discussed later. One clear reason for Norman's survival is that

> WOMAN was indeed the tutelary genius of Norman's wayward fate. Her kindness had preserved his feeble existence, fostered his infancy, and tended his childhood [...] In every felicitous occurrence of his life, Norman could trace the agency of *woman*, – and through so endeared a medium every blessing was to him twice blessed. (314)

Johnstone reinforces her argument by marking the word 'woman' first in capitals and then in italics. The second sentence is predictable, in the sense that he was taken in when he was a newborn baby in a precarious state of health; it forms a standard definition of motherhood. What is not so predictable is the assertion that woman has been the agent far beyond childhood. Consequently it would not be pushing the point at all to suggest that, in terms of contemporary writing on gender, Norman, as subject rather than individual, is an honorary heroine. His experiences and viewpoints are therefore unique, combining the best of both genders. In a way, this tutelage both clarifies and complicates matters, suggesting that in the world there are females, males and enlightened males-cum-females like Norman. Yet that insight makes it extremely complicated to define behaviour since we are left with three types, namely, standard military heroism, heroinism, and heroism-heroinism as carried out by Norman, which is a combination of the traditional military code and Lady Augusta's teaching; inevitably there will be moments when they do not concur.

If my hypothesis is correct, we will witness in *Clan-Albin* a series of parallels that highlight the nature of warfare, whether in its traditional military sense or war between the sexes, as Gilbert identified. Initially, this would seem to be a painstaking task for two basic reasons: first, Lady Augusta's opposition to warfare, and, second, the novel's lengthy disquisition on patriotism.

A national tale is predictably going to contain scenes of warfare, comments and analysis of war, of which *Clan-Albin* is no exception. Again, rather predictably, opinions about war seem to relate to a traditional gender division. Norman's predilection for a military career is accounted for because:

> Educated among a martial people, and taught to consider arms as the only profession worthy of a gentleman destitute of fortune, Norman felt an early and strong vocation to glory. His first lesson had been the military exercise; while yet a child he had been an ideal soldier, the habit of him he fondly called father was military, and all pointed one way. Yet with all the impatient ardour incident to his age and character, with all his impassioned desire to rush into life and action, he cheerfully submitted to the will of her whom it was his happiness to obey. She said he was too young to be left alone, and Norman felt that she was too aged to be consigned to solitude. (69)

The final sentence refers to his desire not to abandon Lady Augusta in her vastly underpopulated glen after it has been cleared, an event narrated in great detail in the first volume. Johnstone stresses that his inclination for the military is a result of the martial nature of the Highlanders. From an early age, from their childish games, the military spirit is inculcated. Later on, in the final chapters of the first volume, and the opening chapters of the second volume, great emphasis will be laid on the destitution of the Highlanders and the ruin that capitalism has brought with it. This will certainly be the end of a sophisticated society, one which, for example, has an ingrained love of music. Nostalgia is not going to occur, as for Johnstone the Highlanders were first and foremost 'a military people' rather than rustics who lived solely for ceilidhs. Similarly, she completely removes the romantic aura of the Highland regiment in what must be one of the most bilious descriptions we could ever come across. When Norman joins up,

> His first disappointment had been, to find a Highland regiment, a name consecrated to glory [...] a promiscuous horde, shaken from the encumbered lap of society, and mingled with the overflowing scum of her morbid ebullition. (253)

This outburst is one of several moments when Johnstone puts herself in the opposite corner to Anne Grant, a subject I will deal with in more detail later on. Juliet Shields comments that 'Grant implies that the army, with its growing corps of Highland regiments, could preserve Highlanders' ethnic purity while also preparing them, should they be so fortunate as to survive the duration of their military service, to assimilate into a civilized society' (2010: 121). Johnstone's desire to show the opposite might be seen as more conceptual than truthful, as studies like John Prebble's *Mutiny* (1975) illustrate that the military's refusal to permit 'ethnic purity' led to mutiny. Her severity is also the result of her tapping into one of the ongoing debates of the period, namely whether the British model of voluntary service was better or worse than the Napoleonic model of conscription. Johnstone comes down firmly against the British model by suggesting that an army based on volunteers will basically attract 'scum'. In early nineteenth-century Britain this runs dangerously close to affronting the national cause and to seditious libel. But that is not the end of the story: Norman, our honorary female, following the edicts of Wollstonecraft, so firmly believes in education that he tries to instruct his illiterate companions, but his literacy campaign is thwarted by their superiors, above all by the most enlightened officers. *Clan-Albin* shows that the officer class are content with illiterates who spend their money on alcohol, as they would feel threatened by a soldier class that destined some of their scanty pay to books and writing materials in order to educate themselves.

Lady Augusta is explicit about warfare. In her educational exchanges with her young pupils, when asked whether she believes wars will ever cease, she replies that she hopes so (174), which is not as evasive an answer as might appear: she states that progress has been made in other areas, such as the virtual disappearance of the Inquisition, the Slave

Trade Act (1807), education and several other causes dear to liberal thought. She hopes that the memory of the horrors of the French Revolution will not become an obstacle to progress. The causes of war might eventually be abolished, as progress in other areas of life would indicate.

It is no wonder that Lady Augusta, if not quite a pacifist, is openly sceptical about warfare. The citation describing Norman's early years suggests that her educational system replaced the traditional martial one, which presumably explains her disapproval of playing with toy swords. She did not want Norman to become a soldier; she would have preferred 'a medical education' (68). Having insufficient funds, this is not possible; she simply hopes his education, which is almost entirely her instruction, will enable him to survive in a world inhabited by scum. Her preference therefore obeys the traditional gender distinction between warrior and healer.

As constantly occurs in Johnstone's writing, just as she builds up one convincing set of arguments, she then puts together another which sits at odds. When Norman first approaches the military camp, 'all his patriotic enthusiasm' is so aroused by military music that 'his tears burst in an agony of pleasure' (240). Johnstone then proceeds to describe the phenomenon as it affects all classes and both genders. This is made most explicit in the pages dedicated to the inspection of the troops by General Sir John Moore. Moore is certainly put on a pedestal but the review itself is prefaced by the narrative's stressing it is really a 'rehearsal for murder' (292). As we will continually see, Johnstone is yet again engaging in an ongoing political argument. In a novel on the Peninsular War, it is initially odd that no mention is made of the person most closely associated in the popular imagination with that conflict, Arthur Wellesley, Duke of Wellington. Instead, Johnstone decides to present Sir John Moore as the great military figure, not only in this brief incident here, but in most of volume four, which describes the retreat to Corunna which led to Moore's death, celebrated in Charles Wolfe's (1791–1823) vastly popular poem 'The Burial of Sir John Moore after Corunna'. The argument here is about the skills of both generals and about politics. Wellington was an extremely controversial figure for his – and his brothers' – high political profile. After his victory over the French troops at the Battle of Vimeiro on 21 August 1808, very generous conditions were offered to the French, so much so that many people in Britain viewed them as an act of betrayal, and particularly a betrayal of the troops themselves; as Johnstone pithily puts it, '[w]hat had been gained by courage was thrown away by mismanagement' (423). The ensuing outcry provoked an official inquiry which absolved Wellington (Muir 1996: 50–9). The other military figures mentioned in passing in the novel, such as Lord William Bentinck or General James Fergusson (a veteran of Vimeiro and the retreat to Corunna), are all of the reforming school. So, Wellington's fame as a brutal disciplinarian, that is to say the polar opposite of Moore and other generals in favour of military reform, results in his elimination from the text. The Iron Duke is clearly a *persona non grata* for Johnstone. Moore, in contrast, in what is a distinctly provocative move by Johnstone, is presented as 'the first SOLDIER of his country' (293). Again, we see her use of typographical devices, capital letters, to hammer home distinctions. Moore is a soldier, not a scheming career politician – like the Wellesleys – is the implicit comparison, with the added insinuation that he died as a sacrificial victim. So the gender argument does not work as well as it initially seemed, because a clear distinction is drawn between different generals and different causes. A war to liberate Spain, above all, is seen by Johnstone to be a just cause which deserves universal support.

The answer lies in the idea of patriotism. This word has a gendered and generational origin in the etymology of the father. As I have already noted, the emotions that Norman feels on approaching the camp are a deep manifestation of his patriotism. That is hardly unexpected in the bosom of a volunteer, but there are two things which are not so immediately obvious. The first is that his strong reaction is naturally emotional because it is the result of what he hears before he realizes what constitutes the army: scum, ferocious discipline and so on. Volumes three and four describe Norman's developmental education, a fundamental part of which is the realization that military life does not correspond to his ideals. Initially, that might suggest that he was either too young or too innocent, but, as we shall shortly see, the parallel career of Bourke illustrates a lot more than the fate of two fictional characters. Second, as the events after Vimeiro indicate, political rivalry is as present in military as it is in civilian life. If, by the end of this chapter, *Clan-Albin* looks like a liberal manifesto, which is more or less the truth, one reason derives from its positioning towards the armed forces.

During Moore's visit, all the main characters congregate; in fact, Johnstone goes to some length to point out that patriotism attracts everyone from 'the fantastic votary of fashion to the pale mechanic' (292). Although in this particular instance the intention is again to cast votes for Moore's status – people from all walks of life admire him – Johnstone interpolates the narrative with a rhetorical question, 'for who so debased as not to share in the glory of his country, and who so exalted as not to feel that his highest boast is to be called her son' (292). In short, only the oddest of human beings lies outside its reach. Women are inside: '[i]n compliment to the day, or rather to the officers, the ladies wore a sort of military costume' (293). It is possible to note a certain disdain in this flirtatious activity, and one can only wonder what it really looked like. Monimia alone is dignified in her dress, as she is in life: 'she wore the bonnet of Scotland' (293). Furthermore, in another gender modification, it is the female civilian in uniform who stirs desire. This would seem to suggest that despite patriotism being an integral part of our thinking, it is available in many forms and guises, as varied as fashion itself, some dignified, others not.

Therefore, in trying to define what heroism is, making headway is onerous. At some moments gender distinctions are clearly defined, but at others, certain facets are seen as universals. This clearly makes for confusion. However, two subjects certainly permit farther understanding, one is the love-plot, the second is the case of Phelim Bourke.

As was the case of the scene where the word 'heroinism' is used (waiting to hear news of the court martial), in all other spheres a woman's role is bound to be limited, though not necessarily confined to waiting. There are active females: Flora is one example of positive, humanistic values, whereas Archibald Gordon's mother, a schemer of the aristocratic mould that Brunton portrayed, leans more towards the Machiavellian, using the patronage network to solve her problems. Yet it is she who draws the most explicit parallel between a war between sexes and military campaigns. After the military parade, Gordon refuses to let Monimia speak, to which his mother pointedly replies, 'O tyrant! [...] we must just yield to military despotism' (295). Johnstone does not give religion the importance it had for Brunton and late Ferrier, so comfort or justification will have to come from other sources.

At certain moments, Johnstone seems to be deeply romantic: the marriages of Monimia and Flora might suggest that love conquers all and is therefore the reward for overcoming the trials and tribulation of war-torn societies, a template corresponding very much to Bakhtinian models of adventure time. Flora's traumatic experiences include not only witnessing the Peninsular War at first hand, but a gruesome series of events involving an amputation. Her husband's left arm has been shattered; being brave, he urges the surgeons to proceed with the operation, taking no heed of 'the alarming [surgical] instruments' (427) on display, a description intended to communicate intense anxiety. In a most macabre fashion, Flora rushes to his side only to faint on seeing 'the severed arm of Craig-gillian, imperfectly covered, – the arm which that morning had clasped her to his bosom when he blessed and left her' (428). In the end, they live happily ever after, which would suggest that in this case a hypothesis based on gender does not always work. Love has given them the power to endure extreme adversity.

The central love-plot would seem to be pretty conventional too: Monimia, like Dora, the intended rape victim, is pursued by Gordon, and in both cases the power his social standing gives him is of no avail. The romantic side is present in the fact that both lovers are orphans: Norman has no inheritance of note, and Monimia's is being frittered away by her guardian. Their marriage is therefore a match which directly contradicts the dictates of the Earl of Courtland at the beginning of *Marriage* when he laid down the law that marriage is a financial and political transaction; love marriages are for the *canaille*. Monimia is, however, not an ordinary bride. In what must be one of fiction's most unbelievable set of circumstances, she is a virgin widow of a man who was '[m]y father, my friend, my guide, my husband' (110). Of course, the only attribute which is not literally true is the first one. This strange situation is brought about after her own revulsion at having to perform socially as 'the heiress of a Nabob' (108); she has already frequented fashionable Bath, Brighton, Tonbridge and London, and so is fully aware of how the marriage market operates for the wealthy. It is therefore interesting to see how Johnstone describes the troth-plight scene, giving it plenty of local colour while simultaneously putting distance between herself and the romance she describes. For example, the scene contains descriptions like, '[s]he made a feeble effort to disengage herself from his embrace. She slowly raised her face, beautiful in the paleness of overpowering emotion' (346). There is talk of '[t]he first raptures of bliss' (346), all set in an idyllic, pastoral Irish scene. The two distinctive Johnstone touches come from the mind and mouth of Monimia. First, while Norman is still on his knees avowing his love at great length, 'Monimia felt that her preference had already been sufficiently manifest' (346). In other words, Norman's declaration has gone on far too long; conventional wooing is so wearisome! Second, when she takes his hand, she says, in an overtly Foucauldian utterance, '[m]y day of power is past' (346). Consequently an interesting parallel emerges from her two marriages. In the first, she had no way of protecting her inheritance from her guardian; and in the second case, the idea of being given away in marriage is not a metaphor but a statement of fact. The male in the first case is unscrupulous and in the second case is virtuous, but the outcome, or potential outcome, is exactly the same. Therefore heroism becomes almost an impossibility. In the fiction of

Brunton, for comparison's sake, there were clear indications that wives had a function in married life, and an extremely important one at that. Here, we hear nothing at all. It is simply, like Vimeiro and afterwards, a case of what terms of surrender are offered; some are more generous than others. It would be no exaggeration to say that, viewed from this angle, phrases like the Glorvina solution or union are inappropriate if not completely inapplicable.

Although we shall later return to this scene and to the life-story of Phelim Bourke, the question of patriotism looms large in Norman's and the readers' interpretation of Phelim's desertion to the Napoleonic cause. It is timely to recall the pronouncement that 'for who so debased as not to share in the glory of his country, and who so exalted as not to feel that his highest boast is to be called her son' (292) has a corollary, namely that the most debased form of behaviour is therefore betrayal, to be the son who turns against his country. Norman meets Phelim after his desertion, first in a skirmish, and second in prison, before witnessing his death on the scaffold. At the first encounter, Norman does not recognize him, which might be because of his magnificent uniform and Andalusian horse, which would reinforce the importance of uniforms and icons as essential for modern myths, a process which, as Roland Barthes so rightly recognized, tends to deprive subjects of their history (1989: 132). Norman has been temporarily blinded by military splendour, without that necessarily placing him in the same situation as the spectator's at Moore's military parade. Nevertheless, reading a deeper significance into the episode is unavoidable not solely in terms of the novel's plot and structure, as they were bosom buddies, but because Phelim plays the role of his double; in other words, here, the self cannot recognize the other. Johnstone forcefully recounts Norman's feelings as ambivalence: 'Norman looked on this *traitor*, Bourke, with a mixture of vexation, pity, and astonishment; his heart recoiling, and yet drawn towards him by the force of sympathies' (442). The key word is repeated in the same paragraph with a different emphasis, '[y]et let it not be imagined that he thought himself a traitor' (442). Although Johnstone deeply sympathizes with the Irish political situation and draws parallels between the death of Phelim and Wolfe Tone after the 1798 rebellion, these political links will be put on hold briefly. For Johnstone sees no contradiction in Irish soldiers fighting for the British army while professing intense love of Ireland, and unlike Tone, neither Johnstone nor Phelim openly advocate an independent Ireland. Furthermore, Johnstone's remarks about the central role of patriotism are placed during the military review held in honour of General Moore, himself a

Scot, which takes place in Ireland where the two central characters of the novel, an Irish and a Scottish orphan, fall in love.

It is understandable that this all sounds puzzling. However, what will concern us here is the more abstract notion of patriotism as much as each individual case. That said, Phelim's life-story not only has parallels with Tone's but also serves as an illustration of Johnstone's involvement with one of the burning issues of the day, corporal punishment. Leigh Hunt was tried several times, most famously for his supposedly libellous remarks against the Prince Regent. Yet he was involved in another major case, namely one dealing with corporal punishment. The seditious libel law meant, contrary to the commonplace idea that evidence is the basis of conviction, that the jury only had to be convinced of the tendency of the potentially libellous article, which was read out in court, before returning its verdict. *The Examiner* had published several articles on the subject. For example, in the 2 September 1810 edition, Hunt reprinted a short article from the *Stamford News* entitled 'One Thousand Lashes' which detailed a sentence of that number. Another, penned patriotically by an Englishman, appeared on 16 December 1810, and argued that Britain's belief in its civilized society was undermined by the cruelty of flogging its soldiers with 800 or 1000 lashes, thereby sentencing 'the unhappy victim [...] to a premature grave' (Anon. 1810: 796). The article suggests that rather than leaving such matters to the discretion of court martials, punishment should be legislated. This was not an original article in the sense that it fitted into a bitter debate about the state of the army. One argument used by opponents of corporal punishment, which illustrates how deeply people felt about it, was the analogy with slaves. Britain had freed them from such punishment but had not done so with its soldiers, who, in spite of heroically defending Britain and its colonies, were therefore treated even worse. Another was the insinuation that if Napoleon did not use this form of punishment, it was because he was not a barbarian; perhaps Britain should reconsider its own practice. In the end, Leigh Hunt was cleared. His lawyer, Henry Brougham, argued that what was at stake was not solely the question of the army but that of free speech. Just as free Englishmen could speak of taxes, they should be able to speak of the army. The link between the two subjects is clear, as income tax had been introduced in 1798 to pay for the war, making Brougham's line of argument extremely persuasive; it touched two issues that lay central to Britain's conception of itself as a modern, tolerant state. In other words, what was at stake was not solely the fair treatment of soldiers but the whole ethos of the British nation, those constituent parts that comprise patriotism.

The abolition of corporal punishment, or at least its codification within law which would require a vast reduction in the number of lashes and in the power of court martials, was a cause which liberals were deeply concerned with. The details outlined above, as well as many others which liberals so objected to, are integrated into the life of Phelim in chapter 27. Johnstone mentions three points of interest: first, the obligation of young drummer-boys to witness punishment; second, the presence of a doctor, whom she nicknames 'the flogometer' (251), whose job it is to stop proceedings when needed, this necessity taking the form of holding-over, that is, delaying the completion of the sentence to a later occasion if the victim is physically not able to withstand all the lashes in one session. The chapter was reprinted almost word for word some 17 years later in *The Schoolmaster and Edinburgh Weekly Magazine* (4 August 1832) preceded by a short introductory article – 'Flogging in the Army' – which includes the central argument that this is a specifically British custom which the French army does not use. The story of Phelim thus becomes a parable which deals with a facet of army life which was deeply controversial, as Leigh Hunt's trial demonstrates. Third, it is made clear that flogging is a form of violation worse than death, as the liberals insistently argued, which highlights its parallel standing to rape, the fate that Phelim's lover Dora narrowly escaped from. Archibald Gordon's presence in both cases draws the two incidents together, but the question remains unanswered: to what purpose? Is it justifiable to search for reasons beyond the political arguments of the time, which Johnstone herself writes about in her journalism?

It would be easy to dismiss the parallels as simply part of Johnstone's encyclopaedic method. However, I would argue that the intentionality is there, as the following patterns emerge. First and foremost, both the attempted rape and whipping are assaults upon the body. The sex of the intended victim is different in each case, but both share Irish nationality. Neither act necessarily leads to physical death, yet are perceived in many quarters as worse than death. This is made explicit by Phelim in the text itself, both in the earlier chapter describing the punishment itself and in the later one which narrates his death, and by Johnstone in the 1832 article mentioned in the previous paragraph. The connotations of dishonour and death are so obvious and extensive in the case of rape, that no farther comment is required. Both activities are unacceptable in peacetime, in civil society, yet their status in wartime has been acknowledged as relatively normal. Those who argued against the abolitionists regarded it, or at least the threat of it, as necessary for the maintenance of discipline; the figure most closely associated with such vehement discipline is, again, the liberal bugbear, the Iron Duke. However, the evidence he later gave in 1845 to a parliamentary commission investigating military punishments shows a more conciliatory figure, aware of both sides of the argument. At the same time, Wellington's beliefs expressed to the commission in 1845 might have been rather different from those he held 30 years previously. The idea that rape is part of military practice used against civilians with strategic significance, that is to say it is not simply the result of random violence, alcohol or drugs, is extremely controversial. Recognition usually takes the form of saying it occurs in the developing world, in brutal wars such as in the Democratic Republic of Congo or Sri Lanka, or else it is confined to the ethics of medieval codes of war.[2] However, we should remember Carl von Clausewitz's dictum that 'the advance of civilization has done nothing practical to alter or deflect the impulse to destroy the enemy' (1993: 85), and that includes the rape, mutilation and murder of civilians. The attack on Dora, likewise, if seen no longer as Gordon's excess but as a weapon of war either in the battle against Irish resistance or in the battle of the sexes, moves it into another sphere of importance. The remark 'we must just yield to military despotism' could no longer be contained within the realm of female small-talk.

The final task in this account of patriotism within heroism is to try and pinpoint the narrative's attitude to Phelim Bourke's fate. It is important to bear two points in mind: the first is that Phelim's life history is clearly laid out. The English, his own term, in the form of Archibald Gordon, yet again have destroyed his family's fortunes and his own body, therefore his 'traitor' status is explained as a situation with comprehensible symptoms, yet it is clearly not condoned. Johnstone, by setting the military review in Ireland and through the comments that surround it, sees participation in the war against Napoleon as a unifying policy that incorporates Ireland. The way both narrative and Phelim's own remarks are articulated in chapter 51 points towards the idea that if he had not encountered Gordon and had consequently not been sentenced to flogging, he would have continued more or less happily as a British soldier, thus reinforcing the point that corporal punishment is a fate worse than death.

It is revealing to note how Johnstone narrates his reaction to events. 'The torturing [...] had stung into a thousand strengths that busy devil which national prejudice and family wrongs, remembered too well, and resented too keenly, had first admitted into a heart which nature had fitted for the resting place of a very different inmate' (538); this is not the first time Johnstone has used the term 'national prejudice'. Earlier in this same volume four, Norman finds out that the French were not 'the fierce savages that newspapers of the day represented them' (482); in so doing, he overcomes his national prejudice. The term itself is the title of a short essay by Oliver Goldsmith, a writer who Johnstone uses in several epigraphs, particularly in the first volume, in order to draw a parallel between the deserted glen and 'The Deserted Village' (1770). Goldsmith finds it hard to understand that national prejudices are so prevalent among the educated; he makes two important points that Johnstone has picked up. The first is that love for one's country is one thing, but it is fallacious to state that this inevitably grows into prejudice. He parallels this with a distinction between religion and superstition: the latter is not necessarily a product of the former. Let us recall that Flora's Catholicism was not, to use Johnstone's term, theological, that is to say impervious to reason. Second, again with a clear emphasis on rationalism and moderation, that contemporary nationalism has taken us so far, according to Goldsmith, 'that we are no longer citizens of the world [...] we no longer consider ourselves as the general inhabitants of the globe, or members of that grand society which comprehends the whole human kind' (1840: 495). In terms of both time and ideology, this is very much the line taken by Lady Augusta throughout the novel, and which explains the vital difference between the condemned (Phelim) and the hero (Norman). The former behaves in a way which leads only to violence, the other, in a way leading to reconciliation. This would suggest that a certain scepticism exists in Johnstone towards the emerging nineteenth-century state and arguably the national tale itself as the cultural tool used to promote and encourage its establishment. Although similar arguments about universal love and reason can be found in Mary Wollstonecraft and although Johnstone's views on education share much common ground, there is another vital difference between the two thinkers, which inclines me to opt for Goldsmith as the ideologue here. Wollstonecraft's universalism is always directed towards God, undeniably the source of the possible perfectibility of humankind. Johnstone's inspiration is more material.

Left as such, this would be a convincing argument, placing Johnstone simultaneously as part nineteenth-century liberal or radical and part Augustan. The contradictions such co-existence causes might explain the extraordinary ambivalence in this novel. Yet, this is, to a certain extent, a dissatisfactory statement because it does not sufficiently obey the match of the war between opposing sides and the war between the sexes, as Gilbert lays it out. Johnstone does so by reverting to the perennial debate on the rationality – lack of rationality – in men and women.

As this argument stretches back at least to the Greeks and to whether who listens or who can read maps, there is little point in engaging in such debates here, other than to point out that Johnstone's central hypothesis is that, in a complete reversal of Rousseau's thinking, men are the more emotional creatures. As every reader soon realizes, the ideological centre of the text is Lady Augusta. Her own life is narrated in chapter 20, a story of love, religion and violence that takes place in France. In the following chapter, its moral is explained; it is not a condemnation of perfidious, scheming Catholics, but a lesson showing 'the fatal effects of passions, however laudable, indulged in defiance of reason and prudence' (170), a moral which shares the same ground as Brunton's dedication of *Self-Control*, discussed previously. Again, the emphasis is placed on reason. But this is not simply the reason of the Augustan age, this is reason as exercised in the highly gendered world of *Clan-Albin*. Flora is not a theological Catholic but a reasonable one; her father was not a rational Presbyterian, but a theological one. Phelim was a totally passionate Irishman, and however laudable his aims were, he acted in defiance of reason and prudence. It is men, therefore, according to this text, who turn patriotism into a passion with fatal effects, in short, into war. Phelim is therefore Norman's double because he has not had woman as his tutelary genius. This sober message is sometimes difficult to balance with Johnstone's own sympathy with Ireland's plight, as we shall soon see. To conclude, there is not only the war between sexes, based on irrationality and oppression, hence despotism, but the war between nations, based on a similarly unsustainable prejudice fostered in the hearts of men. Heroinism could be defined as the struggle to sustain a rational view of the world which heroism is incapable of achieving; likely achievers are those who have had the right tutelary genius. Consequently, when Peter Womack talks of the 'women's Highlands' (1989: 133), he is certainly right.

Parents and education

Clan-Albin begins with an episode that is common to many novels: the birth of an orphan on a stormy night in November, the month which is the 'highpoint of the "reading season"' (Garside 1991: 36). The original touches Johnstone adds to the foundling *topos* have a certain thematic likeness to Burns's narrative poem *Tam o' Shanter*: a villager, Ronald, is reluctant to return home after a cattle fair once his 'leave of absence' (3) has expired. He does not encounter warlocks and witches on his return but a woman in childbirth. The first two footnotes on the opening pages supplement the information given in the text on Highland customs. The elderly Moome looks on the newborn baby with memories of a 'dalt'. The note explains: 'DALT, a foster child. The custom of fosterage still subsists in the Isles, and some parts of the Highlands, in primitive force. By the lower class it is clung to with Hibernian zeal. It promotes their interest, flatters their pride, and forms the bond of a very endearing connexion between the poor and the rich' (n. p. 11). A few pages farther on, the word 'Calt' appears; Johnstone's footnote glosses, 'CHO-ALT, a connexion by fosterage. All the relations of the *Moome*, or foster-mother, are *Cho-Alt* to the *Dalt*. Devoted to him through life, and but too often a tax on his generosity' (n. p. 13). What is the purpose of Johnstone's footnotes and her ethnographic picture of Highland life?

I would argue that she has four basic aims, all of which result from the desire to inform about Highland customs, following and contesting the views of Anne MacVicar Grant's *Essays on the Superstitions of the Highlanders of Scotland* (1811), which had been published, let us note, only four years previously. The general aim is to position herself as a more faithful 'translator', to use Ferris's argument (1997), who can focus from the margins themselves. Subsequently, Johnstone intends to clarify or correct previously published material or popular, widespread misconceptions. For example, chapter 10 insists that Highlanders 'are the most abstemious of all people' (53), which is an attempt to refute both a national prejudice and Grant's description of drunkenness (1811: 2:117–19). This same chapter includes a description of the Coolin cheese, with an accompanying footnote specifically designed to correct Dr Johnson's 'imperfect account' (n. p. 55) of the same in the chapter 'Castle of Col' in *A Journey to the Western Islands of Scotland* (1775). The third objective is to record details of a society that is passing away due to the Clearances, emigration and the subsequent disappearance of Gaelic. If it is true that all paradises are lost, then Glenalbin would be no exception. Lady Augusta, much in tune with her times, sees America as being the obvious destination for her enterprising Gaels who have been forcefully evicted, not least because 'forced emigration is a far lesser evil than the military service that Grant proposed for displaced Highlanders' (Shields 2010: 124). There, in the land of liberty, they fulfil their potential, and presumably, as Grant herself proposes, have a greater probability of maintaining their native tongue. As a result, one point which is made several times during the book is that the emigrants have no desire to return when the clan's lands have been recovered and its finances put in order. Consequently, recording the old ways becomes a double necessity. The fourth is to foreground the plight of her fictional orphans and the orphan motif as a whole, recurrent as it is throughout her whole work. The first two notes illustrate how these strategies function. Johnstone's text illustrates customs, following Grant's explanation of the *Cho-Alt* (1811: 2:188–202). Johnstone would have noted that Grant's illustrative example of ties takes place during war; hence, her own emphasis on the martial side of Highland life. Recording such an event might enlighten its readers while simultaneously indicating a radically different family structure from the nuclear model of an emerging urban society, which would comprise the vast majority of the novel's readers. The Celtic model privileges kinship over a nuclear model. In the case of Norman, his biological mother dies in the opening pages, but this is not seen as being the end of the matter because he has several mothers who make up his tutelary genius. The most important of these is Lady Augusta: he 'was universally known as "The Lady's Child"' (31). Her educational platform is based on literature, foreign languages, music and religious tolerance. This falls within the requirements for an educated gentleman, but it is perhaps more important to emphasize that a critical part of Norman's upbringing is the maintenance of his Gaelic roots. Shortly after the reference to the lady's child, the narrative continues:

> The Lady wished that he should converse familiarly in English from his earliest infancy, an accomplishment not to be learned in Dunalbin, where the only language was pure Gaelic. She was not however infected with the fashionable fear which now reigns in most Highland families; she was old-fashioned enough to think that there was nothing very horrible or vulgar in a mountain child lisping the language of the mountains; in a Highlander being perfectly acquainted with the energetic idiom of his native land. She even felt something like contempt for those modern renegadoes who pride themselves in real, and often on affected ignorance of all that it should be their boast to know. (32)

Lady Augusta's bilingual educational programme is contrasted to a highly alliterative alternative – infected with the fashionable fear – based on an English-only educational programme for a monolingual Gaelic society. If there is pressure from outside to anglicize society, it meets with little or no resistance from within, otherwise it could never be defined as fashion. In short, these modern 'renegadoes' are writing off their own heritage. Lady Augusta's instruction in language is supplemented by Moome's in folklore. Describing the venerable female, the depository of all knowledge, is beset with the danger of either becoming sentimental or producing a character more akin to new age beliefs.[3] Moome retains knowledge of history, based on genealogies, nature and, most importantly of all, the supernatural. Having mentioned Goldsmith's comment on religion and superstition, it is worthwhile recalling the title of Grant's volumes: *Essays on the Superstitions of the Highlanders of Scotland*, as it implies that superstition, a word quite close to primitivism, was the defining factor of Highland life. Grant herself is often ambivalent in her remarks. When talking about their religious practice, she says that '[i]t was also mingled with superstitions all their own, and entirely distinct from those of popery' (1811: 1:131). Which did she consider worse? In addition, the early pages of the second volume deal with the question of second sight at great length. But in both cases, it is difficult to know where Grant stands, as appreciation of kinship and religious beliefs goes side by side with a strong belief in the ladder of civilization. The superstitions are, in short, relics of a bygone age, but relics certainly have value of some sort. Johnstone, in contrast, has no doubts at all about the worth and validity of old customs, of which fosterage is the first example she gives. Moome is not killed off with the Clearances or even threatened like Crichton Smith's Mrs Scott. She survives in order to play the significant role of closing the final volume of the tale with a blessing which, the narrative points out, is in Gaelic. This is significant for it suggests that Gaelic life and customs are compatible with the present and are condemned to the past through a fashionable infection, or, in other words, a desire to shake them off as quickly as possible. The Celtic twilight Johnstone envisages is a socially, self-induced phenomenon.

While Norman is a small child, it is clear that he does not miss having a biological mother; on the contrary, he is not able to identify his status as an orphan at all, blurting out at one point that he has several mothers (42). One is Lady Augusta and another is Mary, a village girl whose name is the essence of motherhood. Her soldier-lover returns after a long absence and is immediately embroiled in a series of misunderstandings when biology and fosterage overlap. The soldier is surprised to hear first from Norman that Mary is his mother (39); the identical sentiment is expressed a moment later by Mary (40). In this very short chapter 7, Norman will also say that he has no father. Of course, Norman is not the only orphan in Johnstone's fiction; in fact, her fiction is populated with orphans. Monimia is the most obvious case in hand; Elizabeth de Bruce is almost an orphan, in the sense that she has been brought up without seeing or hearing from either of her parents, who only make brief appearances towards the end of the eponymous novel. Elizabeth's husband is also an orphan; in short, the four major characters of her fiction all share this situation; parents have been abolished.

The reason for this peculiar situation is to centre the importance of education in the formation of our personal development. Johnstone opens the first novel with details of ancient customs or fosterage to set the scene for a modern debate on education and motherhood. These very customs, added to Norman's innocent remarks, suggest that nurture is far more important than nature. At the same time, there seems to be a keen awareness that motherhood is something that has to be worked at, and can only be sacred after much effort and hard work. The end result is Norman, brave and gentle, Gaelic speaking and polyglot, a combination of virtues that fashionable infections assign exclusively to one sex or the other. It is tempting to search for Johnstone's influences, especially as she went on to write several interesting educational books, notably *The Diversions of Hollycot; or, The Mother's Art of Thinking* (1828), which includes a very early example of a cloze test. The second half of the title is striking and both an indication of Johnstone's rationalism and a homage to Wollstonecraft's belief in the educated, rational female. There are undoubted similarities, but also notable differences, of which two are fundamental. The first is that *Clan-Albin* still maintains a belief in the importance of social standing and rank: the glens can be recovered if and when the chiefs recover their sense of duty to the community. Second, as previously stated, Johnstone's first novel lacks the pervasive presence of religion and religious love of her predecessors.

In the second novel, *Elizabeth de Bruce* (1827), very little is said about the education of the hero, Wolfe Grahame, other than the fact that he went to school and university (1:17) where he studied law, as becomes 'the eldest son of a Scottish family of the second order of pretence' (1:28). However, he was more interested in extra-curricular activities that led to the suggestive nickname 'Buckish Bob' (1:29). He opts for a military career and becomes a captain. This is narrated in the briefest way possible; a few more details are forthcoming in Elizabeth's case. She learns Irish and Scottish ballads in the nursery (1:95); the Bible became 'her first and only school-book' (1:97), though it is questionable whether her preference for a trio of resourceful heroines, Judith, Jael and Rachel, would meet with her Presbyterian tutor's approval, as Judith and Jael are responsible for two gruesome executions. Elizabeth, also educated by nature, becomes 'hardy and bold as a gypsy's brat' (1:99). The couple's mutual attraction is brought about by their love of books; readers, the narrative informs us, form secret societies like freemasons (1:113). In *Clan-Albin*, the lack of biological parents is more than made up by

Norman's three mothers who instruct him fully in everything, from nature to philosophy. Monimia is educated by the multifaceted man who becomes her first husband. From this illustration, it becomes clear that in this second novel, there is no compensation for the absence of parents; no one is there to stand in. Everything, starting with education, proceeds in a disorganized way in a hostile world. Here lies the marked difference between the texts: the second has a deeply pessimistic view of life. The three mothers at least had the opportunity to participate in the world, but in the gloomy universe of *Elizabeth de Bruce* opportunities and hope are conspicuous by their absence. There will be no Moome to give a blessing or a ray of hope at the end of a long story.

Locations

At this point, we will now turn to *Elizabeth de Bruce*, which, I will argue, is radically different from *Clan-Albin*, best exemplified by their respective treatment of geography. McMillan describes the earlier novel in these terms: '[a]s it proceeds the plot pushes out its circumference and eats up, as it were, a number of different narrative kinds and enables a number of different narrative perspectives' (2003–4: 35). She later describes the novel as voracious. In *Clan-Albin* it would be true to say that world is travelled and experienced with constant scene changes as if we were watching *Antony and Cleopatra*. That ample geography responds very closely to the universalism of Lady Augusta and her concern with correspondingly universal topics, such as religion, war, marriage, education and art. McMillan feels that at certain points the subject matter gets out of control and we are left with 'messy miscellaneousness' (36).

McMillan is stressing that Johnstone's sweep is so large that it cannot be contained within one novel. This is an argument about form rather than ideology. Johnstone promotes her political platform in her fiction but it is not the case that the ideas are messy, rather that she is unable to hone them into a manageable form. In short, McMillan is proposing that Johnstone's fiction is entropic: a massive increase in energy detracts from the reader's ability to process it.

This is extremely persuasive; I will return to her concluding arguments in the next section of this chapter. Briefly, if we examine *Clan-Albin*, McMillan is correct. We start in the Highlands, we are whisked away to industrial England; Lady Augusta recounts her French years; volume three takes us to Ireland and volume four to the Peninsular War. In religious terms, we move between Highland superstitions, theological Presbyterianism and non-theological Catholicism. In terms of social class, we are first among the impoverished Highlanders, then in the salon of pushy, rich incomers, political schemers, French aristocrats, Spanish peasants, Catalan guerrillas and so on. What McMillan is saying, I believe, is that universalism is not sufficiently strong as an idea to bind together these different parts, which therefore become irredeemably disparate, perhaps most obviously in terms of length – why this number of pages for one subject and a lot less for another? – and in importance: is one particular theme supposed to be more important than another?

This argument about form can be taken one step further, because I would propose that it is specifically the question of Ireland which most seriously challenges Lady Augusta's universalism, highlighting its inadequacy as a valid epistemology in a similar way, as argued previously (pp. 13–14), that the Irish question casts a shadow over Colley's definition of Britons. To put it another way, Lady Augusta prophesied progress and peace, she expressed the hope that war might be phased out, yet the Ireland that Johnstone herself devises, at some length in *Clan-Albin* and more extensively in *Elizabeth de Bruce*, renders this project impossible.

Three of the motifs, already developed in *Clan-Albin*, the army, the love-plot and the question of national prejudice, account for this situation. In this section, I will concentrate on the army as the subject which most damagingly counteracts Lady Augusta's optimism. Having talked about the iconic status of the Highland regiments, it is important to add some factual information. First, the army was a career option: '[p]erhaps one in four regimental officers in the mid-eighteenth century was a Scot' (Colley 1992: 126). The reverse side of the coin is that other openings in the labour market were limited. Second, raising troops could be a first step forward to recovering land confiscated under the 1747 Vesting Act. Robert Clyde highlights the case of Simon Fraser, whose family were active Jacobites and consequently lost their property. The Lovat estate was returned to him in 1774 after he raised Fraser's 79th Highlanders. As far as soldiers, as opposed to officers, are concerned, Clyde tells us that:

> Between the beginning of the Seven Years' War in 1756 and the end of the Napoleonic Wars in 1815, over 48,300 men were recruited from the Highlands and islands to serve in twenty-three line regiments and twenty-six fencible regiments of the British army, not including the Black Watch, which first saw service in 1743. This figure is remarkable given the total population of the region, which rose from about a quarter of a million in 1755 to 350,000 in 1830. (1995: 150)

Clyde's point is simple but nevertheless highly impactive: the population of the Highlands is minuscule but its contribution to military life
is huge. *Clan-Albin* takes up this all-important point about the fencible
and line regiments: the former are basically for defence, whereas the
latter are more likely to be destined for service overseas. In the case of
Norman, he is going to serve in the Peninsular War and therefore is a
member of a line regiment. Yet, the troops are stationed for a time in
Ireland which causes us to ponder the crunch question: does this suggest that Ireland is an integral part of the union? That seems to be the
message of the chapter describing the military review, which includes
the remarks about patriotism uniting the inhabitants of all the islands
in a common cause: the liberation of Europe. Yet at the same time,
there are incidents in the text which suggest that Ireland is a foreign
land and therefore rather than form part of the union is seen as being
a distant country occupied by conquering troops. This is evident in
everyday conversation, when, for example, in chapter 36, the highly
offensive term 'bog-trotters' (348) is used to describe possible poachers. Monimia replies, in anger, '[b]ut in future, you need not interrupt
your card and Constantia parties for me.[4] If my Lord's cellars are as safe
from the *poaching* of the civilized English, as his woods are from the
wild Irish, he will lose little game in Ireland' (348). Even Monimia's
servant is terrified of the wild Irish. The fact that this scene describes
'a tedious dinner' (341), added to the conversation just mentioned,
plus the setting of the scene in a big house set in extensive grounds, all
contribute to producing a remarkable similarity to a colonial setting,
where Sahibs and Memsahibs take tiffin and play croquet. The word
'poaching' rebounds on itself, suggesting that the Irish are not the real
poachers but that Ireland itself has been poached rather than admitted
to the union on equitable terms, as the word union continually covers
and uncovers itself. In short, Johnstone's balancing-act of universalism
becomes undone when dealing with Ireland, as it is incompatible with
parts of the narrative that describe the political situation in simple,
unequivocal, colonial terms.

    To paraphrase Yeats, in *Elizabeth de Bruce*, Johnstone's universal
centre, the utopian Voltairean setting at the end of *Clan-Albin* cannot
hold, and the terrible new beauty which is born in the following novel
is the shattered, hostile territory, seething with violence and cruelty.
Elizabeth de Bruce centres on a set of characters whose lives and deaths
lay bare the central, but often unanswered, question that haunts the
national tale: if Ireland and Scotland have both signed up to the union,
what brings them together and what separates them? Or, if phrased in

slightly different words, in the plot, many journeys are made between Ireland and Scotland, between one periphery and the other – instead of to or from England, from the centre to the periphery – but what is the significance of this sideways movement? On all accounts, this radical novel is a peculiar choice, ideologically speaking, for a Blackwood publication.

The two novels, nonetheless, do share many features, as contemporary reviews noted. In a very brief notice, the *National Magazine, and General Review* states that 'the plots [are] intricate, and very much spun out, but the delineation of character very excellent' (Rev. 1827: 315). Similarly, *The Literary Chronicle* protested 'against the insertion of a succession of chapters, containing merely a few incidents, most of them extraneous to the main plot' (Rev. 1827: 49) but believed the novel had more beauties than faults. If the wayward plot is an example of the latter, the novel's eloquence would be an example of the former. In neither instance is there any awareness or declaration along the lines I am anticipating, which are built on the very solid foundations laid down by Ian Duncan in 'Ireland, Scotland, and the Materials of Romanticism' and *Scott's Shadow: The Novel in Romantic Edinburgh*. Why is something which is easily demonstrable nowadays so invisible to Johnstone's contemporaries? There is no straightforward reply to this, as is the case on any conjecture about absence. Several material answers will be given in the following section of this chapter, but several speculative ones assert themselves immediately. One emerges from the dissatisfaction about the plot which the two reviewers found convoluted. Similar objections were made by Saintsbury in his analysis of Ferrier, when he remarked on her inability to construct a cohesive story. It is also useful to visualize Ferrier's fiction as *commedia dell'arte*, with a large cast of characters whose idiosyncrasy is of much greater concern to the author than the interdependence of one character on another. Johnstone's technique lacks Ferrier's desire to cause laughter and derision, but she is deeply involved in drawing types, of which in both novels garrulous Irishmen, with a limited stock of set phrases and exclamations, comprise the most relevant example. This is only one step away from Scott's pronouncement on Edgeworth's 'gay and kind-hearted neighbours of Ireland'. Those familiar words from the 'General Preface', which so heavily promote the political dimension of fiction, should not distract us from its emphasis on the representation of character, or, more precisely, of national character as lying at the centre of fiction. At this juncture, according to Scott, it is through appreciation of local colour rather than plot that union is promoted. Scott's formulation was published two years after Johnstone's novel *Elizabeth de Bruce*, but that in no way detracts from the fact that the national tale, including the Waverley Novels, functions in the same way as the motto on the Great Seal of the United States, *e pluribus unum*. The central question is whether Johnstone's Ireland and its inhabitants' eccentricity, in the basic sense of out of the centre, are contained within this grand sentiment, which naturally encompasses the national tale as a subgenre. The point is that to our contemporary view, Johnstone's landscape and characters live beyond the pale which Scott and his contemporaries' fiction have delineated.

There might be a slight awareness of that at the beginning of *Elizabeth de Bruce* which opens with an apocalyptic scene in Edinburgh, a huge fire, but that feeling, like the fire, is soon put out by the pastoral beauty of the first volume, which so enthralled the *Literary Chronicle*. That this is not going to be a fire that burns and cleanses is evident in another incident in the tenth chapter of volume three when Hutchen's mansion is burnt down and several deaths, including his own, ensue. What is not very clear from the text itself is the true nature of Hutchen's villainy. Is it simply the case that pure evil makes him the Gothic manipulator of the unfortunate de Bruce family? Or, does it have more to do with the fact that he represents a way of behaving closer to modernity? Hutchen, as banker, is the herald of a newer, more commercially oriented society, illustrated by the mob's murmuring before the arson attack. For example, the comment that '[t]he Banker's siller is like the coin which the de'il paid the witches langsyne' (3:231) is sufficiently abstract to cover both Hutchen's own dastardly behaviour and the Scottish banking system as a whole. It is not my intention to suggest that this is Luddite behaviour, but to stress more that Johnstone is willing to depict, in a most graphic style, what Simon Edwards (2001) maps out as a geography of violence. The dynamics of mob behaviour recall Scott's *The Heart of Midlothian* (1818), yet however detailed and punctilious Scott is there, and however suggestive it is to place a prison at Scotland's heart, at one moment his willingness to describe horrors stops short: the execution of Meg Murdockson. Similarly, Waverley locks himself in his room at the inn rather than witness Fergus's execution; both incidents will be dealt with in more detail in the next chapter.

My point is that Johnstone does not look askance. Duncan suggests that Ireland acts 'as id, Scotland as superego: sites of antagonistic excess that stabilize a normative Anglo-British history' (2007a: 264). If Ireland is the equivalent to the id then what will be released is an excess of violence. Duncan also argues that '[w]ritten in the wake of the *Old Mortality* controversy, *Elizabeth de Bruce* explicitly invokes the Killing

Time (rather than 1745) as the Scottish analogue to the contemporary conflict in Ireland' (272).[5] If we accept this hypothesis, then not only does this highlight the oppression of the state but the corollary, namely that religious strife is the bloodiest of all. It is interesting to see how Johnstone deals with the state horror that produces nausea. She shows absolutely no hesitation in dealing with a similar incident in a tellingly explicit fashion. We do not see Fergus's head in *Waverley*, but we do see that of an Irish rebel in *Elizabeth de Bruce*:

> The person thus interrogated, without saying one word, took a torch from the soldier who stood next him, and flared its swart rays upwards over a ghastly object stuck under the centre window of the court-room, over the spiked arch-way of the open porch of St. Peter's Keys. It was a human head, blackened and purpled, the eyes starting from their sockets, the muscles of the face strained as if in the last agony of violent suffocation. Such spectacles were at this period not uncommon in Ireland. (2:330–1)

This is an extremely rich passage. Its graphic description of the severed head is closer to Conrad's picture of the trophy heads on stakes in *Heart of Darkness* than to Scott. Why I believe this is so is because of the mundane nature of the execution. The torchbearer has just been asked whether there has been any business today, and such a humdrum word as business anticipates the final statement that this is not 'uncommon'. In other words, such horror is an everyday occurrence, so common in fact that soldiers have simply become inured to it, in an attitude similar to the executioners who prepare the noose for Quentin Durward in Scott's novel (Edwards 2001: 305). What distances this episode from Fergus's death is precisely its lack of epic proportions. The death of a Highland chief may be ignominious, but Fergus is an epic figure whose idealism and valour are of heroic proportions when contrasted to the deeds and thoughts of Talbot or Waverley himself. The same cannot be said of the victim here, Felix Doran, as he is one of many such victims, basically just ordinary people. Johnstone sets the third volume of *Clan-Albin* in Ireland too, but there the similarity ends, as the later novel, unlike its predecessor, shows not the slightest hesitation in viewing the British army as an army of occupation in a colonized land. Whereas Scottish rebellion is reified in the infamous kilted portrait at the close of *Waverley*, no such parallel can be drawn here: violence is still very much alive.

Examples of colonial behaviour are so numerous that I will limit myself to three. One is the desire to change the names of places: the hostelry called St Peter's Keys, according to O'Toole, who is nicknamed the Protestant Flail, should be renamed St George or the Royal Oak (2:361), something closer to Protestant English identity. In a clear slur, O'Toole has already called his new house Orange Grove (2:360). Occupying troops do not simply search for rebels, but continually pester citizens forced to live under curfew:

> The rude taunts of the dragoons, the occasional side plunge of a horse on some unwary and shrinking traveller, the random stroke of a sabre flourished in air, the brutal jests and senseless insults offered by the soldiers to the religion and national feelings of the people, spoke volumes of the state of this unhappy country. (2:327)

Johnstone extends the idea of violence from physical attack into continual harassment in everyday life. It is sometimes not even safe to walk along the road without having a sword thrust at you or a horse forcing you off. Neither should we lose sight of the powerful ambivalence of the word 'state' used in this extract, as it reflects not solely on living conditions but on the entity – the state – that produces them, in short, the union. The third and final example of colonial behaviour is the need to legitimate violence through the presence of the law. In this novel, justice is administered by O'Toole. Johnstone has no time for him and directly calls him in her usual robust language a 'disgusting specimen of that race of reptiles, which, in all ages and countries, are quickened amid corruption by the hot and pestilential breath of party-strife' (2:363). Although the closing words return us to more universal ideas, they cannot subtract from the novel's specificity: this is occupied Ireland where execution is promoted by an unscrupulous judge. Again, in *Waverley*, as in Scott's short story 'The Two Drovers', the judges have an air of authority and gravity, they understand the predicament of the accused, but here, there are only reptiles. If there is a precedent, it might come from the hanging judge Jeffreys, whose notoriety is encapsulated not only in his name but in the punishment of the followers of the defeated Duke of Monmouth at the self-explanatory Bloody Assizes (1685), a coinage retained in common usage. That is admittedly a debatable point but, whatever the case, Johnstone underpins the fact that the mutual hostility is as much religious in origin as it is national, if, in practice, these two concepts are separable.

To conclude, we could adapt Duncan's Freudian metaphor by testing out union rather than Scotland as the superego: union is the concept which restrains the id. From what I have argued, it is clear that

Ireland cannot be disciplined by this overarching political concept. First, because it is an occupied territory, and second, because its violent energy is directed towards other objectives, whether we call them United Irishmen or Irish nationalism. This is why Felix's head still drips blood after execution and why it is eventually stolen; both the head – as an object – and Irish nationalism, the metonym it becomes, are, despite appearances, more alive than dead.

Cul-de-sac

Johnstone wrote two – or possibly three – novels and then concentrated on journalism. In simple terms, this suggests that she jettisoned one genre in favour of another. As we shall see, this is the truth, but not the whole truth. McMillan interprets this move as a solution that obeys certain logic:

> The variety of her concerns can be held together by the identity of the journal, rather than the ultimately unavailing struggles of a fictional plot. Indeed the journalistic impulse is a strong and rather invasive strain already in *Clan-Albin*. When Lady Augusta, for example, discusses the situation of the Highlands over several pages, Johnstone is actually writing an article, not representing a conversation. This refusal of conversational realism is, of course, a feature of most novels of the period other than those of Johnstone, but I have seldom seen such flagrant violations of possible intercourse as in *Clan-Albin*. (2003–4: 40)

Johnstone's perfect journal, following this line of argument, would not be one dedicated to one subject alone, but something more akin to a serious weekend newspaper, complete with various supplements: one dedicated to literature, another to education, another to domestic economy and so on.

Johnstone did not turn exclusively to journalism, in the narrow sense of reporting or writing columns on home and foreign affairs. Nor is her literary activity restricted to writing reviews for the 'Literary Register'. Johnstone 'conducted' – the word that appears in the subtitle itself – *The Edinburgh Tales* (1845–46), a three-volume collection published by Tait. Easley remarks that it 'included selected stories and novellas reprinted from *Tait's*, as well as a variety of new works commissioned specifically for the series' (2004: 72). She wrote approximately half of the material; the other major contributor was Miss Mitford, namely the dramatist and novelist Mary Russell Mitford (1787–1855). More prestigious figures also appear: Carlyle's translation 'The Elves' in the first volume, Robert Nicoll's 'Marion Wilson; A Tale of The Persecuting Times' in the second volume. The longest contribution is Johnstone's 'Violet Hamilton; or, the "Talented Family"' which occupies 220 pages of double columns, closer to a full-length novel than a novella. Of particular interest, in view of her ambivalent stance to religion and her keen interest in national character, is 'The Sabbath Night's Supper' (1:152–66) written to counter the misconceptions about Scotland among those 'who imagine of its people as a cold, sullen, and ungenial race' (1:152). As Burns is specifically mentioned (1:160), I would suggest her aim is to update his most celebrated poem.

The second story, 'Young Mrs. Roberts' Three Christmas Dinners' (1:11–32), also has a culinary echo, in keeping with her interest in domestic economy, which took the form of her most popular book *The Cook and Housewife's Manual*, first published in 1826 and which ran to a sixteenth edition in 1885. Many of the facets of Johnstone's writing which we have previously encountered are transferred here, such as a rational approach in its organization, the inclusion of recipes from other countries and an investigation of national character, which comes to the conclusion that Scotland and England have abandoned their culinary tradition, in part due to the Reformation, whereas France reigns supreme as concerns both its food culture and its economic know-how of how a kitchen should be organized (Monnickendam 2005). Although a typically eclectic Johnstone text, it forms part of the long tradition of cook-books that was so prominent in Britain, starting from the mid-eighteenth century and best known in the form of Hannah Glasse's *The Art of Cookery, Made Plain and Easy* (1747). But Johnstone's trademark voracity is illustrated by her invention of a literary-cum-culinary group who form the Cleikum Club. The literary presence is marked by the fact that it is presided over by Meg Dods, the innkeeper from Scott's *St Ronan's Well* (1823), and that a prominent club member is the Rev. Redgill from Ferrier's *Marriage*. These facts lead me to the conclusion that McMillan's analysis is correct, but the cook-book shows that it stops short. For *The Cook and Housewife's Manual* does not counter the fact that Johnstone turns to journalism as a better solution for expression but that in addition no genre ties her down. This volume contains cultural anthropology, philosophical dialogues, and menus from England and Scotland, from continental Europe and further afield.

Surprisingly enough, a similar semi-anarchic attitude to form is also evident in her educational books, such as *The Diversions of Hollycot*

(1828) and *Nights of the Round Table: or, Stories of Aunt Jane and her Friends* (1832). If the common term for novels in the Edgeworth style is didactic fiction, it is easier to see these two volumes as fictional didacticism, that is to say that the didactic lessons are illustrated by stories; a similar linguistic cocktail is served up by Martineau's contemporary *Illustrations of Political Economy* (1832–34). Hence, the first chapter of *Nights of the Round Table* carries the title 'When I was a Young Girl' in which questions of obedience are described in much the same way as the early chapters of Brunton's *Discipline*. Sometimes the tone is more openly like an essay; for example, in the chapter 'Fashion, and Personal Ornaments' we are topically informed that '[o]f all pieces of female dress, the *veil*, and next in order, the shawl, mantle, or scarf, are the most graceful' (1832: 179). In the ongoing debate on motherhood, Johnstone is more explicit, using a neologism 'name mother', that is to say adult women who share the same name as the children, in order to suggest that education overrides biology. This is a conscious or unconscious reworking of fosterage, so crucial to *Clan-Albin*. Initially, this concoction of styles gives the impression that there is little difference between these volumes and didactic fiction, yet there are two significant ones. First, they are openly didactic in intention; the word 'novel' or 'tale' is absent. Second, as a result, this reduces the role of fiction to little more than a parable; we could even go so far as to suggest that Johnstone sees fiction as now having next to no importance whatsoever as a generic category. My conclusion would be that for her, there is simply prose.

This argument can be reinforced by the apparently fictional *True Tales of the Irish Peasantry* (1836), which is belied by its full title *True Tales of the Irish Peasantry, as Related by Themselves; Selected from the Report of the Poor-Law Commissioners, by Mrs Johnstone*. This is a collection of witness accounts of hardship and hunger. Its title might be a throwback to William Carleton's *Traits and Stories of the Irish Peasantry* (1830), the difference being that Johnstone sees that this is not the time for recording traits and stories, as the economic situation is so desperate. Her volume is divided into sections with titles like 'Stories of Old Men', 'Stories of Widows' and 'Ejected Tenants'. In a typical Johnstone move, poverty is measured in comparison with other European countries, such as Denmark or Prussia. She names and shames the most negligent absentee landlords. A sense of poignancy is increased when bearing in mind that the publication and events predate the Great Hunger by a decade. In this particular instance, we have further evidence of Johnstone's distance from fiction. We could argue that a compilation of first-hand accounts of abjection has nothing to do with fiction at all in a period when fiction dealt openly with these concerns: Disraeli published his landmark *Sybil, or the Two Nations* in 1845. Other than circumstantial evidence there is no indication that Johnstone lost faith in fiction, hence I would argue that it is more important to see that genre boundaries have little or no meaning to Johnstone: all seem equally valid at certain moments. Hence, if we return to Bertram's remark on the literary quality of her journalistic practice (p. 102), it is a much more astute comment on her work as a whole than at first sight might appear.

If we want to argue that Johnstone's distance from fiction is visible from within, then her two novels provide plenty of evidence for this. If we return to *Clan-Albin*'s troth-scene, conflicting, if not contradictory, romantic and anti-romantic motifs make their presence felt. Those which fall within the conventions of the national tale are plentiful. Norman and Monimia are young, in love, and have undergone the trial of separation which strengthens their love and its parabolic significance. Their orphan status, their insuperable education, moral status and honesty place them as carriers of the ideals necessary for the creation of a new society. The evening setting with a backdrop of rain indicates fertility. The political overtones are fairly self-evident when Norman 'wrapped the plaid closely around her, his trembling arm, gliding beneath its cumbrous folds, entwined her waist. In the rapturous delirium of that moment he fell at her feet, he drew her towards him with a constraint, strong, gentle, irresistible' (346). The irresistible conclusion is that the two lovers have become one, as the trope of union would inevitably insist upon.

So what is wrong here? The union is not between the stronger and the weaker, but between two weaker parts. Consequently any political reading that pushes a Glorvina solution or a *Waverley* union ends up locking Ireland and Scotland together as victims of an inequitable ideology of progress. I use the word ideology with care, as Johnstone's most evil character is Archibald Gordon, an Anglo-Scot, who victimizes Norman, Monimia, Phelim and even Norman's dog. In short, the love-plot collapses. This is compounded by certain other features. The first is that, as in Brunton and especially Ferrier, the adversity that the major characters experience goes far beyond that which would be necessary for a *Bildungsroman*. This would explain, I propose, the reason for the idyllic conclusion, where all-comers live happily in Voltairean seclusion, or in what Judith Wilt formulates as an outlawed retreat, like Sherwood Forest. Norman, perhaps even more so than Donald Bean Lean, the Highland robber in *Waverley*, will truly be 'the manager-king of a hidden but emphatically civil society' (Wilt 1985: 32). This idea is extended by Shields, who argues that 'Norman's rehabilitated Highland community welcomes those who have suffered in the service of British imperial power, and those who, like Monimia, simply seek an escape from metropolitan corruption' (2010: 128). That only strengthens the suspicion that the retreat simply becomes a utopia, a non-place with no existence other than on the written page and in the imagination. The subplot of Phelim Bourke obliges us to ditch such fantasies as Sherwood Forest and equivalent locations, ensuring that one of the inevitable casualties is the Glorvina solution. The traitor's story cannot be contained within a national tale; fictional equivalents to Simon Fraser will fit in, but equivalents to Wolf Tone will never be able to do so.

Cracks in the traditional structure of the national tale are evident in *Clan-Albin*, whereas their presence is much more powerful and unsettling in *Elizabeth de Bruce*. This is why, in Duncan's words, it 'reads, much of the time, like a pastiche of Scott and his Blackwoodian contemporary Susan Ferrier, with startling infusions from current Irish fiction – a *Guy Mannering* featuring United Irishmen instead of gypsies' (2007a: 261).

Given Duncan's use of pastiche, is it licit to propose that through a process of estrangement this novel is so deeply subversive that, in formalist language, it writes against itself? Duncan has rightly pointed out that this is very much the case in that the lovers are already married at the novel's outset, the significance of which cannot be underestimated. If the national tale comprises the private and public sphere, removing its conclusion or objective or *raison d'être* or whatever term we use can only result in implosion. A national tale harnesses future and fertility as synonyms, yet the plot of *Elizabeth de Bruce* revolves around trying to understand Elizabeth's mysterious birth, explained in chapters 13 and 14 of volume three. The marriage between her Scottish father, de Bruce, and her Irish mother, Aileen O'Connor, is foiled at the last moment through a violent abduction. It is virtually impossible not to read an overt political message in this situation that undermines any idea of union; instead, and at the risk of repetition, the colonial dimension of both countries takes on greater credibility as a convincing explanation of the political status quo. Although Elizabeth will name her own daughter Aileen, a decision which suggests belief in continuity and therefore the future, the novel concludes perfunctorily with a series of deaths: no catharsis is present; there will be no brave new world. The novel ends when the curtain comes down, and, in a similar fashion to the end of Ferrier's novels, there is nothing else to add. In fact, if Robert Tracy's influential article (1985) places the question of legitimate rule at the heart of Edgeworth's and Lady Morgan's work, there is little legitimacy in Johnstone's final novel. The whole question of biological legitimacy is brutally thrown up in the air by the discovery that Elizabeth's birth is the culmination of a long story of abduction and violence rather than the fruit of a harmonious union. British rule is imposed in Ireland by force, by the army and O'Toole, the Protestant Flail; consequently there is no political legitimacy in any sense the word might have other than through an imperial imperative. In short, in writing *Elizabeth de Bruce*, Johnstone has produced a novel which has so radically modified its fictional parameters that it becomes stubbornly recalcitrant in Ferris's (1997) terms. Johnstone has written a national tale that lays out why she can never write another national tale; to go one step farther: it is a national tale to end all national tales.

4
Question Time: The Debate on Fiction

> – What are you reading now, Captain? Dixon asked.
> *The Bride of Lammermoor?*
> – I love Scott, the flexible lips said. I think he writes
> something lovely. There is no writer can touch sir
> Walter Scott. (Joyce 1992: 247)

The final chapter of this study bases itself on an idea close to the heart of modernism, located most forcefully in Ezra Pound's war cry that we should make art new. This ambitious programme reorients our perceptions through estrangement; the object is newly viewed rather than being a product created or recreated through romantic genius. To draw such a parallel would be presumptuous on my behalf: there will be no verbal violence or fragmentation, but I do earnestly believe that having foregrounded the work of Brunton, Ferrier and Johnstone prior to analysing Scott will produce an engagement with and even a challenge to some basic critical beliefs, as concerns both Scott himself and his so-called satellites. We will not have a new Scott – which would be the presumption – but one who is slightly different in some fundamental aspects. An analysis of the closely related subjects of religion, desire, violence and union provides the basis for a truer understanding of heroinism. The Scott text I will refer to most frequently is *Waverley*, its foundational status being the prime reason, another being its date of publication: it came out around the time of the texts I have analysed (1814). Brunton's *Self-Control* precedes it, and she also comments on Scott in her correspondence; Johnstone published *Clan-Albin* a year after, and Ferrier follows and extensively parodies the mode of Scottish fiction which he put in place. This chapter's underlying motif is 'whereas', which is to say, if his female contemporaries write in this way about a particular subject, how does Scott go about it? How do they shed light on each other?

Religion

The first subject is religion. A provocative polarity is produced if we contrast Hogg's quip with Lockhart's testimony. Hogg states of Scott that:

> He was no great favourer of religion and never went to church that ever I heard of excepting once or twice on King's fast days as we call them [...] True he wrote two very indifferent moral sermons but he was no religionist. He dreaded it as a machine by which the good government of the country might be deranged if not uprooted. (1999: 14)

This is a hard-hitting exclamation, not only in its insistence that Scott never went to church but that his strong dislike stemmed from the belief that religion and 'good government' were at odds with each other. Notable also is the language of the final sentence in its use of disorder and madness (deranged) and revolution (uprooted). It is also telling that Hogg attaches an industrial simile 'as a machine' to the man whose major fault was, according to Hogg himself, such a persistent attachment to the aristocracy that supposedly the killer-blow was, literally, the Whig ascendancy; in other words, all that democracy and reform were doing to end old patriarchal ways. This is exactly what Lukács identified in the much-quoted adage that 'Scott ranks amongst the honest Tories of England of his time who exonerate nothing in the development of capitalism, who not only see clearly, but also deeply sympathize with the unending misery of the people which the collapse of old England brings in its wake' (1981: 32–3). However, unlike Lukács, Hogg's language contains some devilish strategies which reverse revolutionary impulses: it is not the case that religion upholds the *ancien régime* and therefore is deeply repressive, but for Scott, according to Hogg, it is contemporary religion which threatens 'good government', making it as potentially dangerous as an infuriated mob marching on the Bastille.

In contrast, Lockhart states that:

> Sir Walter received a strictly religious education under the eye of parents, whose virtuous conduct was in unison with the principles they desired to instil into their children. From the great doctrines thus recommended he appears never to have swerved. (1900: 5:446)

As a result, Scott's

> works teach the practical lessons of morality and Christianity in most captivating form – unobtrusively and unaffectedly [...] The sanctities of domestic love and social duty were never forgotten; and the same circumstance that most ennobles all his triumphs, affords the best apology for his errors. (5:447)

Initially, the emphasis on morality and Christianity places Scott precisely in the area that the Ferris thesis removes him from: the writings of Brunton and Ferrier. Surely it would be perfectly feasible to argue that a keen sense of morality and Christianity is what their fiction strives to achieve; it is precisely this high moral tone in the frequent discursive byways to which, as the previous chapters have demonstrated, generations of readers have taken exception. For example, Lockhart's words could be read as a gloss on the Mrs Douglas section of *Marriage* or of the triumph of Laura in Brunton's *Self-Control*. Has Lockhart, unwittingly, turned Scott into a feminine writer?

That is possible, but there are other options. It is one thing to say that these two men are engaged in a struggle to create radically different versions of Scott's literary persona, but their own sincerity in this matter is open to discussion. For example, Lockhart's pronouncement seems extremely formulaic, in the same way that obituaries insist that all soldiers die gallantly on the battlefield or that all people who have passed away will be sorely missed. Hogg's and Lockhart's responses highlight their rivalry more than anything else: Hogg's role as a trickster, as a subversive; Lockhart's self-created role of high-priest and guardian of a national treasure, or, in less abstract terms, editor-cum-author of Scott's biography. Therefore, at the same time as they are talking about Scott, they are continually speaking against each other in their ongoing feud which reaches great intensity, as the following brief examples suggest. On Hogg's death in 1835, Lockhart says of him that 'it had been better for his fame had his end been of earlier date, for he did not follow his best benefactor until he had insulted his dust' (5:451). Two years earlier, according to Blackwood, the manuscript of Hogg's *Memoirs of the Author's Life and Familiar Anecdotes of Sir Walter Scott* had the following effect on Lockhart:

> Mr. L[ockhart]. knowing well what a bundle of lies the whole would be, at first declined to look at it, but McC[rone]. pressed him so much that he opened the scroll. The very page he glanced at contained such

> beastly & abominable things that he could not restrain his indigna-
> tion, and poured his indignation against Hogg in such unmeasured
> terms that his poor auditor was quite dumbfoundered. He however
> left the M.S. for Mr L's consideration. He went over it, and was filled
> with utter disgust & loathing. (Mack 1983: 6)

What can cause such histrionics? What exactly were these beastly and
abominable things? The view that Lockhart saw 'the nation as comprised of several well-defined classes' (Morgan 1975: 28) and that only
the leisured classes could be literary is satisfactory to a certain extent,
yet something more than a class war underlines the ferocity of these
exchanges. Whether Lockhart, with Blackwood's assistance, is exagger-
ating his response is moot, but certainly Hogg really knows where to
direct his blows against the body of the man who aspires to write the
great biography of the great literary figure of his time. Lockhart's life
and work seemingly represent a most vivid example of Harold Bloom's
theory of the anxiety of influence. In a deft sentence, Hogg delivers a
knock-out punch:

> Of Lockhart's genius and capabilities Sir Walter always spoke with
> the greatest enthusiasm more than I thought he deserved for I knew
> him a great deal better than Sir Walter did and whatever Lockhart
> may pretend I knew Sir Walter a thousand times better than he did.
> (1999: 67)

Hogg is mocking his rival when he plays with the word 'genius' by
affirming that Lockhart is overrated as a writer, he is not a genius at all;
Hogg naturally sees himself as undervalued. He adds that Lockhart lacks
the sufficient factual knowledge to write a biography, whereas he suggests that he himself and William Laidlaw are far better equipped for the
task. In other words, the biography lacks content and style; the project's
entire validity is hence called into question. So deep is this engrained
antagonism that Hogg extends the spat into Lockhart's role in the family
set-up: Lockhart may be the son-in-law who wishes to play the role of
guardian, but Hogg regards Scott as 'an elder brother' (73), and therefore
reckons he is better placed to make judgements. To complete the demo-
lition, Hogg's life of Scott is a short chatty volume entitled *Anecdotes*
which pretends to contest the ground with Lockhart's mammoth production; in short, the conflict extends into the question of genre, in fact
to practically every aspect of life. The gadfly buzzes around Lockhart,
stinging him continually in an attempt to deride his authority.

Scottish literary history has shown that Hogg's version of events had not had much influence over our understanding of national tales until the recent Hogg revival. Therefore, in the light of that phenomenon and in the light of the fiction I have been analysing, my point of departure here is that Hogg is close to the truth. How many times Scott actually went to church is not an issue of great importance in that it would not, in itself, prove very much. To take an extreme example, going to church has a very specific function for Lovelace in *Clarissa*: he sees Sunday service as a delightful spectacle because of the presence of large numbers of attractive, well-dressed women in one public space. With Hogg's comment in mind, the seemingly secular slant of Scott's fiction appears more apparent.

What is not in question is that Scott wrote at great length on religious subjects without being a 'religionist'. At no moment will we find the Bible sustaining the female from the attacks of the Richardsonian rake in order to prepare the ground for a marriage based on mutual respect, companionship and fortitude, as in *Self-Control*, nor will religion be the basis for union as happens in the above-mentioned novel and in Ferrier's *The Inheritance*. At the same time, statements like David Craig's 'Scott himself was a Moderate at heart; he became an Anglican' (1961: 181) may be factual but do not contribute to the question I have identified.

Craig's chapter 'Religion in Scotland' has two striking characteristics. First, it does not focus on any of the female religionists I have been discussing; instead, it focuses on Scott, Galt and Hogg. Second, the three novelists are bound together by their handling of the Covenanters; Craig, following his Marxist principles, bases his criticism on the comparative nearness or distance to judging Covenanting as a manifestation not primarily of religion but of the Scottish demotic under attack. As I stated in the introduction, this idea has been farther developed by Duncan (2007b), the result of which is a major shift in our perception of heroic or epic moments. Epics describe pivotal moments of national victory or defeat; as an example, Jane Porter's *The Scottish Chiefs* deals with both victory at Stirling Bridge and defeat at Falkirk but will envisage Bannockburn. In military and historical terms, it would be difficult to say which battle had greater consequences, but in mythical terms, Bannockburn reigns supreme. In a parallel movement, by highlighting the Killing Times as the great epic moment, the historical and mythical status of the Forty-Five is modified.

The 29 September 1832 number of *The Schoolmaster and Edinburgh Weekly Magazine*, which Johnstone co-edited with her husband, published an obituary of Scott followed by a lengthier eulogistic article titled 'On the Political Tendency of Sir Walter Scott's Writings' (Anon. 1832: 129–33), presumably written by Johnstone, either on her own or in collaboration with her husband. It is fundamentally a high-spirited exposition of his authorial status. Like Hogg, Johnstone points to Laidlaw, Lockhart and James Ballantyne as potential biographers. She surmises that the potential memoirs may portray Scott as the embodiment of 'the Philosophy of Humanity, and the spirit of our own national history, with that finer spirit, expansive as Life, and enduring as Time, which pervades all that he has written' (129). Scott's talent is therefore that of a universalist whose foundations are national; only once we understand our own circumstances, can we branch out to grasp a larger reality. This is a trifle optimistic, yet what surely is noticeable, especially in the light of Lockhart's comments, is Johnstone's definition of Scott as primarily secular. As I have analysed elsewhere (Monnickendam 2000), her valediction has a very clear message, which might, presumably, be an attempt to lessen the weight of hagiographical accounts that she must have known would shortly follow. She argues that Scott is not a Tory at all; in fact he is a liberal, sometimes a revolutionary, accordingly, in most emphatic terms, she labels him 'this *universal leveller*' (131) (italics in the original). This strongly anti-Blackwoodian sentiment stems from her belief that, in marked contrast to Hogg's assertion of his admiration for the aristocracy, Scott's portraits of figures in authority – kings, churchmen, aristocrats, lawyers and so on – are all extremely critical. Johnstone's unwavering contention is based on a syllogism. Scott's portrayal of older societies highlights corruption, intrigue and immorality; second, he steered clear of writing about contemporary events, above all the Regency; third, 'What a scene for the pen of Sir WALTER SCOTT, had he lived a century later, the sycophant, court-haunting churchmen, courtiers, and harridans of the late years of the late reign!' (131). In other words, the excesses of the London court would have made the perfect scenario for a Scott novel – a hundred years since – as he would have levelled all its members. The logical consequence of Johnstone's reasoning is to propose that historical fiction locates evil societies in the past as a strategy which in part allows the fullest exposure that only distance in time can permit while simultaneously exposing the decadence of contemporary life and its corrupt institutions. In short, Johnstone writes about religion but is no religionist in exactly the same way as her much-admired Scott.

It might seem far-fetched to envisage Scott as a radical, yet this is Johnstone's belief. To transfer critical pictures of past ages and cultures onto contemporary society gives his antiquarianism a completely new function, arguably challenging the deeply held belief that he is first and foremost an antiquarian; following Johnstone's logic, that label would stick only to his creations. That said, it is again noticeable that she draws a distinction between 'court-haunting churchmen', that is, self-seeking career bishops, and Scottish religious history. Religion in history or fiction is not restricted to religion as history. She makes a very brief reference to Jeanie Deans (*The Heart of Midlothian*), but not to the religious context; Johnstone then states that:

> In *Old Mortality*, where we have worthy Tory Lady Ballenden, with her high-flown and fantastic loyalty, and her 'Throne,' contrasted with the old blind widow, sitting, like her of Zareptha, alone by the wayside, to warn the people of God from the snares of the oppressor, – she who had seen both her sons fall in defence of the purity of the Church of Christ, and of the independence of Scotland. (132)

In the light of her strongly liberal views which display a deeply sceptical view of traditional institutions such as the monarchy and the judiciary, in fact all those targets which she claims Scott directs his fiction against, it is significant that these lines show no trace of criticism or irony. Therefore the conclusion follows the line of previous remarks: that the Convenanters, even and especially from this liberal angle, remain inextricably linked to political independence and therefore their suppression represents the primary epic event in the literary representation of modern Scottish history.

Popular nomenclature alone – the Killing Times and the Forty-Five – reveals a remarkable contrast. One suggests murder over a long period – we are dealing with 'times' in the plural – whereas the Forty-Five, linguistically an abstract term, is a date in history which must best be understood by knowledge that is present everywhere save in the word itself. It is curious that the Forty-Five, by referring to one year only, excludes Culloden, 'Scott's watershed', as Lamont (1991: 26) so cogently argues, which took place the following April, and surely Culloden is a firm candidate for the defining moment in modern Scottish history; it is only mentioned in passing in *Waverley*. As a term which states little but implies a lot, the Forty-Five is therefore open to all sorts of interpretation which hide or refuse to explicitly mention violence. Consequently, its romanticization, its focus in popular manifestations on the glamour of Charles Stuart, give it an epic nature through a tragic hero; nevertheless the whole movement is secular. If we do not find the following analogy out of place, this is why Charles Stuart could be placed on a shortbread tin while neither the Covenanters nor Oliver Cromwell could easily be commercially linked to biscuits.

Put simply, I am suggesting that perhaps the foundational Waverley novel is secular and that reading these novelists in regard to their secularism or religiosity is as fruitful or arguably a more rewarding set of paradigms than, for example, the contrast between the Enlightenment and Romanticism, which clarifies something about Johnstone, but next to nothing about Ferrier or Brunton. In order for this to be a coherent argument, it is necessary to focus on the text from the moment that Waverley's allegiance to Jacobitism wanes under the relentless psychological pressures exerted by Colonel Talbot. Before their encounter occurs, in the preceding Edinburgh chapters, even though the city may be upon the hill (in other circumstances this would be a predictable religious topography), its castle is impregnable, while the major event, the ball, takes place in the ghostly palace of Holyrood. Other geographical features mentioned – the Canongate, Arthur's Seat and so on – lack any notable religious dimension: whether consciously or unconsciously, religion seems to have left scarcely any trace in *Waverley*'s transitional Edinburgh, hence the scenes set there can yield to the burlesque (Duncan 1992: 77). In contrast, even Johnstone, so much more openly sceptical towards the effects of religion on society, in the penultimate chapter of *Clan-Albin* has Flora visit Greyfriars Kirk before embracing Catholicism. This facet of Scott's Edinburgh landscape is significant, as surely one of the great generalizations about the Forty-Five is to identify Catholicism with the Stuarts; after all, Henry Benedict Stuart, otherwise known as Henry IX, was a cardinal. The degree of truth in these assertions is less important than the realization in the Edinburgh chapters that confrontation has been whittled down until little is left but its dynastical dimension, which, as previously stated, is a form of identity which belongs to the politics of pre-nation-state Europe.

Therefore, the first major conclusion of this chapter is to extend an argument which is commonly applied to the Waverley Novels' reification, commodification or aestheticization of the Highlands. All three terms are similar in that they uphold the hypothesis that Scott turns what was once a political and military threat into romance, the most revealing example of which, in *Waverley*, is the portrait of Waverley and Fergus in Highland dress, and which, in terms of cultural and national politics, would be the king's jaunt; both legitimize Highland dress as British artefacts, that is to say, henceforth as nothing other than artefacts.

This same process, I would argue, is what happens to Scottish religion in the same novel, as concerns the disruptive potential of both Catholicism and the Cameronians ('the more strict and severe Presbyterians' (Scott 1985: 260)). In what seems uncannily similar to the remarks made about Flora in *Clan-Albin*, Fergus assures Waverley that religion may be an obstacle to his proposed match to his sister Flora (*Waverley*), nevertheless, he adds, 'we are not bigoted Catholics' (211). Whereas Johnstone sees non-theological religion as akin to tolerance and understanding, the presence of Catholicism in the behaviour and lifestyle of Fergus and Flora within the history of *Waverley* itself is practically negligible. Duncan's assertion that *Waverley* manages to make rebellion 'a reactionary adventure' (1992: 53) is cemented from within the novel itself by the clergyman Morton's words that 'at the time of the Union [the Cameronians] had nearly formed a most unnatural league with their old enemies, the Jacobites' (261). Both are twinned as equally irrelevant to modern life and therefore meet for the discourse of romance. Hogg's disagreement with Scott over their divergent fictional rendering of the Killing Times fits these parameters perfectly.

If the hypothesis that modern Britain is essentially a successful combination of Hanoverianism and Protestantism – which is most persuasively argued by Colley (1992) and omnipresent in studies of literature and culture of this period – is correct, then it would be logical to see how, in pyramidal fashion, Waverley is exposed to rival ideologies. The rising movement is represented through his encounter with Jacobitism; but what about the descent, which I would indicate as first taking place in chapters 47 and 49 with their ironical titles 'The Conflict' and 'The English Prisoner' respectively? The former refers to the crisis of identity that Prestonpans causes in Waverley's mind and the latter may literally be Talbot himself but figuratively it is a reflection of Waverley's confused ideas at this juncture.

Talbot is Fergus's counterpart, that is to say, an alternative ideological pool; Scott draws some fundamental distinctions between them that merit considerable attention. The first is to highlight how they exercise, or try to exercise, power. Fergus would do so by marriage and feudal patronage; Talbot would use patronage of the eighteenth-century model, based more on the exchange of favours between the ruling elite than on blood-ties; consequently when a problem arises for Waverley, Talbot 'had smoothed the way' (478), a turn of phrase with such deep bureaucratic reverberations, that it is impossible to imagine Fergus employing such methods. Surely Talbot is the ancestor of Sir Humphrey Appleby (BBC TV: *Yes Minister*). In addition, for Talbot, marriage is primarily for extending property rather than a passport for entry into a particular sphere of influence. But more significant than this is the fact that both characters are portrayed as representatives of a national type. Talbot, the case in hand, becomes as mythological an Englishman as Fergus is a Highlander; two examples demonstrate this. The first is the suppression of emotion in chapter 55, which, I hope to demonstrate, should be a notorious episode. Waverley hears 'a suppressed groan' (382) from Talbot's rooms and goes to investigate. The narrator informs us that:

> As if ashamed at being found giving way to such emotion, Colonel Talbot rose with apparent displeasure, and said, with some sternness, 'I think, Mr. Waverley, my own apartment, and the hour, might have secured even a prisoner against –'
>
> 'Do not say *intrusion*, Colonel Talbot, I heard you breathe hard, and feared you were ill; that alone could have induced me to break in upon you.' (382)

In addition to the suppression of feelings, Scott jokes with another national cliché: an Englishman's home is his castle, even if it is his prison! By bringing to the fore Scott's use of irony, Talbot's stance as a representative national type is not questioned, but irony necessarily leads to the exposure of his narrow views, making his role as spokesman for 'what is correct and logical for and in the novel's own present' (Makdisi 1998: 87) untenable. It is the logic of expansion that is revealed, not that rationalism which undermines Waverley's romantic view of the Highlands and its people. Yet even more is going on here than might at first appear. The narrative qualifies the genuineness of Talbot's behaviour at two moments: first, the conditional 'as if', the second, displeasure, is qualified by 'apparent'. I would propose that Talbot is play-acting here. He is fully aware that Waverley will respond more to a manifestation of a projected English identity, which, after all, forms his cultural roots, than to anything else. At the risk of being irreverent, Talbot, at many points, behaves like an extremely sinister caricature of those humorous pictures of English manners and attitudes which made the Hungarian comic writer George Mikes so popular in books such as *How to Be an Alien* (1946). If this hypothesis is correct, then hopefully the instances that follow will increasingly appear simply formulaic or satirical or even funny. The first of these is that the suppressed emotion and the visible tears result from strong feeling: 'I was only thinking of home' (383). Is this credible? Or can we detect any irony in the sentences '[b]ut Colonel Talbot was in every point the

English soldier. His whole soul was devoted to the service of his king and country' (365), that is to say, irony emerging from the hackneyed language it employs. Has Scott forecast Rupert Brooke's emotive patriotism of 'The Soldier': 'If I should die, think only this of me: / That there's some corner of a foreign field / That is forever England'? In isolation, Talbot's words would look as if they have been taken from a guide to model citizenship, but as he is not reluctant to publicly expose his national attributes, we should at least question whether the ideas expressed reveal cracks in his sincerity and subsequently their veracity as patriotic aspirations.

In the novel itself, his actions do not correspond to such lofty ideals. Scott might have allowed Talbot's perceived English perfection to fall by its own weight, but at the same time, he is openly described as having two very strong prejudices. First, the ladies dislike his misogynist streak, described by the narrator as 'spleen and prejudice in the excellent Colonel' (366). More emphatically, Talbot expresses one fundamental dislike which Scott emphasizes on several occasions: Talbot, we are told, is an erudite person 'tinged [...] with those prejudices which are peculiarly English' (366), the first of which is a virulent hatred towards the Highlanders. When given parole by Charles Stuart, he wages into a diatribe against Highlanders that would have pleased John Wilkes: 'what business have they to come where people wear breeches, and speak an intelligible language? I mean intelligible in comparison with their gibberish, for even the Lowlanders talk a kind of English little better than the negroes in Jamaica' (387). This vitriolic attack is followed by the predictable remarks on Edinburgh's sanitation of the 'gardez loo' type. Scott's insistence on Talbot's roots in chapter 71, with clear allusions to Shakespeare's *Henry VI*, emphasizes how deep-rooted this Scotophobia is, pinpointing how closely it is linked to territorial conquest. Just as his ancestors occupied France they now administer Scotland; in both cases they have no qualms about the legitimacy of their presence. Clearly, the comparison between Fergus and Talbot discloses figures from different cultures; but in terms of humanity, in Fergus there is some while in Talbot there seems to be none at all. It is easy to overlook that the contrast here between two people from different cultures is totally unlike that of 'The Two Drovers', which is based on the presence or lack of mutual understanding, whereas understanding Scotland is something which does not concern Talbot at all.

This critical view of Talbot inevitably clashes with his role in securing the recovery of the Bradwardine estate. Still, it would be ingenuous to see him as disinterested or generous. During closure, two interesting remarks are made about the value of Scottish land, an irrefutable reflection on the effects of the sequestration of estates after Culloden. The first might be ironic; at the end of chapter 70, we are informed that 'Edward Waverley and his lady, who, with the Baron, proposed an immediate journey to Waverley-Honour, should, in their way, spend a few days at an estate which Colonel Talbot had been tempted to purchase in Scotland as a very great bargain' (482). The initial irony is that the narrative is referring to the ruse whereby the estate has been transferred to Waverley. At the same time, in any postwar setting, much land truly was available 'as a very great bargain' for the victors. Talbot himself clarifies the situation a few pages on: 'I have so much of that same prejudice in favour of my native country, that the sum of money which I advanced to the seller of this extensive barony has only purchased for me a box in —shire, called Brerewood Lodge' (486). Talbot has once more openly confessed his allegiance: it is to England not to Britain. In addition, English real estate is more expensive and more desirable than a Highland barony. It must also be noted that Brerewood is precisely the place of Waverley's childhood and education, as outlined in chapters 2 and 3. This gives *Waverley* a circularity which remains enigmatic and little discussed in criticism, greatly due to the emphasis on progress that dominates the novel's conclusion.

So what does this incident tell us? I would point out two important, interrelated themes. First, Talbot's openly declared dislike does not mean he has no interest in Scotland. Quite the contrary, his role throughout the novel is that of advancing policy as an official administrator for the expanding English state, as he would define it. If *Waverley* or similar Scottish novels are open to postcolonial readings, then it is precisely the manipulative figure of Talbot who corresponds to the model of colonial officer; his outstanding qualifications come from his double career of serving his country both militarily and diplomatically. Would puppet-master be too strong a term for someone who advances Waverley's cause? I think not. His role as Waverley's mentor accounts for his keenness that his disciple occupy a northern estate whilst he can retire south – now that his job has been done – to the land of Waverley's roots. From a national point of view, Waverley's and Rose's presence, through the former's origins and the latter's name, indicate anglicization; along similar lines, from the angle of social class, the new ruling elite of Scotland will consist of Talbot's protégés or like-minded agents, as far as is humanly possible. What occurred 60 years since, both as explained in the postscript and in the historical process itself, would demonstrate the validity of that assertion. The recovery of the estate demonstrates that cash and smoothing the way are by far the most powerful weapons. It is no coincidence that neither Waverley nor Talbot has shone as a traditional, valiant hero, a sure indication that the modern world requires proficiency in other spheres.

In *Waverley*, Scott sketches in a minor ideological partner for Talbot whose monstrosity simply increases our awareness of Talbot's real self: this is Mrs Nosebag. She enthuses over how 'her regiment had cut the petticoat people into ribands at Falkirk' (418). The dress metaphors, Talbot's use of breeches, petticoats and ribands, all dehumanize, showing an absence of consideration for the other. What is being suggested here is that if Mrs Nosebag is, for Waverley, just a hag, then her beliefs are not all that different from the superiorly educated, much eulogized Talbot, who is therefore revealed as just 'a bigot' (Hart 1966: 29). In short, Mrs Nosebag and Colonel Talbot have different class origins but share the opinion that no war crimes occurred during the Forty-Five.

This is a deeply disturbing or revealing parallel, as it suggests that intolerance, if not hate, guides both the views of the uneducated and the policy of the ruling elite. It is arguable that the incessant urge to find binaries in the text has obscured the shared ideological platform of bigoted female and bigoted male, yet this conclusion can be sustained from evidence within the text, as has been put forward, and by recalling two other texts which are more explicit on the subject. Talbot's views would not have surprised Goldsmith; as previously stated, his essay on national prejudice focuses on its widespread presence among the educated classes, and, closer to Scott's time, Maria Edgeworth's *Essay on Irish Bulls* (1802) expressed similar disquiet, whether feigned – in order to highlight its extent – or genuine; in either case, the message remains clear: the enlightened are unenlightened.

At this point, it might seem that we have wandered away from the religious question altogether. But that is not the case: it is *Waverley* that has wandered away, in the sense that the novel, in the terms that I have presented it in these paragraphs, does not follow the Colley hypothesis at all, as the only aim of Talbot and his contemporaries is expansion rather than incorporation. Clearly, in terms of influence, Scott has no rival, but it is curious to note how his fiction inhabits an almost godless world, which puts him into a minority here, in comparison to the fiction of Brunton, Ferrier and, to a lesser extent, Johnstone. If the postscript predicts prosperity and if the 'General Preface' sets out a platform for fiction, neither requires divine sanction of the type defined in the United States by the name of Manifold Destiny.

If we follow up Johnstone's remarks about Scott's critical pictures of past societies, then two institutions will necessarily be continually under scrutiny or, if we fully accept the Johnstone line, we would have to phrase it differently, under attack: the monarchy and the Catholic Church. The distinction that Johnstone draws between theological and non-theological religion, between fanaticism and accommodation, is not one that adapts itself easily to Scott. In Johnstone's terms, Scott's mixture of class concerns with the Killing Times exiles Convenanters to the fringes of both civil society and reason. As stated in the previous chapter, Johnstone dedicates the fourth volume of *Clan-Albin* to the Peninsular War, thereby bringing into contact British, French and Spanish peoples. Johnstone employs several strategies to reduce the power of national prejudices: the first is to draw the occasional parallel between landscape and peoples; for example, the idea of there being certain common customs among mountain people of different countries. The second is the relationship between prisoners and their capturers, the Talbot–Waverley paradigm; however, in this case the reverse happens, in that the French soldiers turn out not to be so bad as they should have been! The most significant example of all is to place Phelim in Napoleonic rather than British uniform, which opens up a polemic which is never resolved, as I have argued, in *Clan-Albin*. Most startling is Flora's encounter with Catholicism which will eventually lead to her conversion. The narrative emphasizes her background is 'the strictest sense of Presbyterianism', but in a moment of distress she 'pined for the soothing comfort of social worship' (2003: 474). The fervent individualism that dictates that every herring must hang by its own tail, if we are to believe Mr Struthers in George Douglas Brown's *The House with the Green Shutters* (1974: 32), provides no spiritual comfort, whilst the beauty of the Catholic service does, especially the singing with its 'celestial strains' (475) which offers enormous emotional release: this is well and truly an epiphany which has few if any parallels in literature of that time and which, one would assume, Mary Brunton would also have understood. The question we are left with is how to solve a seeming paradox. True religious feeling provides the female writers' heroines with a purpose to life, while its absence in the life of Scott's heroes is not, I have tried to argue, compensated with anything that might take its place. Hogg might be right in his comments on Scott's religious practice, but, I would propose, neither he nor Lukács are fully aware of the sceptical nature of Scott's views on the workings of power, on good government. The fact that Johnstone is so emphatic about Scott's radicalism is therefore no coincidence at all but the result of what she believes to be political empathy between Scott and herself based, at the risk of repetition, on secularism.

Desire and the insipid heroine

There is another remarkable difference between Scott and his female contemporaries, which chapter 55 amply demonstrates. If disbelief is suspended so that Waverley can hear Talbot's groan from his own apartments, then we notice that a strange game is taking place:

> he was awakened about midnight by a suppressed groan [...] he opened the door of communication very gently, and perceived the Colonel in his night-gown, seated by a table, on which lay a letter and a picture. He raised his head hastily, as Edward stood uncertain whether to advance or retire, and Waverley perceived that his cheeks were stained with tears. (381)

This is followed by the sentence describing Talbot's displeasure at the invasion of his privacy, which was discussed a few pages back. The game consists, I believe, in describing this event as if it were a deeply erotic one, a case of voyeurism. Edward acts as a voyeur while the Colonel dressed in his night-gown is seated and is gazing at a picture. Although written in such suggestive language, it can never be truly erotic, simply because not only does Talbot lack all religious feeling, unlike the Colley model of Englishness, but he is also devoid of libido.[1] This partly accounts for his pejorative remarks about the novel's two heroines and his exaltation of the family, surely the most powerful trope of nineteenth-century fiction. The exact purpose of this incident is hard to trace, as the major figures in the novel likewise seem to be almost sexless or else transfer their desire on to another person or project, as argued by Dennis (1997) in his adaptation of René Girard's mimetic triangle as forming the template of historical fiction. This is all in stark contrast primarily to Brunton, and to a lesser extent to Ferrier. It is clear from the first page of her first novel that Brunton conflates military and erotic prowess in the same person, Colonel Hargrave, which is a Clarissa trope save for one fundamental difference. The Brunton rake has one advantage over Richardson's: namely the respect that society gives to rank, not civil rank, but to the military, in short, to the fact that Hargrave is, like Talbot, a colonel. Again, in contrast, the world of Waverley seems increasingly to be an inhospitable space, emptied at first of faith and now of desire. It is difficult not to agree with Nicola Watson when she argues that 'the erotics of the novel of sensibility' are evacuated (her phrase) 'in favour of a novel of social consensus' (Watson 1994: 68). What is in doubt is whether an umbrella term such as consensus is applicable to Scott.

It may easily be objected that what I am trying to suggest inevitably clashes with the way that *Waverley* concludes in the very specific manner outlined by the postscript, which is sufficient to override the impression of the ravaged Scotland Waverley witnesses: a wasteland whose desolation is heightened by an accompanying lack of belief in any fulfilment in political, religious or sexual terms. However, if this wasteland, as a trope for describing modernity or post-Forty-Five Scotland, convinces, that must be the result of comprehending that Scott's contemporaries do believe in a Scotland where one, two or all of these forms of fulfilment are achievable. At the same time, the nexus between the military and the sexual forms one of the central pillars of Scott's essay on chivalry and of some of his later novels, particularly *The Talisman*. The essay is of particular interest for the forthrightness with which it deals with the subject. It is a critical commonplace to accept that the Jacobite novels are built on a structure of history written just before now, or in Stephen Parrinder's concise coinage, 'intimate tradition' (2006: 153), which therefore shapes the present, an irrefutable illustration being *Waverley*'s subtitle *'Tis Sixty Years Since*, the final words dragging the events of previous generations into the present. The essay on chivalry is rather different: it imagines a brief period when possibly principles were 'pure' (1834: 11) before things took a turn for the worse, primarily due to the offices of the 'Romish clergy, who have in all ages possessed the wisdom of serpents' (12). Being of the devil's party is one matter, but it is clear that chivalry under the slogan of 'Deus lo Volt' leads to indiscriminate violence against enemy troops, civilians and above all females: 'the respect due to ladies of high degree, gave way when they chanced to be infidels' (15). Readers unfamiliar with this text are possibly taken by surprise at Scott's blistering dismissal of the Crusades as 'hare-brained' (11) and his focusing on one ideal above all that is responsible for both their failure and their indiscriminate use of violence: celibacy.

In a move that is a textbook example of Freud's theory of displacement, Scott states that 'the Knights Templars and Knights of St. John of Jerusalem, who, renouncing (at least in terms) the pomp, power, pleasures of the world, and taking upon themselves the monastic views of celibacy, purity, and obedience, did not cease to remain soldiers, and directed their whole energy against the Saracens' (17). All energy is directed towards violence, as celibacy, purity and obedience become deadly weapons for those on the receiving end. A similar remark occurs later on, when we are told that chivalry, in its celibate form, increased 'license and debauchery' (43). It might be argued that Scott's critique is primarily directed towards two orders, and it is true that many pages talk at some length of idealism in a more positive light, yet there is one pivotal moment, when he talks about Joanot Matorell's 1490 romance *Tirant lo Blanch*, '*Tirante the White*, praised by Cervantes as a faithful picture of knights and ladies of his age, seems to have been written in an actual brothel [...] may lead us to suspect that their purity is that of romance, their profligacy, that of reality' (41). For a writer himself so closely linked to romance, that is surely a very remarkable reflection not only on medieval romance but, more pointedly, on the nineteenth-century recovery of romance for which he himself was greatly responsible. Furthermore, Scott may or may not be questioning his own stance, but what is certain is that his critique stands in opposition to two of the most influential texts on civilization and history published in his lifetime, Chateaubriand's *Le Génie du Christianisme* (1802) and *Itinéraire de Paris à Jérusalem* (1811), which together glorify Christianity and the Crusades. Scott's reflections on chivalry seem to be an admission about the received nature of romance, in part a result of his ignoring the fact that the romance love-plot is adulterous, yet it leaves us with the extraordinary task of deciding whether such remarks can shed light on his own epics in which references to female desire and brothels are conspicuous by their absence.

One major objection has yet to be overcome. It is difficult to counter the idea that Brunton adapts Richardson's formulas for her first heroine. The terrible doubts that the deeply religious Laura expresses about the nature of her deeply felt sexual desire might seem far-fetched to those unfamiliar with *Clarissa*, but the process of attraction leading to doubt leading to hate follows Richardson's design. That said, Brunton's fiction is different in three aspects of which only the final one seems to me to be of major importance, and I shall soon turn to it. These are, in ascending order, length, the replacement of the epistolary by other methods of narration, and a happy ending. In addition, the prospect of adulterous desire in *Discipline* is described in terms of frankness and physicality that are unmatched in Scott. In short, Scott's female characters' lack of desire might have more to do with the idealization of either or both national identity and bourgeois domesticity. If the contrast is limited to Scott and Brunton, this may or may not be an acceptable argument. It is possible to counter that females such as Queen Berengaria in *The Talisman* are aware that female desire in the West is as tightly policed as in the mythical East, but such polemics would seem to be more the exception than the rule. Perhaps the fact that Berengaria came from Navarre and never set foot in England might account for her different slant on sexuality. For surely there is a whole body of criticism analysing how questions of desire are deliberately sidetracked or avoided, above all in the case of Rebecca in *Ivanhoe*.[2] Such discussion, interesting as it might be, has a more formidable obstacle, which is that many female readers, starting from Johnstone herself, believe that Scott's detailed descriptions of female characters contribute to the claim that he is a universal genius, and Scott could hardly be universal if he excluded half of the world's population from his fiction.

Johnstone's eulogistic 'On the Political Tendency' concludes:

> Sir WALTER'S heroines are Revolutionists, or in the Opposition. *Flora MacIvor* wishes to overturn the Hanoverian line. *Minna Troil* is bewildered into a dangerous maze, by a grand but visionary scheme of revolutionizing the isles of Zetland. *Edith Bellenden* is in love with a fugitive leader of the party of the Covenant. *Rebecca*, the high-souled Jewess, is the alone, and eloquent, and bold defender of her oppressed race, against the rapacious and dissolute aristocracy of that dark and tyrannical age. (Anon. 1832: 133)

Johnstone is overtly trying to convince readers of two points that I have previously highlighted: the first, that Scott is not a Tory at all; second, that his pictures of the past are really portraits of the present, which can be deduced by a couple of her turns of phrase. Surely, the term 'in the Opposition' is an acceptable phrase for the discussion of a contemporary parliamentary debate but somewhat anachronistic for *Ivanhoe*. 'That dark and tyrannical age' could similarly be applied to the violence meted out by Normans on Saxons in that same novel or to the turbulent events that scarred Britain in the Peterloo years.

What is at stake here is not simply the question of desire in its erotic sense but what exactly is the presence and role of heroism in Scott's fiction and how this contrasts to the heroism described by his contemporaries. It is certain that Brunton generally and Ferrier, particularly in *Destiny*, show deep interest in describing female sexual desire, but that cannot be the end of the story, as union is such a central trope in Scott and his legion of European followers; the overlapping of the political and the personal cannot occur if the personal level is completely eradicated. If post-Culloden Scotland is a wasteland, then perhaps the economic progress outlined in the postscript is insufficient to make the country a land of opportunities for those outside the ruling elite. If Scott were writing the economic or social history of Scotland that might make sufficient sense, but what Scott is writing is fiction in which the two levels intertwine. After all, the language of conquest is redolent with such terminology: virgin territory is but one example; a 1620 publication calls Ireland 'a young wench that hath the green sickness for want of occupying [...] And betwixt her legs (for Ireland is full of havens) she hath an open harbour, but not much frequented' (Barker 2001: 152). As 2010 marked the four hundredth anniversary of the Plantation of Ulster, the recognition of the sexually violent content of such language is surely as relevant as ever. Again, the ur-text in this respect is the final act of Shakespeare's *Henry V*, which in straightforward fashion displays that fertile France requires the rapturous embrace of the youthful, virile Plantagenet.

Yet to draw the comparison between medieval France and eighteenth-century Scotland could be seen as an attempt to push through the colonial and postcolonial readings too forcefully without sufficient consideration of the evidence Scott provides, despite the Shakespearean echoes – in the lineage of Talbot – that I have previously analysed. Surely, the courtship between Rose and Waverley is based on some mutual attraction rather than mere submission by the vanquished to the victor? Some solution to this knotty problem can best be achieved if we recall how controversial the role of Scott's heroines and handling of heroinism can be. But before dealing with that matter, another principle has to be set down. Binary interpretations of Scott – Dekker (1987) is a particularly lucid example – are legion; one which affects this subject directly is the polarity – the supposed polarity – between Flora and Rose. Flora's famous dictum on Waverley's sentimental inclination has been internalized not only by Waverley but by generations of readers and critics. Flora recommends that '[t]he woman whom you marry ought to have affections and opinions moulded upon yours. Her studies ought to be your studies; – her wishes, her feelings, her hopes, her fears, should all mingle with yours' (215). These familiar words set up one of a series of polarities, as George Dekker and others have laid out: desire as opposed to marriage, passion to domesticity, Highlands to Lowlands, law as against lawlessness and so on. Waverley's subsequent marriage to Rose would indicate that he has taken in the lesson, but it is noticeable at this point that Waverley replies: 'And why will not you, Miss Mac-Ivor, who can so well describe a happy union – why will not you be yourself the person you describe?' (215). The conflation of private and public makes its appearance in 'a happy union' whereas Flora's disdain for the private places her in opposition to Rose. That is surely too simple a reading if we bear in mind that whatever description we make of the two potential wives, the one thing that they share is that both their names are floral. In other words, has the binary reading produced a more simplistic interpretation than the text itself suggests? Let us recall that it is Fergus who warns us of reading too much into the written word when he asks, 'are we in the land of romance and fiction?' (211).

Two Victorian readings throw up intriguing suggestions. In a highly intertextual scene in *The Mill on the Floss* (1860) that purposefully recalls Waverley and Flora's exchange, Maggie Tulliver and Philip meet each other far away from the eyes of society to discuss romance and fiction. Maggie tells Philip:

> I'm determined to read no more books where the blond-haired women carry away all the happiness. I should begin to have a prejudice against them. If you could give me some story, now, where the dark woman triumphs, it would restore the balance. I want to avenge Rebecca and Flora Mac Ivor, and Minna and all the rest of the dark unhappy ones. (Eliot 1973: 314)

The irony here is that Maggie will herself experience passion and death, without being able to 'carry away all the happiness', at least not in this life. Maggie is suggesting that any attempt to step outside the path to marriage and domesticity leads to punishment, though whether that is as accurate a mid-century reading of fiction in general as it is of Maggie's various attempts to be different, by cutting her hair or by attempting to learn Latin or love the wrong man, is questionable; that said, it is patently obvious that Scott's females have a fuller life than can be experienced in St Ogg's. This is surely why Maggie is so envious of Flora's freedom of action manifested in her rejection of Waverley, a decision that displays the right to choose, especially when this decision runs contrary to the wish of the brother as patriarch, another meeting point of both novels.

John Ruskin, in contrast, suggests that Scott's females are superior to their male counterparts in certain quintessential aspects. He argues that in Scott's

> true works, studied from Scottish life [...] there are but three men who reach the heroic type – Dandie Dinmont, Rob Roy, and Claverhouse; of these, one is a border farmer; another a freebooter; the third a soldier in a bad cause. And these touch the ideal of heroism only in their courage and faith, together with a strong, but uncultivated, or mistakenly applied, intellectual power. (1903: 96–7)

The first reaction to this highly provocative statement is that Ruskin's definition of what are 'true works' is highly subjective, yet surely it is remarkable that only three men, who form an odd assortment, can begin to be considered heroic; but even here, this seems at odds with intelligence. In short, there are few heroes and they all lack grey matter. In stark contrast, Ruskin states that Scott

> in his imaginations of women, – in the characters of Ellen Douglas, of Flora MacIvor, Rose Bradwardine, Catherine Seyton, Diana Vernon, Lilias Redgauntlet, Alice Bridgenorth, Alice Lee, and Jeanie Deans, – with endless varieties of grace, tenderness, and intellectual power, we find in all a quite infallible sense of dignity and justice; a fearless, instant, and untiring self-sacrifice, to even the appearance of duty, much more to its real claims; and, finally, a patient wisdom of deeply restrained affection, which does infinitely more than protect its objects from a momentary error; it gradually forms, animates, and exalts the characters of the unworthy lovers, until, at the close of the tale, we are just able, and no more, to take patience in hearing of their unmerited success. (97–8)

Ruskin definitely does not separate the blond and the dark heroine; for this reason Diana forms part of the same group as two women often seen as belonging to different hemispheres: Flora and Rose. In numerical terms, Ruskin is proposing that in the Waverley Novels the number of true heroes is proportionally small and the number of intelligent women proportionally large. It is also significant that one of the main figures in debates about Scott's females, Rebecca, is absent at this stage. However unpredicted that may be, like Johnstone, Ruskin sees the female sex as basically the rational one. This is worth emphasizing because Ruskin's remarks about female patience and self-sacrifice might otherwise be read as patronizing, a periphrastic way of saying that they simply stay at home waiting for their menfolk in Griselda fashion. But that is not the case, as women have the wisdom which men rarely possess; this is why the male, he emphasizes, is unworthy even at the end of the tales, by which time a process of learning – the *Bildung* – should have concluded. Union must therefore be seen as an event or a conclusion, but definitely cannot be considered a reward. Ruskin goes on to affirm that consequently women are not simply healers to their Iron Johns but guides, an attribute which Ruskin claims Scott inherits from Shakespeare's portrayal of sexual difference. Ruskin has no hesitation in affirming that women therefore fulfil the role that reformers of the Wollstonecraft era had campaigned for.

In the light of Eliot's heroine and Ruskin's remarks, it is not surprising to hear Merryn Williams (1985) claim that the energy presented in Scott's female characters is discontinued in mid-century fiction, as Maggie Tulliver intuits: hence for her, there is no release from the hateful world of St Ogg's other than the archetypal female death-by-drowning. Two points have to be made here. First, the light–dark heroine divide is present in Scott but also has a much longer life-story; therefore, for example, to say that Fenimore Cooper incorporates this polarity solely from his reading of Scott is precipitous. Second, Eliot, as others, is aware that the relative freedom enjoyed by some of Scott's heroines diminishes as the century progresses. The journey trope or, in Wilt's most precise coinage, 'the psychogeography' (1985: 8) is essential to the Waverley Novels and is also used extensively by Scott's female contemporaries, even to the extent of absurdity in the case of Brunton's transatlantic escapade, with or without the overhanging threat of ruin, rape or death; in contrast, Maggie Tulliver receives the first and third of these as her seaward journey is a prelude to her death.

Another standard mid-century trope is that the fallen woman dies or requires a miraculous reincarnation to survive. The fate of Nancy in *Oliver Twist* additionally shows that having a heart of gold is not enough to guarantee survival. But such violence against women is also present in Scott and therefore predates its location as necessarily a product of the chaos that rules the metropolis that London would soon represent; it cannot be upheld that such violence is a product of modernity. Williams's sympathetic chapter on Scott in her survey *Women in the English Novel* starts with the premise that his characterization of the female, both light and dark women, must be set in the context that female vulnerability is the result of violence. For her, *Ivanhoe*, rather than being primarily jingoistic or patriotic fiction, is an exposition of violence, primarily meted out by Normans on women from other races. She would therefore disagree with Twain's claim that the novel restored faith in chivalry; admittedly, it is difficult to know to what extent his statements should be taken at face value. What draws Rowena and Rebecca together is not simply the fact that they are women but 'belong to a subject race and can expect no mercy' (1985: 57) from their Norman jailors. Williams also highlights Scott's description, in the last-but-one paragraph of chapter 23, of how the Normans systematically raped Saxon women in the eleventh and twelfth centuries: many were therefore sent to convents for their own safety. Scott emphasizes that even such a royal figure as the future Empress Matilda was not exempt and had to assume the veil. Williams suggests that rape is therefore one of the major motifs in *Ivanhoe*: Ulrica's fate is not simply an indication of what Rowena might have suffered but that it was also 'the common fate of Saxon women' (Williams 1985: 57). Whether that is a correct assumption is open to debate, nevertheless Williams reminds us that such strategies are not simply part of a violent, mythical past, but also affect the present, marking, notably, the character of Helen MacGregor. Such analysis recalls Johnstone's picture of Ireland and the use of rape as a military strategy, as expounded in the previous chapter. Perhaps the emphasis on union as the endgame of the Waverley Novels has somewhat obscured the violence of the main body of the preceding text; in other words, a reinforcement of the idea that closing chapters do not always provide convincing closure. However, Williams's emphasis on violence and rape represents a valuable contribution, more so, if we can answer two questions which her brief study of Scott does not.

The first of these would be whether this awareness of violence, and especially violence perpetrated against women, is simply what occurred in the past rather than in modern Britain. The answer is that is not the case. The new Britain is distinctly barbaric: such a strident conclusion is easy to uphold if we consider the punishment meted out to the Jacobites. The irony of '[t]he verdict of GUILTY was already pronounced' (464) in the opening paragraph of chapter 68 of *Waverley* unequivocally indicates that the decision was taken before the trial began, as all Jacobites are born guilty, but some are guiltier than others. The emphasis in the following chapter on the Tudor origins of Carlisle castle forces us to consider, if not accept, that eighteenth-century Britain treats its rebels with as little concern for justice and fairness as we could expect from an authoritarian Tudor monarch, a judgement which surely contradicts the message of progress since those times that informs the novel's postscript. The second would be whether this violence of 60 years since is evident in a more modern, civil society, that is, one not engaged in warfare. The answer would again be in the affirmative, as *The Heart of Midlothian* amply demonstrates. Its title fits a Foucauldian understanding of the world to a tee, as it suggests that the modern state has a prison at its centre which, like a panopticon, surveys the lives of its citizens. But this particular novel is explicit in its description of injustice and violence against females. The debate about illegitimacy and punishment and the fate of Effie Deans are resolved by a fairy-godmother figure of the Queen, which should not obscure the fact that another anachronistic, medieval form of punishment is exposed in chapter 39. There are significant details: again we are back to Carlisle, the punishment is barbaric, and the mythology of witchcraft more appropriate to the Middle Ages than progressive, commercial Britain. One highly significant moment is when Jeanie 'turned her head to the other side of the carriage, with a sensation of sickness, of loathing, and of fainting' (Scott 1999: 390). It would be wrong to limit her reaction to the purely personal circumstance that Jeanie is witness to what nearly happened to her sister, as the narrative informs us, for there is surely more. The barbarity shown here, with its textual similarities to the fate of Fergus and his followers, suggests, to paraphrase Williams, that both Jacobites and women expect no mercy because they are aware they belong to subject races. Jeanie's refusal to look at such a horrifying event is presumably an attempt to evoke a similar sense of shock and outrage in the reader by inferring that not only is the punishment so terrible it cannot be reproduced in print but that we also live in a society that condones it by placing a curtain in front of the stage, itself a word that locates the scaffold as the place where the modern state performs for its public. *The Heart of Midlothian*'s final chapter narrates the sordid history of the Whistler ('Effie's unhappy child' (502)), slavery and death, which contrasts with the familial and financial prosperity of the happy ending. In addition, there is a note, written in the moralizing language associated with Brunton, and the final word is given to Jedediah Cleisbotham. To decide which is the message or messages the reader takes home is therefore a complicated matter, yet what is easier to argue is that in a fashion similar to *Waverley*, Scott's endings are not straightforward. This leads me to conclude that tandem Scott-progressive history does not fully correspond to the Waverley Novels, where numerous doubts pepper the texts. At certain moments, it seems that Scott is back-pedalling. Perhaps an alternative pattern of non-progressive or even regressive history emerges.

Insipid heroism and heroinism

What Johnstone and her contemporaries identify is that for subject races to survive in whatever period of time is little short of miraculous. Heroinism demands fortitude, which is provided in the Brunton and Ferrier model through religious faith; in the Johnstone model, through humanism and tolerance. In contrast the Scott hero, has, from his inception, been seen as rather wooden and indecisive, though both Alexander Welsh (1992) and Duncan (1992) regard this as evidence of Scott's understanding of how the modern state works; its good citizens are necessarily submissive and nondescript. Scott's heroines, in contrast, can be read as stronger and more active, whether or not we follow Ruskin completely. For example, if we simplified *Waverley*, we could propose that the hero has made a journey, messed things up and achieved little; in contrast, the heroine of *The Heart of Midlothian* has made a journey, cleared up other people's mess and achieved a lot. The risk of extending this gender basis is voiced by Williams when she makes the assessment that at the close of *Rob Roy* 'she [Diana Vernon] is revealed as a completely traditional woman [...] acting under father's orders' (1985: 59) and also by Duncan, 'women hold power [...] in order to give it up to men' (1992: 71). Agreement or disagreement is of less importance than the recognition that it highlights the fact that most heroines in historical romance hold deep loyalty to the family and in particular to the father; it certainly can be no exaggeration to call this devotion the Cordelia syndrome. It stems from two literary sources; one, obviously, is Shakespeare. The similarities and differences between Jessica and Shylock in *The Merchant of Venice*, on the one hand, and Isaac and Rebecca in *Ivanhoe* on the other are immediately apparent to any attentive reader; similarities of plot extend farther into the characters of Portia and Rowena, the question of exile, and so on. Brunton's second novel alludes at certain crucial points to *King Lear*: Ellen's father's bloody corpse is something she cannot contemplate or describe, in similar fashion to Jeanie Deans's or Waverley's refusal to witness horror. The second tradition is Richardson, and again, this is most evident in Brunton. Clarissa, even when her father most virulently refuses to accede to any of her wishes and even when she is irredeemably in Lovelace's clutches, maintains that her father's wishes are most sacred, over and above all her desires, including the choice of husband. The fact that such unshaken loyalty, in contrast to Waverley's wavering, is fundamental to the heroines, contributes to reading them as characters with a set of principles which they will cling to, whether they are based on religion, or, in the case of Flora, on dynastical loyalty. This itself is one consequence of the Cordelia syndrome, as *King Lear* is a play notorious for its lack of catharsis, a phenomenon that offended eighteenth-century sensibility imbued in classical idealism; no phoenix would arise from the ashes. This again is close to interpretations which question the concordance of the *Waverley* postscript with the rest of the final chapters. At the same time, it would seem a fitting way to summarize the end of *Redgauntlet*: the cause is lost for ever.

The central thrust of my argument is that the female tradition shows heroines with a purpose in life that Scott's heroes lack and only some of his heroines have. Religious faith provides part of the explanation, as does loyalty to the family or belief in education. Put in the briefest of formulas, this would initially seem to set up a contest between the didactic novel – let us not forget Scott's unbounded admiration for

Maria Edgeworth – in opposition to romance. But the situation is more complicated than that, as Waverley's 'education' is described in the third chapter. To my line of argument, there are two elements that stand out above the canonical content of the Gothic library. One is the narrative's insistence on Waverley's intelligence, which stands in contrast to the critical commonplace that the hero is rather dull (a more restrained remark than Scott's own words on Waverley's imbecility): '[h]is powers of apprehension were so uncommonly quick, as almost to resemble intuition' (46). Of course, the remarks immediately following, added to the comments about how he read voraciously only what pleased him, suggest the lack of direction central to Ferris's female reader. In a secular novel this guidance will not come from religion, hence the importance of the second element, namely that 'his mother died in the seventh year after the reconciliation between the brothers' (49). In the context of Brunton, Ferrier, Johnstone or any other didactic writer, this comment would certainly account for the waywardness of their heroine's education; for example, it is explicitly articulated in the case of Ellen in *Discipline*, consequently it is legitimate to ask whether Scott's objective to distance himself from feminine writing has failed. Linking Ellen's loss to Waverley would definitely steer us in that direction, as would some critical remarks on the low quality of contemporary education, which are worth citing in order to show that this proximity is intentional and significant:

> I am aware I may be here reminded of the necessity of rendering instruction agreeable to youth [...] but an age in which children are taught the driest doctrines by the insinuating method of instructive games, has little reason to dread the consequences of study being rendered too serious or severe. The history of England is now reduced to a game at cards, – the problems of mathematics to puzzles and riddles, – and the doctrines of arithmetic may, we are assured, be sufficiently acquired, by spending a few hours a-week at a new and complicated edition of the Royal Game of the Goose. There wants but one step further, and the Creed and Ten Commandments may be taught in the same manner, without the necessity of the grave face, deliberate tone of recital, and devout attention, hitherto exacted from the well-governed childhood of this realm. (46–7)

These indisputably stern words from *Waverley* form an extremely moral condemnation; this contempt of modern mores could easily have been delivered from Dr James Fordyce's pulpit; nevertheless, their influence in criticism has been surprisingly minimal. That said, the reference to the Creed and the Ten Commandments is one of the few explicit religious references in the text. The consequence of his self-guided, intuitively based formation is the inability to judge how his individual deeds affect his family, in short, the incapacity to distinguish adventure from reality, fiction from real life, which is apparently a consequence of his 'vast store of literary knowledge' (Sroka 1980: 147). Edward's education is therefore flawed by a lack of moral guidance, itself hardly a novel idea. It would be a very neat argument to place his self-taught literary education in opposition to fervent religious faith, yet I would posit that the guide to life he lacks could easily have been supplied by Rousseau.

In my chapter on Ferrier, I discussed the view that Wollstonecraft greatly influenced *Marriage*, particularly in its treatment of motherhood, education and religion. It is easy to place Rousseau and Wollstonecraft in opposite corners of the ring, but at the same time it is worth bearing in mind that, according to Janet Todd, 'she was, she later said, half in love with Rousseau' (2000: 102). Wollstonecraft's disagreements with Rousseau form the foundations of *A Vindication of the Rights of Woman* (1792) basically because of his lack of an openly declared religious faith, his views on the libido and, most importantly of all, his belief in unmovable sexual difference. In *Vindication*, Wollstonecraft, like Rousseau, consciously decides to concentrate on the education of middle-class females (1993: 77), but their programmes share little in common.

Half in love maybe, but the other half is in complete disagreement. For Wollstonecraft, Rousseau is a sensualist who places sexual pleasure as the ultimate goal in place of the love of God. Neither would she approve of the fact that he stresses that boys should learn about life through contact with nature rather than through books, receiving no religious instruction before 15. It is quite clear that not only Wollstonecraft but all three authors stress both explicitly and implicitly the importance of literacy in their fiction and other prose, and therefore share nothing in common with Rousseau here. Perhaps they also interpreted the following sentence, presumably aimed at convent-educated females, as a slight on their own beliefs:

> For my part, I am much afraid that those little saints who are compelled to spend their childhood in prayer will occupy their youth in a very different manner, and will do their best, when they are married, to make up for the time which they feel that they have lost when they were girls. (Rousseau 1964: 226)

Rousseau basically argues in *Émile* that women should use their natural cunning to make their husbands believe they are free when in fact they are devoted to the care of the family. Sexual difference is present in some highly provocative remarks, for example that girls love playing with dolls, as it is 'a taste clearly based on their life-work' (222) or that 'she [the generic wife] ought to learn betimes to submit even to injustice, and to bear oppression from her husband without complaining' (225). Clearly, no such idea would ever be condoned in the didactic fiction I have analysed.

Yet, where Wollstonecraft is more than half in love with Rousseau is in the primacy given to reason, thus the second paragraph reads: 'In what does man's pre-eminence over the brute creation consist? The answer is as clear as that a half is less than the whole; in Reason' (1993: 81). Wollstonecraft's disgust that Rousseau's complete educational programme is, in essence, directed only towards males is apparent even in this briefest extract. The pointed use of 'man' as restricted to sex is presumably intentional, hence 'a half is less than the whole', as is the barbed term 'brute creation', an allusion to the idealization of developing societies; Rousseau stresses that peasants are dull, they are little better than machines, whereas 'savages are remarkable for their strong sense and keenness of intellect' (1964: 122). Wollstonecraft, in contrast, believes more in the perfectibility of both men and women through education and religion. For Rousseau, education brings man to reason, and therefore for Wollstonecraft this search for perfectibility should also be applied to the other half, otherwise they will simply pass on the little they have learnt from instruction based on precepts that leave women with 'all the follies and vices of civilization' (1993: 137) but with none of its virtues.

Perfectibility incorporates reason which crosses both gender and class lines among the well-educated; perhaps only the aristocracy, corrupt through ill-breeding and vice, are beyond redemption. Waverley's education shows a complete lack of any of those elements which Rousseau believed are necessary for the male and which Wollstonecraft believed should be available to women to allow them to break out of a vicious circle of breeding beautiful girls to become beautiful mothers of yet more beautiful girls. It would not be fair to say that Waverley is a *tabula rasa* before he sets out, as, after all, he has a good knowledge of the classics and European canonical literature. What he clearly does not have is reason, or to use a contemporary term taken up by Welsh, 'prudence', which in most cases has a religious origin and which in its secular form is personified by the figure of Lady Augusta in *Clan-Albin*. Waverley therefore appears to be a character based on absence, in that he seems to have absorbed very little of the ideological and educational tools that constitute character for Scott's female contemporaries. Waverley's wavering could have been corrected by a moral or religious education which is available to all citizens and comes in a wide variety of forms. Consequently, his secularism gains greater prominence, as his lack of religious belief comes to be somewhat an anomaly. Scott's account of his education ensures that he is neither a believer, like his contemporaries, nor an agnostic, like Rousseau; instead he appears an atheist, devoid of any concerns, in short, an insipid hero. Such scepticism or disbelief in the value of literature is similar to that which drove Scott's literary relations into a cul-de-sac.

Brunton, Ferrier, Johnstone and Scott all set up military men as husbands for union. Within this common trope there is plenty of diversity, from the wasted figure of Lennox (*Marriage*) to the ambivalent figure of Waverley. Hargrave's military rank is seen by Laura's father and, one supposes, by extension by society at large, as a guarantor of status and virtue, thereby making him a perfect catch. Of course, there is a counter tradition. Wordsworth's poetry portrays a destitute countryside; 'The Ruined Cottage' is a paradigmatic poem in which poverty is not caused by poor harvests alone but by the army supplying the only possible alternative, or arguably the last resort for the poor. It is difficult to gauge whether the medicine is worse than the illness, but the poem clearly shows disquiet with the consequences of an increasing militarization which necessarily glorifies the virtues of the mutilated and the dead. Scott's lifetime activities in the militia are complemented in his fiction by a whole gallery of glorious heroes and a punctilious attention to the description of uniforms, heraldry and so on. What, as a matter of fact, could be more deeply romantic than Bonnie Prince Charlie? Yet even in the first novel, seeming contradictions manifest themselves.

Waverley does not attend the public spectacle of execution at Carlisle, instead, 'he rushed into an apartment, and bolted the door' (476). The noise and atmosphere generated by the procession is sufficient in itself to create that indelible impression of horror, the very words which open the next chapter. This is, by the way, the only major incident he will not contemplate, a sure indication of its barbarity. This exceptional refusal lends itself to several interpretations. Those centred on character studies could argue that it is perfectly reasonable for anybody to refuse to witness the excruciating pain inflicted on someone to whom he has been very close, as Ian Dennis's application of the triangle of mimetic desire would corroborate. This argument can be extended into a critique of how Hanoverianism handles its affairs: it might purport to modernity in theory but the Carlisle incidents belie the claim by illustrating what really occurs. This argument can be farther strengthened by connecting it to episodes in *The Heart of Midlothian*, even if the logical consequence of that is to read the two incidents in gendered terms: that Waverley is demonstrating traits taken more from heroinism than from heroism, which would go some way to clarifying the bizarre nature of Waverley's behaviour in battle. My next conclusion is that by dropping the masculine role of soldier, he assumes the female role of protector in the Ruskin mould.

Violence, non-violence and regressive history

Given the enormous attention that generations of scholars have given to chapter 47, 'The Conflict', I will limit myself to drawing several conclusions that show that Scott's descriptions of military action share much of Johnstone's scepticism about war. First, it is useful to see that Prestonpans has certain features that substantiate or at least encourage a Freudian reading. Initially, the misty atmosphere – 'The vapours rose like a curtain' (339) – is a theatrical metaphor announcing the unfolding of action, yet it also indicates a certain dream-like approach that will contrast to the very physical presence of violence, destruction and death. In the following description, mist will be replaced by smoke as an impediment to a clear view of carnage. In trying to save Colonel Gardiner, Waverley sees him receiving 'more wounds than would have let out twenty lives. When Waverley came up, however, perception had not entirely fled. The dying warrior seemed to recognize Edward, for he fixed his eye upon him with an upbraiding, yet sorrowful look, and appeared to struggle for utterance' (341). There is some strength in his former commander, but it is insufficient for a coherent utterance, hence, as in a dream, interpretation relies on gestures and fragments of discourse. If we accept that Gardiner was his commander and father-figure – as is made clear in the novel's early chapters – responsible for his military education, what we are witnessing is an incident reminiscent of Hamlet's ghost. The youth is aware of the pain of death but is unable to divine what form his future action should take.

Waverley's path has been to save rather than take life with the alacrity that Colonel Talbot and Mrs Nosebag would promote. This is most graphically illustrated when his act of heroism takes the form of preventing Dugald Mahony's battle-axe delivering a deathblow to Talbot. The wildness of the Highland troops in Scott's description is highlighted by their love of plunder and their use of the broadsword in contrast to the order of the English troops 'trained in Flanders' (340), whose knowledge of modern warfare is ineffective in this case but not, by implication, in any future conflict. Axes and plunder really belong to earlier times, suggesting that due to their technical inferiority in the long term the Jacobites have no possibility of overcoming the regimented modern state and its organized army, despite their success in 'personal struggles' (340), of which modern warfare provides less opportunity than before. In a binary reading of past and present, there is no doubt as to who represents that past and who represents the present, but I will propose that Scott's strategy points elsewhere.

Hanging, drawing and quartering, which involves the use of multiple ways of inflicting pain and death, is both a forbidding example of state power and a public demonstration of the many different ways it has to torture and murder. One important instrument is precisely the axe, the same weapon yielded by Dugald and by the executioners of Fergus; the multiple wounds received by Gardiner emphasize the ferocity of battle but also the multiple wounds inflicted on a victim of treason; they are parallel examples of extreme and excessive suffering. The account of barbarism in this chapter emphasizes the violence of the Highlanders, the violence of warfare in general, but at the very moment when it is tempting to use this as an unequivocal indication of how Jacobitism belongs to the past, it also necessary to envisage the existence of similar sadistic practices in the modern state, with Carlisle as its public arena. Thus a peculiar symbiosis is put in place whereby each indication of the outmodedness of the Jacobite army mirrors an equal if not greater cruelty in the modern state. This hypothesis conflicts with Welsh's assertion (1992: 203) that Scott positions torture in the past.

I have previously noted the dubious nature of Talbot's language, which seems to create both an ideology of English nationalism while simultaneously calling it into question. In a classical Bakhtinian formula, this is a fine example of the literary discourse of the novel subverting itself. Does a similar process take place in the battle scene itself? I believe it does, when we consider Scott's description of its conclusion:

> Loud shouts of triumph now echoed over the whole field. The battle was fought and won, and the whole baggage, artillery, and military stores of the regular army remained in possession of the victors. Never was a victory more complete. Scarce any escaped from the battle, excepting the cavalry, who had left it at the very onset, and even these were broken into different parties, and scattered all over the country. (341)

The irony emanates from a probable allusion to *Macbeth*: the second witch's celebrated words in the opening scene: 'When the hurlyburly's done, / When the battle's lost and won', suggesting perhaps the smoke-filled setting. Battles are presumably fought to be won in the name of honour, patriotism, glory, for some noble cause, but here the scale of the victory is quantified by the wholly successful appropriation of material goods, as the second sentence states: baggage, artillery and stores. The exclamatory third sentence emphasizes either that fact or narrative irony or both. The description of the cavalry borders on the absurd, as they were safe from harm having missed the battle almost completely! Again, these ironic accounts of events could arguably emphasize the backward-ness of the Jacobites, as, for example, the taking of stores is fundamental to *Henry V*; it is an exercise in gratuitous aggression by the French army, 'expressly against the law of arms' (4.7.1). Again, if the connection suggested by Dugald's axe is true and for the nexus to hold, then the modern state would somehow have to palimpsestically recur to similar plunder in the near future. The origins of this future lie in the narrative's remarks on the organization and firmness of the Hanoverian army, as well as their technical superiority: they recur to weaponry rather than charging wildly as if they were extras in *Braveheart*. Hence the result of Culloden is announced in the language of Prestonpans, where the result, the temporary result, is different. What strengthens the link between the rapacious Highlanders and more efficiently rapacious modern state is that it will likewise be extremely interested in the 'whole baggage, artillery, and military stores' of the losers: in short, Talbot's expansionist policy for Scotland. Surely, by substituting France for Scotland, he would wholeheartedly share Henry V's sentiment that England loved Scotland so well that it would not part with a village of it.

Such analysis brings to the fore a deeply sceptical world-view expressed between the lines or in the lines themselves in the first of Scott's monumental novels. These attitudes are not unique to *Waverley*. As I have shown elsewhere (Monnickendam 2009), a similar episode occurs in chapter 11 of *The Talisman*. This time, the intervention does not occur on the battlefield but in a terrible argument about nationali-ties and national symbols. Scott draws an extremely bluff and brawny Richard I, so lacking in intelligence and charm that he is at the most distant point from images of nobility and chivalry; Johnstone's take on Scott as a leveller puts down firm roots here. Just after Richard has defi-antly torn up the Austrian flag, Kenneth – in order to ward off a deadly blow from 'a gigantic warrior from the frontiers of Hungary' (Scott 1897: 126), that is, an equivalent to Dugald, on the commander-in-chief of the Third Crusade, that is, a superior version of Gardiner and linked to Kenneth by military loyalty – positions his shield, as had Waverley, to protect an English military chief. If the two episodes have incidental similarities what do they suggest? That brawny Richard can only kill whereas others have the additional heroism which manifests itself in the prevention of the death of others. The embryonic nation states are ineluctably xenophobic.

Scott's *The Siege of Malta*, unavailable in a complete edition until 2008, while not describing individual acts and thoughts after its early chapters, reaches a notable level of pessimism about the human condition, basically because of humanity's obsession with war. There is little left of belief in the art of war in such statements as 'But the relentless shower of heads which was thundered into his entrenchments, seemed to infer that the war was to be continued on the same relentless principle, until one of the two armies had totally ceased to exist' (2008: 115). However, it does seem to predict the policy of General Grant in the American Civil War. Towards the end, the narrator mulls the possibility that '[c]onquest [...] seemed to be as irretrievable calamity as defeat itself' (156), an aphorism that could have come from the pen of that most influential of modern theorists of war, Clausewitz. Both *The Talisman* and *The Siege of Malta* sustain a view that history is not progressive at all, and possibly regressive.

Military glory is questioned in the first book of *The Iliad*, so Scott is hardly an original in the field, but the oddity resides in such scepticism being located in the foundational historical novel which inspired a large corpus of Victorian epic poems and much European historical fiction. Milton, in the invocation to the ninth book of *Paradise Lost*, dismisses

> Wars, hitherto the only argument
> Heroic deemed, chief mastery to dissect
> With long and tedious havoc fabled knights
> In battles feigned; the better fortitude
> Of patience and heroic martyrdom
> Unsung. (9:28–33)

Milton therefore will not write an Arthurian epic for England but one which emphasizes the possibility of inner fortitude – the paradise within – the virtue which is needed to overcome the horrors of war and destruction which he so graphically depicts in the gloomy vision of the history of the world, basically a picture of death and woe, recounted in books 11 and 12. Brunton and Ferrier would seem close to Milton here in their belief that inner fortitude provides the means to overcome the hardships of life. Scott is close to Johnstone's belief in the horrors of war, but, as stated previously, at least Lady Augusta seems to believe that war can eventually be eradicated in the same way as such a powerful institution as the slave trade had been in 1807. The date is vital, as its proximity turns what might otherwise be considered a mere pipedream into something tangible. Lacking both the religious core of the first two writers and the explicitness as sometimes expressed in Johnstone's writings leaves Scott, by comparison, somewhat in limbo. In fact, it could be argued that his intellectual concerns move from disquiet about the human condition, as illustrated in the ambivalent relationship of *Waverley*'s final two chapters and, as another example, in the difficulty in resolving the fate of Rebecca in *Ivanhoe*, towards the ideas exposed in the preceding paragraphs concluding with the quasi-nihilism of *The Siege of Malta*. To plot such a development is risky but undeniably plausible when the emerging presence of fatalism in Scott's work becomes even more evident when placed alongside the more positive ideological certainties expressed in the writings of his female contemporaries. The conclusion is a simple one: Scott's position as a doubter is ever strengthened when juxtaposed with the fiction of his contemporaries.

Union

This study closes with the subject of union. Initially, it would seem a rather fruitless task to try and dismantle its presence as a positive force in the work of Scott. After all, recalling his sonorous promotion of Edgeworth's achievement in the 'General Preface' leaves no room for doubt: 'she may truly be said to have done more for the union than perhaps all the legislative enactments by which it has been followed up' (1985: 523). Scott has not the slightest qualm in submitting literature to the service of political aims; neither does he express the slightest doubt about union: his remarks on native foibles suggest that Scotland is joining a superior organization, or even, perhaps, that a subject once fit for comedy is now fit for history. This casts an interesting light on his own aestheticization of the Highlands. That said, it is tantalizing to inquire which were the 'legislative enactments' between 1800 (the Union) and 1829 (the date of publication of the 'General Preface') Scott judged as having less impact than Edgeworth's prose. In a similar fashion, Scott's desire to follow her cultural policy would suggest that less has been achieved for the case of Unionism in Scotland since the 1707 Act of Union than in Ireland during the much briefer period of 1800–29.

It is important to recall Trumpener's assertion that:

> The empirewide influence of the Waverley Novels lies in their ability to harmonize Scottish materials with British perspectives, as they reconstruct the historical formation of the Scottish nation, the simultaneous formation of the Britain that subsumes it, and a cultural nationalism that survives because it learns to separate cultural distinctiveness from the memory of political autonomy and can therefore be accommodated with the new imperial framework. (1997: 246–7)

Trumpener extends Scott's belief in the power of fiction to promote the union from the British Isles to the empire, which hence performs as a living example of a worldwide union. I have previously proposed that if the concept of union comprises the sexual and the political, Scott tends to diminish concerns about the nature of desire, which necessarily results in an increase in the political dimension. Scott's own words on Edgeworth and the vast scholarly tradition, with Trumpener as my example here, follow this pattern. I am not going to argue that the question of union deconstructs itself within the Waverley Novels, something which is an absurd supposition, but I will suggest that if the union is cemented by romance, there are some notable faultlines which are identifiable through a contrastive analysis with his contemporaries. The cracks are not limited to the acknowledgement that the union is between unequal partners.

Hart recognized that Scott's endings were both melancholic, a term which he uses several times in his study, and polemical, for example in Scott's description of 'the large painting of Fergus and Edward together in Highland dress, thus giving the force of legend to an image of reconciliation that exists only through art' (1978a: 57). 'Only through art' indicates a certain disparity between art and life, fiction and reality, which almost borders on deceit. I would therefore like to try and build on this hypothesis and suggest why they are distant from 'reconciliation'. Most emphatically, an acute problem of coherence is identifiable in the political or symbolic dimension of that weaker vessel, Rose. If union is to be the magic formula that discursively brings together family and state, a union must have a certain promise for the future. Arguably, that is precisely the function of the postscript, yet if that is the case, it seems so detached from the preceding chapter that Scott's own comment that it should have been the preface makes perfect sense. In either case, the separation of the private from the public spheres is reinforced. This disparity is farther highlighted in the other examples of union that I have referred to and which I will very briefly recap. As previously stated, the Shakespearean representation of the ur-union of England with France is imbued with the language of fertility; rather than courtship, it is a mating dance where virility in the figure of Henry imposes itself over fertility in the figure of Catherine with an irrefutable aim: impregnation. The end of *Discipline* stresses through Ellen's own words that she is still coquettish and desirable, illustrated by the presence of children and the existence of certain experiences that cannot be articulated in English, that is in print. It is easy to attest that the end of literary works tend to be conventional: tragedies end in catharsis, comedies in marriage, but predictability is essential in reminding us of the ideological importance of closure. In addition, it is striking to note that what Brunton will not write about is fulfilment, whereas what Scott will not write about is cruelty; the contrast reveals radically different mindsets.

If we turn our attention to Ireland, the formulation of productive union in the Glorvina solution, as articulated by Tracy (1985), is meaningless without the promise of the future. There is no point in a union, of a better understanding between the unequal relationship of core and non-core cultures, to use the terms of Cairns Craig in *Out of History: Narrative Paradigms of Scottish and English Culture* (1996), if there are to be no progeny. Surely, this partly explains the selection of the younger over the older suitor in Owenson's *The Wild Irish Girl*. Ferris's use of the term 'incomplete union' in *The Romantic National Tale and the Question of Ireland* (2002) might seem to indicate that incompleteness invalidates the union but that presupposes that postcolonial or feminist subtexts were written into romance, something which Trumpener's analysis of empire questions if not refutes. The situation responds more to the Bakhtinian belief that novelistic discourse is naturally hybrid: any attempt to impose a single viewpoint will certainly fail or, by reduction, in purely formal terms, not produce a novel at all. The marked orality of romantic-era fiction prevents this occurring; therefore the articulation of a union will always be incomplete to differing degrees. At the risk of repetition, Bakhtin would argue that the language of romance is just one voice that opposes another: in this case, the officialese of both Talbot and the postscript. If this were not the case, then union would hardly escape the connotation of rape or, in milder terms, an example of sleeping with the enemy, with or without collusion. One powerful reason why Johnstone marries her young lovers so early on in *Elizabeth de Bruce* is her acute awareness of the implications of the linguistic-cum-political battlefield of union and in doing so purposefully challenges the Glorvina solution.

Although Scott's 1814 romance ends in union and shows little resemblance to the pedestrian ending of Johnstone's tale, Rose certainly remains a major enigma at the end of *Waverley*. Precisely at the culminating moment of a romance, her voice and very presence itself are even more negligible than in previous chapters. The mundane words, '[t]he marriage took place on the appointed day' (481), which open the closing paragraph of chapter 70, are hardly promising. We might expect there to be some account of female thoughts, anxieties and state of being on the marriage day, surely one of the most predictable episodes in any tale, yet the only mention of female presence is Lady Emily's – Talbot's wife's – ill-health. Poverty, debt and fear of offending the authorities account for a toned-down wedding, but there is additional poverty of description. Rose is mentioned twice, once in relationship to David Gellatley, and then in the details of the marriage contract, but we never get a word from her. There is not even a toast to Rose or the happy couple.

Her absence in the closing pages would surely consolidate my argument that Scott erases the question of female desire in his account of union, but does that necessarily mean that that implies an increased focus on the political side of union? Is this simply an example of another incomplete union? The answer to this question depends – yet again – on how much importance is given to the closing words of chapter 71 (see below) and how much corresponds to the postscript. In the history of criticism, the postscript wins by a knock-out, but it is worth considering the end of the preceding chapter. In a remarkable replay of chapter 11, instead of toasting to violence, the toast is now for peace, but rather than toasting the newly weds, the Baron addresses, in the first place, Colonel Talbot, then the prosperity of the two houses. Prosperity is reduced to whatever the estate might produce; no mention is made of what might arrive in nine months' time or any similar example of what is toasted or joked about at a wedding. One only has to look at Manzoni's *The Betrothed* (1827) to see how peculiar *Waverley*'s conclusion is: 'Within twelve months of the wedding a fine baby was born to them [...] As the years went by, other children arrived, some boys and some girls – I forget how many' (Manzoni 1987: 719). Such happiness is close to *Discipline* but light years away from *Waverley*. Rose might well be 'of the fertile valley' (Duncan 1992: 83), but it is debatable whether the wedding guests, other than her father, view her in that way. Perhaps the oddest thing of all is that if there is an overlap between plot – as land – and plot – as storyline – then it is reasonable to expect that the marriage fulfils the dictum outlined by the Earl of Courtland, whose giveaway name is another terrible Ferrier pun, that marriage is for the aggrandizement of family and wealth. My next conclusion would be that it is difficult to tell who is the victor, the new Briton, at the book's conclusion: Waverley or Talbot, who seems to believe in certain rights of inheritance? Either or both? In any case, the very purpose of marriage and romance is called into question. Waverley, as estate-owner and husband, is the obvious choice. Yet, Talbot has demonstrated that he, if not the owner of the largest purse, controls the purse strings. The new economic set-up divulges that money is as efficient as arms, and, crucially, both need an administration in order to operate effectively.

The final paragraph of chapter 71 is even more perplexing:

> It only remains for me to say, that as no wish [for the union of the Bradwardine and Waverley houses] was ever uttered with more affectionate sincerity, there are few which, allowing for the necessary mutability of human events, have been, upon the whole, more happily fulfilled. (491)

Interpretation necessarily includes a dose of subjectivity; nevertheless, the use of six commas in a single sentence interrupts any fluidity and must surely estrange its content, in true formalist logic. The happiness desired is simply financial, overriding any mention of the couple's well-being: life is reduced to a simple formula of happiness equalling influence in the Talbot-dominated world. Consequently, the postscript presumably now has a logical place in the scheme of things, as it forecasts what happiness means to the new Briton. Whether this is another example of Scott's postmodernism, to add to those analysed by Jerome McGann (2004), is questionable, but if that were the case it certainly points to a world as sterile as Welsh's allusion to Kafka would corroborate. The bourgeois idealism of Brunton or Manzoni therefore farther highlights the despair in Scott's narrative voice, whose jerky syntax calls its subject matter, happiness, into question. I would even propose that this is one of the bitterest and most sarcastic paragraphs in Scott's early work, if not in all his work.

Landscape and tradition

The marked contrast between secular Scott and his female contemporaries is unequivocally marked in their description of landscape. Volumes have been written on the implications of Scott's evocative description of the defiant Highlands of Perthshire as marking a 'stupendous barrier' (1985: 73). Whether we make more of the sublime mountains than of the miserable cottages is of less importance than noticing that this barrier, a term imbued with probation and impossibility, draws a Highland line which gives Scotland a geographical pattern similar to Edgeworth's Ireland, where magnificent houses stand beside miserable cottages, both within and outside the pale. In contrast, Brunton's description of homecoming in *Self-Control*, analysed in Chapter 1, which predates *Waverley* by three years, elevates the piety of Sunday to such a degree that the landscape owes its beauty to its worshippers: its sublimity responds to the God of love rather than the God responsible for an abrupt and terrifying nature. Brunton and Ferrier most certainly, and Johnstone to a lesser extent, as I have repeatedly argued throughout this study, view religious activism positively, and establish it as the foundation of personal happiness, which includes material prosperity and physical well-being. This combined with a certain degree of optimism indicates a degree of faith – no pun intended – in the future which *Waverley* might not indicate for anyone other than Talbot and company.

Ian Watt's seminal *The Rise of the Novel* discusses Richardson at some length and provides several significant clarifications for this study. The inordinate length of the latter part of *Clarissa*, that is to say after her death, is accounted for by the fact that it 'belongs to a long tradition of funeral literature' (1997: 217). Instead of restricting our focus to that of form alone, it is important to see that the conclusions graphically illustrate why a Brunton heroine can and will survive. Arguably, a Brunton conclusion might just read as formulaic a conclusion as a fairy story, were it not for one vital point. Watt adds: '[i]n *Clarissa*, however, a similar unawareness of sexual feeling on the heroine's part, which by others may be interpreted as gross lack of self-knowledge, if not actual dishonesty, becomes an important part of the dramatic development, deepening and amplifying the overall meaning of the story' (228). Brunton's heroines' battle for survival is brought to crisis from precisely what Clarissa lacks: an awareness of sexuality and hence of the real nature of sexual harassment. To put it another way, it is possible to argue that Brunton's engagement with Richardson, her desire to find an answer to both Pamela's and Clarissa's entanglement with men, makes her sense of a distinct Scottish location hinge solely on the degree to which it can maintain its distinctive religion.

Watt argues that '[t]he reason for the emphasis on death seems to have been the belief that the growing secularization of thought could best be combated by showing how only faith in the future state could provide a secure shelter from the terrors of mortality' (217). Initially this might seem to have virtually nothing to do with Brunton or her contemporaries or, for that matter, with Scott, if we accept my argument about the secular nature of his texts. But for nineteenth-century Scottish fiction it does have powerful implications. If we remove plot, if we remove sexuality, as they are presented in Brunton; if we remove wit, if we remove social criticism, as they are presented in Ferrier; if we remove reason, if we remove Ireland, as they are presented in Johnstone, what do we have left? An understandable reaction would be the belief that we are left with practically nothing of interest, but that would be too hasty. What we have left is that sentimental, religious literature of the late nineteenth century, in short the Kailyard. For surely if Scott is secular and if he draws such a firm Highland line, his link to the Kailyard is difficult to map out. In contrast, if we decaffeinate the writings of Scott's contemporaries, in removing the vigorous spirit of their prose, what remains is necessarily mawkish. Laura's return to Scotland or the closing pages of *Clan-Albin* taken out of context and read in isolation are certainly proto-Kailyard texts. In other words, I would conclude that by decaffeinating the work of these three women writers, the Kailyard is exactly what we end up with.

Am I suggesting that Scott's agnosticism or atheism rule him out as instigator of the Kailyard? That question is best answered by considering Anthony D. Smith's assertion that '[t]hough [...] nationalism is a fundamentally secular ideology, there is nothing unusual about a religious nationalism' (1991: 49). Here, Smith is widening his view that modern nationalism is basically a product of the Enlightenment in order to include countries such as Sri Lanka, Armenia, Poland and Ireland where ethno-religious communities are built on this particular exchange of concepts. Therefore it is tenable, with Scott in hand, to suggest that nineteenth-century Scottish identity is not only indelibly marked by its religion, which reinforces the case for the Killing Times becoming as epic a moment as Bannockburn, and arguably more so than the Forty-Five. Religion as a sign of identity was exactly what the Kailyard advocated, yet if we dismiss the Kailyard as a historical irrelevance, then the representation of the Covenanters and the Killing Times as the epic moment become even more central. If this argument can be sustained, it must be because *Old Mortality* is more deeply concerned with good government than Hogg's account of the same period in *The Brownie of Bodsbeck*. But then, as I have repeatedly done, if we view Scott in the light of his female contemporaries, his purposefully secular identity is more and more identifiable at every point.

Cairns Craig observes that all the major Scottish novelists are as much, if not more, associated with a region than with the country as a whole (1998: 221). If we think of writers such as Lewis Grassic Gibbon, Neil Gunn or more contemporary artists, such as Jessie Kesson, this rings true. The more recent development would be the increasing importance of the city – Glasgow in the case of Alasdair Gray or James Kelman – taking over the role of region. This would seem to be a reliable guideline which Scott's stupendous barrier would predate and guarantee, were it not for these three writers. Although it is true that religious nationalism locates much of their fiction in a remote Highland setting, this is a response to an underlying fear: that envisaged by Richardson, of an ever-encroaching secularism. In other words, that term so beloved of the nineteenth century, national character, for Brunton and company, resides in religion. Without it, Scotland is a spiritually barren country with no distinguishing features; Hargrave's presence in Glenalbert indicates that there is no real stupendous barrier left to cross in 1811, three years before Waverley reaches Perthshire.

How does Scott relate to this context? Initially as an enigma, once we take into consideration the Malachi episode. For P.H. Scott, the letters represent the foundation of Scottish nationalism; key for him is the belief that Scott more or less called for 'the repeal of the Union' (1976: 252). Sutherland represents a body of thought which believes that the letters 'were out of character' (1995: 306) and are the result of his distressing personal circumstances at the time. A brief look at Scott's *Journal* for February 1826 reveals his deep concern and care in their preparation, characteristics which clash with a much more widespread image of a slapdash, hurried author. Such a contradictory state of affairs could be explained away by resorting to the antisyzygy, or it could be the final piece of proof to indicate that Scott is not only wracked by metaphysical doubts about human existence but is also contradictory in his beliefs. With Brunton and her contemporaries we at least know in which direction their fiction points, but Scott, at the end of the day, seems to have none, or at least he has left his compass in the drawer alongside his fishing tackle. However, it is precisely in the case of identity that I believe we can find the only ideological certainty in Scott.

Anthony D. Smith points out that there are two basic trajectories in nationalism. The first is lateral and aristocratic, marked by the elites' capacity 'for self-perpetuation to the extent that they can incorporate other strata of the population within their cultural orbit' (1991: 54). Although this model is centuries old, its development led to nation building, 'the outcome of a vigorous programme of political socialization' (61). This is a top-down model, in which the ruling elite extend both their ideas and influence down the social structure. In contrast the nineteenth-century model, adapted by subject races in Europe, builds its political platform on the demotic, turning ethnic members into citizens. Of course, there is no guarantee that what is seen as advantageous by one form of nationalism is viewed in a similar fashion by the other. *Waverley* would seem to illustrate several aspects of these two models. One outstanding exemplification would be that Scott is perfectly aware that the union will never allow Scotland's ethnic members to become citizens, as illustrated by Talbot's pejorative remarks about Highlanders, gibberish and so on. An individual can thus simultaneously hold conflicting views of what constitutes the national interest. Again, this highlights the role of Talbot: his manners may be considered aristocratic, but, as I argued, they are those of the new nationalist English ruling class, the administrative elite. The Malachi episode, I would propose, is not that different from *Waverley*, even though one has been associated with union and the other with its repeal or something similar; in short, we are dealing with two seemingly irreconcilable sets of ideas in one location. In both cases, what is occurring is that the lateral trajectory does not act in accordance with the demotic; the rub is whether we are talking about rules or exceptions. This is the tension which underlies the Waverley Novels and pushes Scott both in his first novel and in his unpublished works into moments of intense debate and gloom which lead, in *The Siege of Malta*, to the abandonment of the human factor in fiction. The importance of the Caledonian antisyzygy is not simply that it provides a feasible cultural theory for Scotland, but that its 'zigzag of contradictions' (Smith 1919: 4) do not come from a struggle between native and outside influences but from the two templates for identity as Anthony Smith articulates. The passage from the Scottish Enlightenment to the Scottish Romanticism, or the tensions between Scott and Hogg, are full of enactments of the lateral/demotic at work and being productive, or at play, and wreaking havoc.

Many scholars use modernity in relationship to Scott as part of a strategy to understand the mechanics employed by Scott to set up a hero who is, in his creator's own notorious words, something of an imbecile. The passivity shown by Waverley has convincing explanations, such as that supplied by Welsh – modernity implies becoming a member of society rather than a hero – and also by Duncan, in his analysis of gender and the 'female-quixotic manner' (1992: 79). Modernity is also present in another, equally precise fashion once we consider his military career. Which is the first modern war is an open question; firm candidates include the Napoleonic War, for its use of mass armies, the Crimean War, for its rapid communication of news between battlefield and the home front, the American Civil War, for its use of technology and its targeting of civilians, the Boer War, for its incarceration of civilians in camps, and World War One, where traditional heroism is eclipsed. It is not a difficult task to find some of these features in *Waverley*, not simply because Scott is a prophet, but the process of modernity is just that, a process.

That does not discount the possibility of identifying the emergence, disappearance or modification of certain concepts at certain moments, the most important of which is the hero. The presence of writers like Siegfried Sassoon and Wilfred Owen in the canon as the essential war poets results in making the pity of war the one unavoidable subject of war poetry. Consequently trench warfare and the Western Front become practically the only recognized scenario in the representation of war for British writers and readers. The hopelessness that their poetry so eloquently narrates stems from the virtual impossibility of heroism, save on those rare occasions when, as in Waverley's case, heroism comprises rescuing combatants from a certain death. This kind of behaviour, along with other ideas, led Mark Rawlinson in *British Writing of the Second World War* (2000) to assert that '[t]he human subject of twentieth-century war literature is not a hero but a witness' (11). In terms of form, this would coincide with the rise of reportage and documentaries, but it also obeys the logic that individual human intervention in warfare is very much a thing of the past, save for live-saving rather than life-taking acts. At the same time, it provides a fitting conclusion to this study because it sheds a different light on *Waverley* – as a subject-exercise both in romance and in ethnography, itself a predecessor to reportage – and on Waverley himself, a figure whose wavering personality therefore becomes the perfect weapon for survival which permits him to live in both camps; this is why his last meeting with Fergus reads as a media interview between a journalist and a victim, the former searching for some pithy remarks with which to immortalize the latter. Therefore, I would conclude that the modernity identifiable in Scott is that of the passive hero, who is modern in his knowledge that traditional heroism is henceforth impossible and in his quest for and/or ability to witness and record; in brief, Christopher Isherwood's witness famously jots down, in the opening of *Goodbye to Berlin*, 'I am a camera', an epithet that perfectly suits Waverley. He also shares some features with Isherwood's 'Truly Weak Man: no matter whether he passes it [the test] or whether he fails, he cannot alter his essential nature' (2000: 207). This leap forward in time from 1814 to 1939 should be seen as an attempt to clarify and pinpoint the nature of his sneaky imbecility.

My analysis of Scott's female contemporaries would also suggest, as I have argued throughout, that survival of the female witness is even more miraculous, as *Ivanhoe* might reveal. An extreme example of witnessing comes from the otherwise most bizarre transatlantic escapade in Brunton's *Self-Control*. Ellen reports on the plight of penniless Highlanders and the shallowness of bourgeois life in an uncultured Edinburgh. Ferrier's use of battered heroes and heroines is yet another example, as is her determination to report on the lucre-banished clans in an attempt to strip away romantic Scotland's sheen. Johnstone's career as a journalist makes her role as witness almost a foregone conclusion. But if the witness becomes the human subject, it is not just because of what is reported but because of the hardships reporting requires its witness to go through. This is the function of the many landscapes of *Clan-Albin*, leading Flora to make a heretical move by seeking refuge in a convent. If the seeds of modernity are identifiable here, they call into question one of the most sacred tenets of the history of the novel.

Watt's widely accepted account of the rise of the novel, which shares much in common with Colley, is based on the hypothesis that the rise of the bourgeoisie, the rise of individualism and the rise of the novel intermingle and mutually influence each other. Central to his study is the figure of Defoe, because 'the heritage of Puritanism is demonstrably too weak to supply a continuous and controlling pattern for the hero's experiences' (1997: 80). The novel has therefore moved on from the days of John Bunyan. However, if we turn our attention to Brunton and Ferrier, then religious values certainly are more than sufficient to supply a controlling pattern for the heroine's experience, which would be my final conclusion. It might be a loose pattern but it is certainly there and again, at the risk of repetition, it has been far too present in their fiction for those who disapprove of its disruptive force. Johnstone's complex narrative, complex in the basic sense of multiple plots, landscapes and character, likewise refuses to submit to Watt's prescription. Furthermore, as I noted (p. 152), Brown plays havoc with the question of individualism both in the herring metaphor and later in the way that he invokes classical dramatic devices to put an end to his model village. Scotland's most canonical twentieth-century novel, Lewis Grassic Gibbon's *Sunset Song* (1932), is remarkable for the way in which it negotiates most forcefully between individualism, in the figure of Chris, and the community, in terms of both plot and narrative discourse. How her story diverges from the villagers' as her voice gradually loosens itself from Gibbon's communal narrative voice is well documented. It would be madness to state that Watt has got it all wrong, but it is not absurd to point out that Scott's literary relations do not conform to the rise of the novel in the terms that Watt and several generations of materialist criticism have plotted it out. Whether this makes for a distinctively Scottish tradition, with a predominant interest in the collective and less focus on the individual, presupposes that there are national literatures, itself one of culture's Gordian knots.

Notes

Introduction

1. Lady Morgan's *The Wild Irish Girl* (1806) is a romance set in Ireland which uses archetypal features throughout: a wild landscape, ruins, the harp and so on. The Glorvina solution is a term which refers to the romance's conclusion, where Glorvina, as subject of a poorer, conquered nation, marries Horatio, a citizen of the richer, conquering nation: England. It is easy to see how this situation is open to all sorts of political interpretations, especially if we bear in mind that it was published only six years after Ireland's incorporation into the union. Robert Tracy's 'Maria Edgeworth and Lady Morgan: Legality Versus Legitimacy' (1985) remains the classic account. I will deal with the subject of union in greater detail in Chapter 4.

1   Mary Brunton: From the Soul of the Baroque to Tron Church

1. Brunton's 'Memoir' uses Roman numerals, whereas *Emmeline* and 'Extracts from Journal' use Arabic numerals successively. The fragments stop at page 100 and the 'Extracts' start on page 103.
2. His troops are used as an example of excellence in *Waverley*, 'Six grenadiers of Ligonier's, thought the Major to himself, as his mind reverted to his own military experience, would have sent all these fellows to the right about' (266).
3. Brunton takes a wry view of Wordsworth in the following extract from her journal: 'The celebrated [Tintern] abbey is nothing outside, but within it is very fine' (149). Reversing priorities, it is the building, rather than nature or memory, which she recalls most.
4. This could be, building on a point made by Moers (1977: 132), that the asylum becomes the location for Gothic heroinism, a borrowing from Wollstonecraft's *The Wrongs of Woman*.

2   Susan Ferrier and the Lucre-banished Clans

1. The colloquial usage of the term 'fag-end' is familiar. However, the original end-piece in this use of the metaphor would be from a web of cloth or piece of rope.
2. Margaret Oliphant's *Kirsteen* (1896) is set in the time of the lucre-banished clans. The Laird refuses to consider any untitled suitor for his unmarried daughters, whatever their wealth, something which he desperately needs. Oliphant views such class prejudice as an obstacle to the progress of women and Scotland's economic and social advancement. London, in contrast, is a much more dynamic place, where enterprising Scots are highly successful, as

Kirsteen herself will be. However, although she rescues her family's rickety finances, they still stick to the old ideas and remain ungrateful, farther justifying Kirsteen's voluntary exile.
3. In 1843, the Church of Scotland split over the question of patronage, leading to the setting up of the breakaway Free Church of Scotland which believed itself closer to the ideals of the Reformation. This Disruption should be seen as a major upheaval in Scottish social history rather than as a minor matter of doctrine.

3   Christian Isobel Johnstone: From Centrifugal to Centripetal

1. There is however, an inventory, dated 2 December 1857, which records that John Johnstone died intestate. The value of his estate was £962, which included the copyright for *The Cook and Housewife's Manual*.
2. *Henry V* supplies the perfect example. Henry threatens Harfleur with Armageddon if the city does not surrender. 'What is't to me, when you yourselves are cause, / If your pure maidens fall into the hand / Of hot and forcing violation?' (3.3.111–12). Age will not be respected and 'Your naked infants spitted upon pikes' (3.3.118). The resisting citizens of Harfleur are the 'cause' of this situation as plunder is licensed in medieval warfare when the besieged city refuses to surrender. Henry's threat is omitted from the famous Olivier 1944 film production, leaving Harfleur linked to Harry, England and St George rather than to possible atrocities.
3. Iain Crichton Smith's *Consider the Lilies* (1968) would be an interesting test case. On the one hand, it is carefully set in real circumstances, the Sutherland Clearances, with the notorious factor Patrick Sellar appearing as a character. By ending the novel before the final eviction, the form violence would take on the physically frail Mrs Scott remains unknown and therefore an ongoing threat. Yet the mentally strong heroine stands out as such a beacon of humanity in her treatment of others whilst at the same time so intuitive as to the workings of the law and its language that she seems to be too good to be true. To the suggestion that the novel tends towards a Manichean view of the world, the reply would be that in the Clearances, the sense of justice and injustice is clear-cut, more so than even in a depiction of the Covenanters or the Jacobites.
4. This might be a reference to Constantia wine, so perhaps this is an early version of a sherry party. Another instance of Constantia can be found in Austen's *Sense and Sensibility*, 2.8 (chapter 30), p. 208.
5. The Killing Times refers to the 1680s when the Convenanters refused to accept the imposition of episcopacy in Scotland. This refusal was repressed by force of arms. Like many religious conflicts of that century (we only need to think of the Thirty Years War), it certainly was a bloody, killing time. However, the controversy surrounding the events of that decade stems from whether this resistance is viewed as heroic and demotic, or the work of stubborn, religious fanatics. Scott's *Old Mortality* certainly recognizes the ubiquitous presence of violence, but opts, most probably, for the status quo. Hogg's *The Brownie of Bodsbeck* sides with the Convenanters.

4   Question Time: The Debate on Fiction

1. Hence Mikes's famous epigram, 'Continental people have sex lives; the English have hot-water bottles.'
2. To take a very contemporary example, Joan Cooper's (2011) lucid account of *Ivanhoe* likewise concentrates almost exclusively on the political dimension of Rebecca.

Bibliography

Alker, Sharon (2002) 'The Business of Romance: Mary Brunton and the Virtue of Commerce'. *European Romantic Review* 13.2: 199–205.

Anderson, Benedict (1991) *Imagined Communities: Reflections on the Origin and Spread of Nationalism*. London: Verso.

Anon. (1778) *The History of Eliza Warwick*. 2 vols. Dublin: S. Price.

—— (1810) An Englishman. 'Military Flogging'. *The Examiner* 155: 796–7.

—— (1810) 'One Thousand Lashes'. *The Examiner* 140: 557–8.

—— (1832) 'Flogging in the Army'. *The Schoolmaster and Edinburgh Weekly Magazine* 1.1: 9.

—— (1832) 'On the Political Tendency of Sir Walter Scott's Writings'. *The Schoolmaster and Edinburgh Weekly Magazine*, 29 September: 129–33.

Armstrong, Nancy (1987) *Desire and Domestic Fiction: A Political History of the Novel*. Oxford University Press.

Ashcroft, Bill, Gareth Griffiths and Helen Tiffin (1989) *The Empire Writes Back: Theory and Practice in Post-colonial Literatures*. London and New York: Routledge.

Austen, Jane (1926) *Plan of a Novel According to Hints from Various Quarters*. Oxford: Clarendon Press.

—— (1980) *Sense and Sensibility*. Ed. Tony Tanner. Harmondsworth: Penguin.

—— (1985) *Northanger Abbey*. Harmondsworth: Penguin.

Barker, Simon (2001) 'Dressing up for War: Militarism in Early Modern Culture'. In *Dressing Up For War: Transformations of Gender and Genre in the Discourse and Literature of War*. Ed. Aránzazu Usandizaga and Andrew Monnickendam. Amsterdam: Rodopi, 145–56.

Barron, James (1903–13) *The Northern Highlands in the Nineteenth Century*. 3 vols. Inverness: R. Carruthers and Sons.

Barthes, Roland (1989) *Mythologies*. Trans. Annette Lavers. London: Paladin Books.

Bertram, James (1893) *Some Memories of Books, Authors, and Events*. London: Constable.

Blakey, Dorothy (1939) *The Minerva Press*. Oxford University Press.

Boswell, James (1955) *Boswell on the Grand Tour: Italy, Corsica, and France, 1756–1766*. Ed. Frank Brady and Frederick A. Pottle. London: William Heinemann.

Boucher, Odile (1983) 'The Criticism of Fiction in *Tait's Edinburgh Magazine*, 1832–1850'. *Studies in Scottish Literature* 18: 75–84.

Bour, Isabelle (1997) 'Mary Brunton's Novels, or, the Twilight of Sensibility'. *Scottish Literary Journal* 24.2: 24–35.

Bowers, Toni (2009) 'Representing Resistance: British Seduction Stories, 1660–1800'. In *A Companion to the Eighteenth Century Novel and Culture*. Ed. Paula A. Bachsheider and Catherine Ingrassia. Cambridge: Wiley and Blackwell, 140–63.

Brown, George Douglas (1974) *The House with the Green Shutters*. Intro. J.T. Low. Edinburgh: Holmes McDougall.

Brunton, Mary (1811) *Self-Control*. 2 vols. Edinburgh: Manners and Miller.
—— (1814) *Discipline*. 3 vols. Edinburgh: Manners and Miller.
—— (1819) *Emmeline: with Some Other Pieces*. Edinburgh: Archibald Constable.
Bury, Charlotte Campbell (1908) *The Diary of a Lady-in-Waiting*. 2 vols. London: John Lane.
Buzard, James (2005) *Disorienting Fiction: The Authoethnograpic Work of Nineteenth-Century British Novelists*. Princeton University Press.
Carlyle, Thomas and Jane Welsh Carlyle (1985) *The Collected Letters of Thomas and Jane Welsh Carlyle: 1839*. Volume 11. Ed. Kenneth J. Fielding and C.R. Sanders. Durham, NC: Duke University Press.
Chambers, Robert (ed.) (1875) *A Biographical Dictionary of Eminent Scotsmen*. 3 vols. Glasgow: Blackie.
Clausewitz, Carl von (1993) *On War*. Intro. and trans. Michael Howard and Peter Paret. London: Everyman's Library.
Clyde, Robert (1995) *From Rebel to Hero: The Image of the Highlander, 1745–1830*. East Linton: Tuckwell Press.
Colley, Linda (1992) *Britons: Forging the Nation 1707–1837*. New Haven: Yale University Press.
Connolly, M.F. (1866) *Biographical Dictionary of Eminent Men of Fife*. Cupar: John C. Orr.
Cooper, Joan (2010) 'Ivanhoe. The Rebel Scott and the Soul of the Nation'. *Scottish Literary Review* 2.2: 45–63.
Craig, Cairns (1996) *Out of History: Narrative Paradigms in Scottish and British Culture*. Edinburgh: Polygon.
—— (1998) 'Scotland and the Regional Novel'. In *The Regional Novel in Britain and Ireland, 1800–1990*. Ed. K.D.M. Snell. Cambridge University Press, 221–56.
Craig, David (1961) *Scottish Literature and the Scottish People 1680–1830*. London: Chatto and Windus.
Cullinan, Mary (1984) *Susan Ferrier*. Boston: Twayne Publishers.
De Quincey, Thomas (2003) *The Works of Thomas De Quincey*. 21 vols. Ed. Julian North. London: Pickering and Chatto.
Dekker, George (1987) *The American Historical Romance*. Cambridge University Press.
Dennis, Ian (1997) *Nationalism and Desire in Early Historical Fiction*. London: Macmillan.
Diderot, Denis (1999) *Jacques the Fatalist*. Intro. and trans. David Coward. Oxford University Press.
Douglas, George Brisbane (1897) *The 'Blackwood' Group*. Edinburgh: Oliphant, Anderson and Ferrier.
Doyle, John (ed.) (1898) *The Memoir and Correspondence of Susan Ferrier 1782–1854*. London: John Murray.
Duncan, Ian (1992) *Modern Romance and Transformations of the Novel: The Gothic, Scott, Dickens*. Cambridge University Press.
—— (2007a) 'Ireland, Scotland, and the Materials of Romanticism'. In *Scotland, Ireland, and the Romantic Aesthetic*. Ed. David Duff and Catherine Jones. Lewisburg: Bucknell University Press, 258–78.
—— (2007b) *Scott's Shadow: The Novel in Romantic Edinburgh*. Princeton University Press.

Easley, Alexis (2004) *First-Person Anonymous: Women Writers and Victorian Print Media, 1830–1870*. Aldershot: Ashgate.

—— (2005) 'Tait's *Edinburgh Magazine* in the 1830s: Dialogues on Gender, Class, and Reform'. *Victorian Periodicals Review* 38:3: 263–79.

Edwards, Simon (2001) 'The Geography of Violence: Historical Fiction and the National Question'. *Forum* 34.2: 293–308.

Egenolf, Susan B. (2009) *The Art of Political Fiction in Hamilton, Edgeworth, and Owenson*. Farnham: Ashgate.

Eliot, George (1973) *The Mill on the Floss*. London: Pan Books.

Elton, Oliver (1912) *A Survey of English Literature 1780–1830*. 2 vols. London: Edward Arnold.

Ferrier, Susan (1824) *The Inheritance*. 3 vols. Edinburgh: Whitaker.

—— (1831) *Destiny: or, the Chief's Daughter*. 3 vols. Edinburgh: Whitaker.

—— (1874) 'Recollections of Visits to Ashistiel and Abbotsford'. *Temple Bar* 40: 329–35.

—— (1997) *Marriage*. Ed. Herbert Foltinek. Intro. Kathryn Kirkpatrick. Oxford University Press.

Ferris, Ina (1991) *The Achievement of Literary Authority: Gender, History, and the Waverley Novels*. Ithaca, NY and London: Cornell University Press.

—— (1997) 'Translation from the Borders: Encounter and Recalcitrance in *Waverley* and *Clan-Albin*'. *Eighteenth-Century Fiction* 9.2: 203–22.

—— (2002) *The Romantic National Tale and the Question of Ireland*. Cambridge University Press.

Fletcher, Lorraine (1989) 'Great Expectations: Wealth and Inheritance in the Novels of Susan Ferrier'. *Scottish Literary Journal* 16.2: 60–77.

Flint, Kate (1993) *The Woman Reader, 1837–1914*. Oxford: Clarendon Press.

Foltinek, Herbert (1985) 'Susan Ferrier Reconsidered'. In *Studies in Scottish Fiction: Nineteenth Century*. Ed. Horst Drescher. Frankfurt/Main: Peter Lang, 131–45.

Freud, Sigmund (2002) *Civilisation and its Discontents*. Ed. and trans. David McLintock. Harmondsworth: Penguin.

Garside, Peter (1991) 'Popular Fiction and National Tale: Hidden Origins of Scott's *Waverley*'. *Nineteenth-Century Literature* 46.1: 30–53.

Gates, Henry Louis (1988) *The Signifying Monkey: A Theory of African-American Literary Criticism*. Oxford University Press.

Gilbert, Sandra M. (1983) 'Soldier's Heart: Literary Men, Literary Women, and the Great War'. *Signs* 8.3: 422–50.

Goldsmith, Oliver (1840) *The Miscellaneous Works of Oliver Goldsmith*. Ed. Washington Irving. Philadelphia: J. Crisy.

Gonda, Caroline (1996) *Reading Daughters' Fictions, 1709–1834: Novels and Society from Manley to Edgeworth*. Cambridge University Press.

Grant, A. (1811) *Essays on the Superstitions of the Highlanders of Scotland*. 2 vols. London: Longman.

Grant, Aline (1957) *Susan Ferrier of Edinburgh*. Denver, CO: Alan Swallow.

Green, Katherine Sobba (1991) *The Courtship Novel, 1740–1820: A Feminized Genre*. Lexington: University Press of Kentucky.

Hamilton, Elizabeth (2010) *The Cottagers of Glenburnie and Other Educational Writing*. Ed. Pam Perkins. Glasgow: Association for Scottish Literary Studies.

Hart, Francis Russell (1966) *Scott's Novels: The Plotting of Historic Survival*. Charlottesville: University of Virginia Press.

—— (1971) *Lockhart as Romantic Biographer.* Edinburgh University Press.
—— (1978a) 'Scott's Endings: The Fictions of Authority'. *Nineteenth Century Fiction* 33.1: 48–68.
—— (1978b) *The Scottish Novel from Smollett to Spark.* Cambridge, MA: Harvard University Press.
Hogg, James (1999) *Anecdotes of Scott.* Ed. Jill Rubenstein. Edinburgh University Press.
—— (2000) *The Spy.* Ed. Gillian Hughes. Edinburgh University Press.
Hughes, Gillian (2007) *James Hogg: A Life.* Edinburgh University Press.
Isherwood, Christopher (2000) *Lions and Shadows.* Minneapolis: University of Minnesota Press.
Jameson, Fredric (1991) *Postmodernism, or, the Cultural Logic of Late Capitalism.* Durham, NC: Duke University Press.
Johnson, Claudia L. (2000) 'The Novel and the Romantic Century, 1750–1850'. *European Romantic Review* 11.1: 12–20.
Johnstone, Christian Isobel [Mrs Margaret Dods, pseud.] (1826) *The Cook and Housewife's Manual.* Edinburgh: Oliver and Boyd.
—— (1827) *Elizabeth de Bruce.* 3 vols. Edinburgh: Blackwood.
—— (1832) *Nights of the Round Table: or, Stories of Aunt Jane and her Friends.* Edinburgh: Oliver and Boyd.
—— (1836) *True Tales of the Irish Peasantry, as Related by Themselves; Selected from the Report of the Poor-Law Commissioners, by Mrs. Johnstone.* Edinburgh: Tait.
—— (1840) *The Diversions of Hollycot; or, the Mother's Art of Thinking.* Edinburgh: Oliver and Boyd.
—— (1845–46) *The Edinburgh Tales. Conducted by Mrs. Johnstone.* 3 vols. Edinburgh: W. Tait.
—— (2003) *Clan-Albin: A National Tale.* Ed. Andrew Monnickendam. Glasgow: Association for Scottish Literary Studies.
Joyce, James (1992) *A Portrait of the Artist as a Young Man.* Harmondsworth: Penguin Books.
Kim, Jina (2002) 'Establishing Britishness: The Anglo-Scottish Heroines in Susan Ferrier's *Marriage'. British and American Fiction to 1900* 9.1: 181–96.
Lamont, Claire (1991) '*Waverley* and the Battle of Culloden'. *Essays and Studies* 44: 14–26.
Le Faye, Deirdre (ed.) (1997) *Jane Austen's Letters.* Oxford University Press.
Lockhart, J.G. (1900) *Memoirs of Sir Walter Scott.* 5 vols. London: Macmillan.
Lukács, Georg (1981) *The Historical Novel.* Trans. Hannah and Stanley Mitchell. Harmondsworth: Penguin Books.
Mack, Douglas S. (1983) 'Hogg, Lockhart and *Familiar Anecdotes of Sir Walter Scott'. Scottish Literary Journal* 10.1: 5–13.
—— (2006) *Scottish Fiction and the British Empire.* Edinburgh University Press.
Makdisi, Saree (1998) *Romantic Nationalism: Universal Empire and the Culture of Modernity.* Cambridge University Press.
Manzoni, Alessandro (1987) *The Betrothed.* Intro. and trans. Bruce Penman. Harmondsworth: Penguin Books.
McCracken-Flesher, Caroline (2005) *Possible Scotlands: Walter Scott and the Story of Tomorrow.* Oxford University Press.
McGann, Jerome (2004) 'Walter Scott's Romantic Postmodernity'. In *Scotland and the Borders of Romanticism.* Ed. Leith Davis, Ian Duncan and Janet Sorensen. Cambridge University Press, 113–29.

McKerrow, Mary (2001) *Mary Brunton the Forgotten Scottish Novelist*. Kirkwall: The Orcadian Limited.

McMillan, Dorothy (ed.) (1999) *The Scotswoman at Home and Abroad: Non-Fictional Writing 1700–1900*. Glasgow: Association for Scottish Literary Studies.

—— (2003–4) 'Figuring the Nation: Christian Isobel Johnstone as Novelist and Editor'. *Études Écossaises* 9: 27–42.

Mellor, Anne K. (1993) *Romanticism and Gender*. New York and London: Routledge.

Meynell, Alice (1905) 'The English Women-Humorists'. *North American Review* 181.6: 857–72.

Millar, John (1903) *A Literary History of Scotland*. London: T. Fisher Unwin.

Milton, John (1971) *Paradise Lost*. Ed. Alastair Fowler. London: Longman.

Moers, Ellen (1977) *Literary Women*. London: W.H. Allen.

Monnickendam, Andrew (2000) 'The Odd Couple: Christian Isobel Johnstone's Reviews of Maria Edgeworth and Walter Scott'. *Scottish Literary Journal* 27.1: 22–38.

—— (2005) 'Eating your Words: Plate and Nation in Meg Dod's *The Cook and Housewife's Manual* (1826)'. *Scottish Studies Review* 6.1: 33–42.

—— (2009) 'Guarding the English Flag: The Enigmas of Allegiance in the Talisman'. *Écosse; l'identité national en question*. Ed. Bernard Sellin and Pierre Carboni. Nantes: Centre de Recherches sur les Identités Nationales et l'Interculturalité, 159–66.

—— (2011) 'The Scottish National Tale'. In *The Edinburgh Companion to Scottish Romanticism*. Ed. Murray Pittock. Edinburgh University Press, 100–11.

Morgan, Peter F. (1975) 'Lockhart's Literary Personality'. *Scottish Literary Journal* 2.1: 27–35.

Muir, Rory (1996) *Britain and the Defeat of Napoleon 1807–1815*. New Haven: Yale University Press.

Musgrove, Martha (2007–8) 'Relocating Femininity: Women and the City in Mary Brunton's Fiction'. *Eighteenth Century Fiction* 20.2: 219–44.

'Noctes Ambrosianae 29' (1826) *Blackwood's* 20: 770–92.

'Noctes Ambrosianae 58' (1831) *Blackwood's* 30: 531–45.

'Obituary Notices. Mrs. Johnstone' (1857) *Tait's Magazine* 24: 573–5.

Oliphant, Margaret (1882) *The Literary History of England in the End of the Eighteenth and Beginning of the Nineteenth Century*. 3 vols. London: Macmillan.

Otway, Thomas (2001) *The Orphan*. In *Libertine Plays of the Restoration*. Ed. Gillian Manning. London: Everyman.

Parrinder, Stephen (2006) *Nation and Novel: The English Novel from its Origins to the Present Day*. Oxford University Press.

Paxton, Nancy L. (1976) 'Subversive Feminism: A Reassessment of Susan Ferrier's *Marriage*'. *Women and Literature* 4.2: 18–29.

Perkins, Pam (2010) *Women Writers and the Edinburgh Enlightenment*. Amsterdam and New York: Rodopi.

Pittock, Murray (1994) *Poetry and Jacobite Politics in Eighteenth-Century Britain and Ireland*. Cambridge University Press.

—— (2008) *Scottish and Irish Romanticism*. Oxford University Press.

Prebble, John (1975) *Mutiny: Highland Regiments in Revolt, 1743–1804*. London: Secker and Warburg.

Price, Leah (2000) 'The Poetics of Pedantry from Thomas Bowlder to Susan Ferrier'. *Women's Writing* 7.1: 75–88.

Radcliffe, Ann (1998) *A Sicilian Romance*. Oxford World Classics.
Rawlinson, Mark (2000) *British Writing of the Second World War*. Oxford: Clarendon Press.
Rev. (1816) '*Clan-Albin*'. *Monthly Review* 80: 84–91.
Rev. (1819) '*Emmeline*'. *Blackwood's Edinburgh Magazine* 5.26: 183–92.
Rev. (1819) '*Emmeline and Other Pieces*'. *The Edinburgh Monthly Review* 7.2: 72–92.
Rev. (1820) '*Emmeline with Other Pieces*'. *British Critic* 13: 166–74.
Rev. (1827) '*Elizabeth de Bruce*'. *The Literary Chronicle and Weekly Review* 402: 49–51.
Rev. (1827) '*Elizabeth de Bruce*'. *National Magazine, and General Review* 1.5 (March): 315.
Rev. (1842) 'Miss Ferrier's Novels'. *Edinburgh Review* 74.150 (January): 498–505.
Rev. (1899) 'Miss Ferrier's Novels'. *Scottish Review* 34.67: 70–90.
Richardson, Samuel (1984) *Pamela*. Harmondsworth: Penguin.
Rousseau, Jean-Jacques (1964) *His Educational Theories Selected from 'Émile', 'Julie' and Other Writings*. Ed. R.L. Archer. Great Neck, NY: Barrons Education Series.
Ruskin, John (1903) 'Of Queen's Gardens'. In *Sesame and Lilies*. London: George Allen, 87–143.
Saintsbury, George (1923) *The Collected Essays and Papers of George Saintsbury 1875–1920 Volume 1*. London and Toronto: J.M. Dent & Sons.
Schivelbusch, Wolfgang (2003) *The Culture of Defeat: On National Mourning, Trauma, and Recovery*. Trans. Jefferson Chase. London: Granta.
Scott. P.H. (1976) 'The Malachi Episode'. *Blackwood's Magazine* 320: 247–61.
Scott, Walter (1834) *Miscellaneous Prose Works*. Volume 6. *Chivalry, Romance, The Drama*. Edinburgh: Robert Cadell.
—— (1891) *The Journal of Sir Walter Scott*. Edinburgh: David Douglas.
—— (1897) *The Talisman*. London: Adam and Charles Black.
—— (1985) *Waverley*. Ed. Andrew Hook. Harmondsworth: Penguin.
—— (1999) *The Heart of Midlothian*. Ed. Claire Lamont. Oxford World Classics.
—— (2008) *The Siege of Malta and Bizarro*. Ed. J.H. Alexander, Judy King and Graham Tulloch. Edinburgh University Press.
Shaffer, Julie (1992) 'The High Cost of Female Virtue: The Sexualization of Female Agency in Late Eighteenth- and Early Nineteenth-Century Texts'. In *Misogyny in Literature: An Essay Collection*. Ed. Katherine Anne Ackley. New York and London: Garland Publishing, 105–42.
Shakespeare, William (1980) *Romeo and Juliet*. Ed. Brian Gibbons. London: Methuen.
—— (1998) *Henry V*. Ed. Gary Taylor. Oxford World Classics.
Shields, Juliet (2010) *Sentimental Literature and Anglo-Scottish Identity*. Cambridge University Press.
Smith, Anthony D. (1991) *National Identity*. Harmondsworth: Penguin Books.
Smith, Gregory G. (1919) *Scottish Literature: Character and Influence*. London: Macmillan.
Smith, Sarah (1986) 'Men, Women and Money: The Case of Mary Brunton'. In *Fetter'd or Free? British Women Novelists 1670–1815*. Ed. Mary Anne Schofield and Cecilia Macheski. Athens: Ohio University Press, 40–58.
Sroka, Kenneth M. (1980) 'Education in Walter Scott's *Waverley*'. *Studies in Scottish Literature* 15: 139–64.

Sutherland, John (1995) *The Life of Sir Walter Scott: A Critical Biography*. Oxford: Blackwell.

Todd, Janet (2000) *Mary Wollstonecraft: A Revolutionary Life*. London: Weidenfeld and Nicolson.

Tracy, Robert (1985) 'Maria Edgeworth and Lady Morgan: Legality Versus Legitimacy'. *Nineteenth Century Fiction* 40.1: 1–22.

Trumpener, Katie (1997) *Bardic Nationalism: The Romantic Novel and the British Empire*. Princeton University Press.

Usandizaga, Aránzazu and Andrew Monnickendam (eds) (2007) *Back to Peace: Reconciliation and Retribution in the Postwar Period*. University of Notre Dame Press.

Warren, Maria Lilly (1942) 'The Life and Works of Susan Edmonstone Ferrier'. Ph.D. dissertation, Cornell University.

Watson, Nicola (1994) *Revolution and the Form of the British Novel, 1790–1825*. Oxford: Clarendon Press.

Watt, Ian (1997) *The Rise of the Novel: Studies in Defoe, Richardson and Fielding*. London: Hogarth Press.

Welsh, Alexander (1992) *The Hero in the Waverley Novels with New Essays on Scott*. Princeton University Press.

Williams, Merryn (1985) *Women in the English Novel, 1800–1900*. Basingstoke: Macmillan.

Wilt, Judith (1985) *Secret Leaves: The Novels of Walter Scott*. University of Chicago Press.

Wollstonecraft, Mary (1993) *A Vindication of the Rights of Woman*. In *Political Writings*. Ed. Janet Todd. London: William Pickering, 67–296.

—— (1998) *Mary and The Wrongs of Woman*. Ed. Gary Kelly. Oxford University Press.

Womack, Peter (1989) *Improvement and Romance: Constructing the Myth of the Highlands*. London: Macmillan.

Woolf, Virginia (1992) *To the Lighthouse*. Oxford University Press.

Index

Note: Page numbers followed by *n* and a number refer to information in a note.

flogging issue and Johnstone's work,
117–19
Foltinek, Herbert, 76
Fordyce's *Sermons to Young Women*, 86
Forster, E.M., 6
Forty-Five, 53, 56, 143, 145–6
Foucault, Michel, 161
Fraser, Simon, 127, 137
'fratriotism', 15–16
Freud, Sigmund, 37, 154

Gaelic language
  Brunton's *Discipline*, 51
  Johnstone's work, 23, 122, 123, 124
  and prejudice in Scott's *Waverley*, 149
Galt, John, 3–4, 97
  and Hogg and Scott, 12, 13, 17, 143
Garside, Peter, 2, 3, 20, 46
Gaskell, Elizabeth: *Mary Barton*, 90
Gates, Henry, 16
gender
  anonymity of women in
    journalism, 104–5
  attitudes towards female writers, 103
  and genre division, 7
    and anonymity of Johnstone's
      work, 105–6
    condemnation of romances and
      readers, 85–6
    female reading and feminine
      writing, 4–6
    fiction genre, 28, 64–5, 141
    heroic action in women's writing,
      33–4
    praise for Alexander Brunton's
      writing on wife, 26–8
    Scott's appropriation of female
      territory, 17–18, 65, 98–9, 141
    insipid heroism and heroinism,
      162–8
    male character as heroine in
      Johnstone's *Clan-Albin*, 109–10
  and national tale, 4, 6, 7, 107
  and power relations in literature,
    17–18
  and Highlands in Brunton's
    Discipline, 54–5
  violence and gender in
    Johnstone's work, 118–19

rationalism and the sexes in
  Johnstone's work, 120–1, 159
sexual difference and Rousseau and
  Wollstonecraft, 165–6
warfare and gender relations in
  Johnstone's work, 108, 110,
  112, 113–21
see also education: and gender bias;
  female sexuality and desire;
  heroinism; heroism; male desire
genre *see* fiction as genre; gender:
  and genre division; historical
  novels; romances
George IV, king of Great Britain,
  10–11
Gibbon, Lewis Grassic, 179
  Sunset Song, 182–3
Gilbert, Sandra M., 108, 110
Girard, René, 153
Glorvina solution, 8, 96, 116, 136,
  137, 174
Goldsmith, Oliver, 120, 124, 151
Gonda, Caroline, 56, 58–9
Grant, Aline, 66
Grant, Anne MacVicar, 18, 111
  *Essays on the Superstitions of the
    Highlanders of Scotland*, 122–3,
    124
Gray, Alasdair, 12, 179
Green, Katherine, 45
Griffiths, Gareth, 16
grotesque Scotland in Ferrier's work, 92
Gunn, Neil, 179

Hamilton, Elizabeth
  Cottagers of Glenburnie, 12, 18–19,
    43, 88
  Memoirs of the Life of Agrippina, 18
Hanoverianism, 13, 30–1, 45, 167, 170
harp and national tale, 49–50
Hart, Francis Russell, 76, 97, 173
heroinism, 22, 23–4
  Brunton, 21, 23–4, 33–43, 162, 182
  Ferrier, 22, 72–84, 162, 182
  'insipid' heroines, 83–4, 86
  heroine as witness, 182
  Johnstone, 22, 33, 106–21, 162
  orphan heroines, 108–9, 121,
    122–3, 124–5